The Afterlife of the Platonic Soul

Ancient Mediterranean and Medieval Texts and Contexts

Editors

Robert M. Berchman
Jacob Neusner

Studies in Platonism, Neoplatonism, and the Platonic Tradition

Edited by

Robert M. Berchman
Dowling College and Bard College

John F. Finamore
University of Iowa

Editorial Board

JOHN DILLON (Trinity College, Dublin) – GARY GURTLER (Boston College)
JEAN-MARC NARBONNE (Laval University-Canada)

VOLUME 9

The Afterlife of the Platonic Soul

Reflections of Platonic Psychology in the
Monotheistic Religions

Edited by
Maha Elkaisy-Friemuth and John M. Dillon

BRILL

LEIDEN • BOSTON
2009

This book is printed on acid-free paper.

Library of Congress Cataloging-in-Publication Data

The afterlife of the platonic soul : reflections of platonic psychology in the monotheistic religions / edited by Maha Elkaisy-Friemuth and John M. Dillon.
    p. cm. — (Ancient Mediterranean and medieval texts and contexts) (Studies in platonism, neoplatonism, and the platonic tradition, ISSN 1871–188X ; v. 9)
    Includes bibliographical references and index.
    ISBN 978-90-04-17623-2 (hardback : alk. paper)
    1. Plato. 2. Soul. 3. Plato—Influence. 4. Abrahamic religions. I. Elkaisy-Friemuth, Maha. II. Dillon, John M. III. Title.

    B398.S7A38 2009
    128'.109—dc22

2009014849

ISSN 1871-188X
ISBN 978 90 04 17623 2

Copyright 2009 by Koninklijke Brill NV, Leiden, The Netherlands.
Koninklijke Brill NV incorporates the imprints Brill, Hotei Publishing,
IDC Publishers, Martinus Nijhoff Publishers and VSP.

All rights reserved. No part of this publication may be reproduced, translated, stored in a retrieval system, or transmitted in any form or by any means, electronic, mechanical, photocopying, recording or otherwise, without prior written permission from the publisher.

Authorization to photocopy items for internal or personal use is granted by Koninklijke Brill NV provided that the appropriate fees are paid directly to The Copyright Clearance Center, 222 Rosewood Drive, Suite 910, Danvers, MA 01923, USA.
Fees are subject to change.

PRINTED IN THE NETHERLANDS

CONTENTS

Preface vii
List of Contributors ix

Introduction 1

A. EARLY PERIOD

Philo of Alexandria and Platonist Psychology 17
John Dillon

St Paul on Soul, Spirit and the Inner Man 25
George H. van Kooten

B. CHRISTIAN TRADITION

Faith and Reason in Late Antiquity: The Perishability Axiom
and Its Impact on Christian Views about the Origin and
Nature of the Soul 47
Dirk Krausmüller

The Nature of the Soul According to Eriugena 77
Catherine Kavanagh

C. ISLAMIC TRADITION

Aristotle's *Categories* and the Soul: An Annotated Translation
of al-Kindī's *That There are Separate Substances* 95
Peter Adamson and Peter E. Pormann

Private Caves and Public Islands: Islam, Plato and the Ikhwān
al-Ṣafāʾ 107
Ian Richard Netton

vi CONTENTS

Tradition and Innovation in the Psychology of Fakhr al-Dīn
al-Rāzī 121
Maha Elkaisy-Friemuth

D. JUDAIC TRADITION

The Soul in Jewish Neoplatonism: A Case Study of Abraham
Ibn Ezra and Judah Halevi 143
Aaron W. Hughes

Maimonides, the Soul and the Classical Tradition 163
Oliver Leaman

E. LATER MEDIEVAL PERIOD

St. Thomas Aquinas's Concept of the Human Soul and the
Influence of Platonism 179
Patrick Quinn

Intellect as Intrinsic Formal Cause in the Soul according to
Aquinas and Averroes 187
Richard C. Taylor

Bibliography 221

Index of Names 231
Index of Concepts and Places 234

PREFACE

This collection of essays takes its origin from a series of seminars delivered over the last few years in the Centre for the Study of the Platonic Tradition, in Trinity College, Dublin, which is a subdivision of the Mediterranean and Near Eastern Studies (MNES). We are most grateful to all those who made the journey to talk to us, as well as to all those who participated in the discussions. We selected the topic of the soul as being one that directly engaged, in a problematic way, all philosophically-minded thinkers of all three of the great religious traditions of late antiquity and the middle ages; we then invited a selection of major authorities on the various traditions concerned, and we were not disappointed with the results. Inevitably, in an enterprise of this sort, not all aspects of a given topic can be covered, but we hope that the papers here presented between them give a reasonably comprehensive and coherent panorama of the ramifications of the subject.

We are grateful to MNES, in particular its Director, Prof. Brian McGing, and its former director Prof. Sean Freyne, for supporting this project in all its stages from its inception, and for assisting with the costs of the publication.

LIST OF CONTRIBUTORS

Peter Adamson, Reader in Philosophy, King's College, London, UK.

John Dillon, Regius Professor of Greek (Emeritus), Trinity College, Dublin, Ireland.

Maha Elkaisy-Friemuth, Assistant Professor, Faculty of Theology, Leuven Katholieke Universiteit, Belgium.

Aaron W. Hughes, The Gordon and Gretchen Gross Professor of Jewish Studies, SUNY, Buffalo, USA.

Catherine Kavanagh, Lecturer, Department of Philosophy, Mary Immaculate College, Ireland.

George H. van Kooten, Professor of New Testament & Early Christianity, Faculty of Theology & Religious Studies, University of Groningen, The Netherlands.

Dirk Krausmüller, Lecturer, School of Religious and Theological Studies, Cardiff University, UK.

Oliver Leaman, Professor of Philosophy, University of Kentucky, USA.

Ian Richard Netton, Sharjah Professor of Islamic Studies, Institute of Arab and Islamic Studies, University of Exeter, UK.

Peter E. Pormann, Assistant Professor, Department of Classics & Ancient History, University of Warwick, UK.

Patrick Quinn, Professor of Philosophy, All Hallows College, Dublin, Ireland.

Richard C. Taylor, Professor of Philosophy, Marquette University, USA.

INTRODUCTION

This volume aims to present a study on the treatment of the human soul by a selection of medieval Christian, Jewish and Muslim thinkers. Notably, medieval thought was heavily influenced by Greek philosophy, ever since Philo of Alexandria had first integrated it into his interpretation of the Bible. Church Fathers, and Muslim and Jewish theologians afterwards, found in Greek theorizing an objective logical tool for understanding the world and its creator or originator. Integrating and reconciling Greek thought to one or other of the three monotheistic religions, however, was a great challenge which most thinkers of this period felt it incumbent upon them to face. The reason, perhaps, is that both religion and philosophy claim to possess truth. Some issues, it must be said, found no interdisciplinary solution and remained a subject of conflict, such as the question of the origin of the world, whether it is created or eternal. Others, however, like the question of the 'faculties of the human intellect and the process of thinking, were settled under agreement between philosophy and religion. The nature and the future of the human soul is also one of the most important problems which call for deep study and support from both theology and philosophy. Thus, this volume devotes considerable attention to the problems that arise when studying the nature and the destiny of the human soul, and illustrates some of the solutions which the most notable thinkers of the mediaeval period provided.

We are here particularly interested in theologians who struggled to master both disciplines, and who devoted most of their efforts to gaining philosophical expertise and integrating it into their religious beliefs. In this introduction we will first give a short synopsis of the Platonic concept of the human soul and follow it by an outline of the eleven chapters of this volume which demonstrate the influence of those Platonic principles in the different disciplines, before finally presenting a short conclusion.

Platonic Soul

The doctrine of the soul is a central, but rather complex, feature of Plato's philosophical system. Indeed it might be said that here, as in a number of other areas of his doctrine, he leaves a somewhat confused heritage to his successors. However, from the perspective of later Platonism, perhaps even dating back to the scholarchate of Xenocrates (339–314 B.C.) in the Old Academy, but certainly from the time of Antiochus of Ascalon in the early first century B.C., a reasonably coherent consensus had emerged as to what his teaching was.[1] It is important to grasp, at all events, that the situation appears more complex to us than it seems to have done to his ancient followers.

Basic to the Platonic system, of course, is a strong distinction between soul and body, such that the soul, an immaterial and immortal essence, rules the body, a material and mortal essence, during those periods in which it is connected with it. This soul-body antithesis is set out in its starkest form in the *Phaedo*, but the context, which is the last hours of Socrates' life on earth, may to some extent affect the approach that Plato takes here. At any rate, the soul is presented as the true repository of the personality, whose proper functioning is severely inhibited by its presence in the body, beset as it is by all the demands inseparable from bodily existence.

A somewhat more positive view of the relations between soul and body is manifested in Plato's major work, the *Republic*, generally regarded as having been composed perhaps a decade after the *Phaedo*. Here we find that the distractions to the proper functioning of the soul attributed in the earlier dialogue to the demands of the body are to be blamed rather on an irrational element in the soul itself. In Book 4 of the work (434d–435e), Plato presents an interestingly complex scenario, in which we find a three-way split between a rational element, an irrational element (the passions, such as lust, greed or fear), and an intermediate element, which Plato terms *thymos*, or 'spiritedness', which can join either of the other elements—if the lower, as anger, but if the higher (as it will in the case of a well-structured soul), as something like righteous indignation, or at least self-esteem, which can serve as a counterweight to the passions.

At any rate, this introduces into the concept of soul, not a bipartite, but rather a tripartite division, and this, because of the great prominence of the *Republic* in Plato's oeuvre, persists in later times as a distinc-

---

[1] For a useful summary of later (mid.-2nd. cent. C.E.) Platonist doctrine on the soul, see chs. 23–5 of Alcinous' *Didaskalikos*, or *Handbook of Platonism*, with notes ad loc. (Alcinous, *The Handbook of Platonism*, trans. with comm., John Dillon, Oxford, 1993, pp. 147–60).

INTRODUCTION 3

tively Platonic division of the soul. We also find a division similar to this in two later dialogues, the *Phaedrus* and the *Timaeus*, though in either case with the significant modification that the *thymos*, while still distinct from the passionate, irrational element, or *epithymia*, is firmly separated from the rational element: in the case of the *Phaedrus*, being represented, in mythological terms, as one of a pair of horses (albeit the well-behaved one), as opposed to the reason as charioteer; in the case of the *Timaeus*, being physically cut off from the reason, resident in the head, by the 'isthmus' of the neck, and assigned to the chest, just above the *epithymia*, in the 'nether regions'. The great influence of the *Timaeus* in the later Platonist tradition led to the prevalence in later sources of this latter version of a tripartite division subordinate to a bipartite division.

Another feature of the *Timaeus* led to doctrinal consequences unintended by Plato himself, but fruitful in later times, particularly in connection with the vexed question (which does not, however, appear to have bothered Plato) of the relation of soul to body. At *Tim.* 41E, the Demiurge mounts the souls destined for embodiment onto 'vehicles' (*okhémata*) before sending them down to bodies. Nothing much is made of these 'vehicles' in the narrative after that, but plainly the idea intrigued later Platonists, especially when it was put together with a theory of Aristotle's, enunciated in a well-known passage of the *De generatione animalium*, 736b27ff. Here we are introduced to a special sort of 'innate spirit' (*symphyton pneuma*) residing especially in the blood around the heart, which constitutes the seat of the nutritive and sensitive soul, and which is responsible for the process of image-making (*phantasia*), as well as for purposive action. The substance of this, we are told, is 'analogous to that element of which the stars are made' (736b38)—that is to say, of Aristotle's postulated 'fifth substance', or *aithêr*. So here we have a bridge-entity, notionally capable of receiving immaterial impulses from the intellect, and transposing them, through the instrumentality of the blood, into movements of bones and sinews.[2] This could plausibly be connected with the soul-vehicles of the *Timaeus* so as to make a 'pneumatic vehicle' composed of aether, or pure fire (analogous to the substance of the heavenly bodies), which could serve as a 'cushion' between soul and body, and, in some versions of the

---

[2] Cf. also the intriguing passage in *De motu animalium*, III 10, 703a6ff., where the *pneuma* is related to the whole process of *orexis* and its realisation.

4   INTRODUCTION

theory, as the seat of *phantasia*, 'imagination', or the image-making faculty, and even *aisthesis*, sense-perception. Such as entity could serve, in Platonizing Christian or Islamic thought, as the basis for a doctrine of the 'glorified', or 'resurrection' body. The relation between the vehicle and the irrational soul continues to be a matter of controversy down through later antiquity, since both are concerned with sense-perception and the passions, and both should be disposed of when the soul comes to be free of the body after death.

One feature of Platonic psychology which causes difficulty for all of the three great religious traditions is the doctrine of reincarnation. The Judeo-Christian-Islamic tradition has no problem with the immortality of the soul following upon its creation by God for incarnation in a human body, but for the Greek philosophical tradition, at least after Aristotle had spelled out the implications clearly, immortality for the soul meant immortality *in both directions*, and with that went the implication of repeated—indeed infinitely repeated—reincarnation—even, in some interpretations, into animal bodies (though this latter notion was abandoned in later Platonism, after Porphyry rejected it). Such a doctrine has serious implications for any doctrine of personal salvation, or indeed for the integrity of personal identity,[3] and was resisted forcefully by thinkers in all three traditions. In this connection, there was a tendency among the Christian Fathers to welcome a literal interpretation of Plato's *Timaeus*, according to which the Demiurge created human souls in a sort of mixing-bowl (*Tim.* 41D) before distributing them into bodies; however, any such literal creation of souls, as of the world in general, was rejected even by Plato's immediate successors, Speusippus and Xenocrates, in response to the criticisms of Aristotle (particularly in *De Caelo* I 12), and they were followed in this by all later Platonists, except for Plutarch and Atticus in the Middle Platonic period (first and second centuries C.E.). In general, therefore, Jewish, Christian and Islamic theologians of otherwise Platonist sympathies tend to either elide or explicitly reject the concept of reincarnation, or even of the pre-existence of the individual soul.

---

[3] This latter was also a reason for postulating the resurrection of the body, in some form or other, as we shall see.

INTRODUCTION

Reflection

Monotheistic traditions were indeed directly influenced by these Greek debates on the nature and function of the human soul; some of the religious interpretations of the human condition certainly point back to the main elements of Platonist theory. Let us here draw some connections between the above description of Platonist doctrine and the positions put forward in this volume by the various philosophers dealt with here.

First of all, John Dillon, in his article 'Philo of Alexandria and Platonist Psychology', explains that the first thinker in any of the great religious traditions who drew attention to the Greek understanding of the human soul was indeed Philo of Alexandria. Philo was the first to Hellenize the Bible and to interpret many of what were known as the books of Moses (in effect, the Pentateuch), in full agreement with Greek concepts. Although he accepted the division of the soul into rational and irrational, he related the rational soul to a divine origin, which according to the Bible is the breath of God into Adam's body. The irrational soul he identified with the blood, connecting it to the Bible verses Gen. 9:4, Lev. 17:11 and Deut. 12:23 "the blood is the life". He also adopted the tripartite division of the soul which was widely accepted by Platonists and which became after him the scientific traditional version adopted by most theologians and philosophers of the mediaeval period.

The immortality of the soul is also a concept which attracted Philo's ambition for an afterlife future, however, without accepting the Platonic postulate of the eternal reincarnation of the soul in different bodies. He argues that an archetypal form of the human being must have been in the mind of God eternally, but is brought to actuality through his power of creation. Thus Philo manages here to relate the human soul directly to God and assure its destiny through its primary relationship to God as His own breath. However, the problems that arise from this theory are more thoroughly discussed among the thinkers of the Byzantine period, as will be set out in the article of Dirk Krausmüller below.

St. Paul, subsequently, exhibits interesting analogies to his fellow Jew and contemporary Philo; George van Kooten demonstrates in his article 'St. Paul on Soul, Spirit and the Inner Man' that St Paul's reflection on the nature of the human is mainly Greek. Van Kooten shows through philological analysis that Paul's terminology is related more to Greek concepts than to Jewish Semitic ones when dealing with his understanding of the nature of the human soul and its future. Paul's concept

6 INTRODUCTION

of the inner man, particularly in the *Letter to the Romans*, unveils his Greek understanding of the human soul in its relation to virtues and sin. When Paul made the distinction between the inner man and the man who is a slave to the flesh, he declared that the sinner is the latter; the inner man belongs indeed to another sphere.

However, the most valuable contribution of Paul to our discussion of Platonic psychology and its influence on medieval thinkers is his concept of the pneumatic body. When Paul turns to speak of the afterlife, he borrows the Greek concept of the spiritual 'vehicle' to explain the importance of a spiritual body for the eternity of the individual. This concept goes on to influence the Church Fathers and the whole Christian concept of immortality of the human, as van Kooten argues here.

Philo and Paul thus set the scene for the Christian thinkers of late antiquity, who were confronted with a set of Greek concepts about the nature of the soul which had come by this time to be accepted as basic. One of the problems which they faced in the early medieval period was how to defend the concept of the immortality of the human soul without adopting the Platonic principle of reincarnation. This discussion was connected to their argument against the axiom of perishability, which was accepted at that time as a basic logical principle: 'all that has existed in time must also perish in time', as Dirk Krausmüller sets out in his article, 'Faith and Reason in Late Antiquity'. Christian theologians argued that although the human soul is created and not eternal, it can have immortal life. Krausmüller explains that "late antique Christians were divided into two camps. The first camp had a clear understanding of nature as an autonomous realm based on rational rules, including the perishability axiom, even if these rules had been instituted by God. By comparison, the second camp believed that God could do with his creation whatever he liked." In other words, while the latter camp believed that God bestowed immortality on created souls in accordance with his will and knowledge, the former camp accepted the perishability axiom as a natural law and a condition for understanding the world as it is made by God. However, theologians argued that eternal beings such as the angels are in one sense generated insofar as they come into existence from God and ungenerated insofar as they have come forth not in time. Nevertheless, it is God who decides both of these conditions and therefore the natural law is in fact subject to God's will.

Another strand of thought in this early period is represented by Neoplatonic Christian theologians who adopted the concept of the return of the human soul and its re-unification with God. This ten-

INTRODUCTION

dency is clearly manifested in the writings of 'Pseudo-Dionysius the Areopagite', an anonymous theologian from the late 5th century, who was himself deeply influenced by the Neoplatonism of the Athenian School of Syrianus and Proclus, and who in turn influenced many later Christian theologians, most notably Maximus the Confessor. Maximus' writings on the human soul are strongly influenced by Pseudo-Dionysius' concept of the return of the soul, which he called divinization or *theosis*. Catherine Kavanagh, in her article 'The Nature of the Soul according to Eriugena', introduces to us Johannes Scotus Eriugena, the 9th century Irish theologian, another Neoplatonist who made great use of the psychology of Pseudo-Dionysius. Eriugena's cosmology was a mixture between Platonism and Stoicism which expressed not only an ideal divine world but also an image of a unification between the divine world and the material world in which salvation is the process of reconciliation and return of the whole world to the divine unity and a restoration of its perfect state. Eriugena first established the relationship between the World Soul, which he understands as the source of the human and angelic souls, and the Holy Spirit. By so doing he assures an eternal and immortal status to the human and angelic souls. He also establishes a close relationship between the soul and body by introducing the concept of the archetypal human logos which is a part of the divine Logos. He explains that although humans have two substances, soul and body, both are united in the human logos, and asserts that the material body will be transformed to a spiritual body, through which the human will then be unified into a single spiritual substance. Salvation is a process of spiritualisation and a return to the divine by means of unification, as Catherine Kavanagh explains.[4]

Turning to the teaching on the human soul among Muslim theologians of the ninth century, there can be no doubt that al-Kindī (d. 866) was the first Muslim theologian who integrated Greek philosophy into the Islamic tradition, and therefore is called the first philosopher of the Arabs. It seems that Arab theologians were quite aware of their Christian contemporaries' works, as al-Kindī reports that the logical works of Aristotle and Porphyry had gained great popularity among the Christians of his time. Therefore it is probable that the discussion

---

[4] This mystical understanding of the human soul and its destiny was also adopted among Muslim Sufis of the same period, most notably by al-Junayd, who taught a similar theory in Baghdad.

8   INTRODUCTION

of the problem of integrating Greek thought into religious issues like the afterlife was passed over by them to the Arabs. Muslim theologians such as the Mu'tazilites, though they made extensive use of Greek thought in their cosmology, were reluctant to adopt the Greek concept of the soul which expresses a clear duality between the soul and body. 'Abd al-Jabbār (d. 1024), in his work *al-Mughnī*, presents the conflict between the Basrian Mu'tazilites and the Baghdadis on this issue. The Baghdadi group, while believing that the soul is composed of a very tenuous matter, considered it a separate substance which inheres in the body. In contrast, the Basrian Mu'tazilites believed that the human is a unitary substance and that it is the body with all its different faculties and functions.[5] Al-Kindī was the earliest theologian and philosopher who not only accepted Greek soul-body dualism, but also adopted the incorporeal nature of the soul and listed it under the category of incorporeal substances. Adamson and Pormann's contribution, 'Aristotle's *Categories* and the Soul: an Annotated Translation of al-Kindī's *That There are Separate Substances*', introduces here a first published English translation of a short treatise of al-Kindī under the title *On the Fact That There are Separate Substances*. Here al-Kindī provides logical proofs for the existence of incorporeal substances, central among which is the human soul, using arguments from Aristotle's *Categories*. Al-Kindī is attempting here to attribute to the human soul substantiality through its attachment to the body. When the soul is attached to the body it makes it a living body and therefore it shares its attributes, one of which is substantiality. However, the situation becomes more difficult when he describes only the soul as incorporeal while the body is corporeal. In doing so he uses the Aristotelian *Categories*, arguing that the soul is the form of the body and therefore shares its quality of being a substance, he then defines the *form* of the body as the *species* of the body and argues that *species* are incorporeal. Therefore, only the soul should be credited with incorporeality. Whether we should agree here with al-Kindī in his logic is debatable, but at any rate in this treatise he is to be considered as the earliest Muslim thinker to provide logical argument for the proposition that the human soul is a substance which is incorporeal.

---

[5] M. Elkaisy-Friemuth, *God and Humans in Islamic Thought*, London: Routledge, 2006, pp. 52–4.

INTRODUCTION 9

Included among those thinkers who followed al-Kindī in his description of the human soul and attempted to build bridges between theology and Greek philosophy is an anonymous group of Arab philosophers who were called Ikhwān al-Ṣafāʾ, 'The Brethren of Purity' (flourishing between the tenth and eleventh century). They argued that the human soul is a part of the universal soul and therefore is incorruptible, with an eternal future. Although the Ikhwān are clearly influenced by Neoplatonism, they consider that God is omnipotent and is the only guarantee for the function of this natural system of emanation from the One to the Universal Intellect and the Universal Soul. It is God who bestowed eternal life on these incorporeal beings in accordance with His own plan for this world. Since eternal life is a grace, the Ikhwān are not excluding the possibility that the body possibly will have eternal life after its resurrection just like the bodies of the heavenly spheres, thus supporting the Qurʾanic resurrection. This argument was widely used among Byzantine theologians, as we learned from Dirk Krausmüller above. However, in their treatise *On Death and Resurrection*, this possibility is more or less reduced or not spelled out clearly. But in their treatise *On Life and Death*, they are rather more certain that the life of the soul on earth has the purpose of receiving knowledge and being awakened to its nature as belonging to the spiritual world. Ian Netton in his article, 'Private Caves and Public Islands: Islam, Plato and the Ikhwān al-Ṣafāʾ' introduces here their parable of the two islands, by means of which they express the view that the main task of the soul in its life on earth is seeking knowledge. When the soul departs from its body as enlightened in its nature it joins the world of the spiritual beings enjoying the beatific vision of God.

Moving to another figure among the Muslim thinkers who provided a systematic work on the human soul, we find a good example in Fakhr al-Dīn al-Rāzī (d. 1209). Fakhr al-Dīn, a follower of Ibn Sīnā (d. 1037) and al-Ghazālī (d. 1111), though a Muslim theologian, seems to adopt the Greek concept of the immateriality of the human soul. Al-Rāzī, as we will be informed in my own article, 'Tradition and Innovation in the Psychology of Fakhr al-Dīn al-Rāzī', attempts to reconcile the concept of the corporality of the human soul accepted by Muslim theologians with the immateriality of the human soul as a principle which was adopted by Muslim philosophers like Ibn Sīnā. *Al-nafs*, for al-Rāzī, is the substance which initiates all activities, and *al-rūh* is the inner principle which provides *al-nafs* with sensible information and

10 INTRODUCTION

transforms its orders to the bodily organs. Certainly this is influenced by the Aristotelian concept of the 'innate spirit' (*symphyton pneuma*). *Al-rūh* therefore is a tenuous material substance which resides in the heart, while *al-nafs* is immaterial and is able to perceive both universal and particular knowledge. *Al-nafs*, although it uses *al-rūh* as its mediator with the body, has the ability to perceive material images as they are transferred through the senses. However, al-Rāzī here argues that the images of the material world become immaterial as soon as they enter the body through the senses; e.g. seeing does not mean that the thing itself enters into the eye, but only an immaterial image of it. In this sense al-Rāzī claims that the immaterial rational human soul, as Ibn Sīnā calls it, is able to know the sensible world after the death of the body and therefore remain as an individual soul throughout eternity. Its body will be also recreated by the divine process of bringing its separated atoms together to resurrect the same body into eternal life. Al-Rāzī argues here, as do many of the Byzantine Christian theologians, that the guarantee of this process lies in the divine wisdom which had first created it.

Moving to the Judaic tradition, according to H. A. Wolfson the Jewish philosophical and theological disciplines did not develop until beginning of the ninth century under Muslim rule.[6] The corpus of Jewish philosophy under Muslim rule flourished in the east of the empire through its connection to the Muʿtazilites schools of Basra and Baghdad and in the west of the empire through following the Arabic philosophical discipline in al-Andalus. Al-Masʿ-dī and Ibn Ḥazm refer to Saadia Geon (d. 942) and his teacher Abū Kathīr of Tiberias (d. 932), who taught in Baghdad, as *mutakalimūn*;[7] but though they were strongly influenced by the Muʿtazilites concept of the unity and justice of God, they also had their own contributions to make. Saadia, in his great work, *The Book of Doctrines and Beliefs*, introduces in chapters three and four, and further in chapters eight and nine, his study on the human soul. Here Saadia presents one of the earliest Jewish views on the human soul, which is heavily influenced by Aristotelian and Neoplatonic concepts. His concept that the soul is a substance independent of the body and that it belongs to the celestial sphere shows

---

[6] H. A. Wolfson, 'The Jewish Kalām', in *The Jewish Quarterly Review*, New Series, vol. 57, 1967, p. 545.

[7] Ibid., pp. 554–5.

INTRODUCTION 11

that some of the Jewish thinkers in the east of the Islamic empire were indeed influenced by the schools of al-Kindī and al-Fārābī (d. c. 950). In this respect Saadia is considered to be the first Jewish philosopher of the medieval period, and it is possible that his works were also read by Jewish philosophers in Spain.[8] However, Jewish philosophy mainly flourished in Spain under the influence of the Arabic Aristotelian philosophical school of al-Andalus. We may mention here the figures of Abraham Ibn Ezra (d. 1167) Judah Halevi (d. 1141) and the greatest of all, Moses Maimonides (died 1204—just five years after the death of Ibn Rushd, known in the West as Averroes, who influenced him greatly). In this volume, however, we will concentrate mainly on the Andalusian Jewish thinkers.

Aaron Hughes' article, 'The Soul in Jewish Platonism: A Case Study of Abraham Ibn Ezra and Judah Halevi', discusses thoroughly Ibn Ezra's concept of the soul and follows it by Judah Halevi's criticism, presenting a good example of Jewish theologians who integrate philosophy into religious thinking. Ibn Ezra, though careful in his terminology, adopts fully the Neoplatonic theory of the soul. As a part of the universal soul, the human soul will be individuated and separated from the universal soul and sent to its specific body. The human soul consists of three parts or levels: the vegetative (*ha-nefesh*), the animal (*ha-ruah*), and the human (*ha-neshamah*). *Ha-neshamah* is the rational soul and is the only soul which will be granted eternal life through gaining philosophical knowledge, and therefore only prophets and philosophers are those who will enjoy eternal life. Judah Halevi, by contrast, criticises Ibn Ezra for his relying on Greco-Arabic thought and, in a Ghazalian fashion, shows that the philosophers cannot prove their claims about the nature and destiny of the human soul. Halevi here presents the Jewish example of the theologian who, though he does not differ in the main from a philosopher, argues that only God through his revelation in scripture is the source of true knowledge and the guarantee of the functioning of the natural universal system.

Although Halevi and Ibn Ezra in one way or another were influenced by Greco-Arabic philosophy, it was the master of Jewish philosophy Moses Maimonides, who became a great follower of al-Fārābī, Ibn Sīnā and Ibn Rushd. As a defender of the oral law and the Talmud,

---

[8] I. Dobbs-Weinstein, 'Jewish Philosophy', in *The Cambridge Companion to Medieval Philosophy*, Cambridge University Press, 2003, pp. 122–26.

12   INTRODUCTION

Maimonides claims to have obtained the basis of his concept of the human soul and the afterlife from scripture and oral traditions. Oliver Leaman shows in his article, 'Maimonides: the Soul and the Classical Tradition', that Maimonides holds two positions concerning the nature and the future of the human soul: a philosophical and a religious one. In his philosophical mode he follows Arabic philosophers in asserting that the soul's main activity is intellectual; all moral activity of the body is directed to assist the soul in its task of becoming divine, while in his religious works Maimonides adopts a belief in bodily resurrection, punishment and reward. Leaman argues that the key guide to reconciling his two concepts on the soul is through understanding Maimonides' theory of language. Words and images normally point to our material experience; however, religious language uses material language and images in a figurative sense to express abstract philosophical ideas. The unimaginable experience of the afterlife is portrayed in religious language in order that the mind can perceive its abstract reality; thus, it assists the person to move from the material to the abstract.

Reconciling religion and philosophy remained the main challenge until the end of the thirteenth century when St. Thomas Aquinas, in both his works, the *Summa Theologica and the Summa de veritate catholicae fidei contra Gentiles*, produced the finest arguments for the harmony between theology and philosophy. We end here our discussion on the human soul among medieval thinkers with two articles on Aquinas: 'St. Thomas Aquinas's Concept of the Human Soul and the Influence of Platonism' and 'Intellect as Intrinsic Formal Cause in the Soul according to Aquinas and Averroes'. While the former explains his theory of how the human soul can obtain in this life and in the afterlife a vision of God, the latter presents co-operation between Muslim and Christian philosophers in understanding the different faculties of the human intellect through Aquinas' criticism of Averroes' *De anima*.

Patrick Quinn, in the former article, points out an important text in the *De Veritate*, 13.3, where Aquinas explains how the human soul can obtain a vision of God in this life and in the afterlife. In order for the intellect to reach this experience it has to be totally independent of the imaginative faculty and separated from all bodily senses. By doing this the human intellect reaches a state where it becomes similar to the heavenly intellects and therefore receives the ability of seeing God. This same condition is even more possible to reach in the afterlife when the human soul is totally separated from its body. Here Aquinas explains in the first place a religious experience through the use of the philosophical

INTRODUCTION 13

concepts of the human intellect and its faculties and functions. Reaching the stage of beatific vision can only happen when the mind functions totally free of the sense-based process of knowledge and acts in a purely mental way. Thus Quinn here presents an important fusion between religion and philosophy through the study of Aquinas' philosophical and theological work *De Veritate* 13.3 and a number of other works.

Finally, Richard C. Taylor introduces us in his contribution to another faculty of the intellect, namely the material intellect, explained by Averroes as an intrinsic formal cause in the human soul, and Aquinas' criticism of it. The material intellect is a faculty which enables all humans to think, and is explained by Averroes as the intrinsic ability created in each of us, which is to be considered the formal cause of thinking. Averroes argues that "what is essential to human intellectual understanding —{which is} the abstractive power of the Agent Intellect itself—cannot remain only transcendent but must also be intrinsically present in the individual human soul, and not in an accidental or incidental fashion". This means that the human being has the power and ability of thinking within himself. Taylor in this article examines Aquinas' understanding of the teaching of Averroes on the Agent Intellect, and comes to the conclusion that Aquinas had only a partial understanding of it.

Conclusion

To conclude, Christian, Muslim and Jewish medieval thinkers found a great challenge in integrating Greek concepts of the human soul into their thought without introducing considerable modifications. While Christian theologians easily accepted the duality between the soul and body, since St. Paul declared that the actual human is the inner man, early Muslim theologians did not welcome this duality and considered the human to be the body with its different faculties, which will resurrect and be judged with reward or punishment. However, after al-Kindī's assimilation of Greek philosophy, a change entered into Islamic psychology. Christian and Jewish theologians also did not have difficulty in accepting the spirituality and immateriality of the human soul; but whereas Muslim theologians had great difficulty in accepting the immateriality of the human soul, probably because they believed that the only immaterial being is God, Muslim philosophers argued that the human is an immaterial entity which uses the material body

14   INTRODUCTION

as a window for perceiving the material world. Moreover, it seems that
Muslim, Christian and Jewish thinkers accepted the tripartite division
of the soul and agreed that the rational soul is the closest to the divine
world. Furthermore, most medieval theologians found in the Aristotelian concept of 'innate spirit' (*symphyton pneuma*), or the Platonist
concept of the vehicle of the soul, a solution for how the immaterial
soul can have a relationship to the body. In addition, they also found it
useful for explaining the resurrection of the body, which they considered
essential to assure the eternal survival of the human being.

The immortality of the individual is another issue which occasioned
a conflict between theology and Greek philosophy for thinkers from
all three monotheistic religions. Muslim theologians in general insisted
on the resurrection of the body and attributed eternal life to it as an
inseparable part of the human being. However, the Ikhwān al-Ṣafā'
argued for accepting both the spiritual and bodily resurrection. While
Christian theologians found in St. Paul's concept of receiving a spiritual
body in the afterlife a good solution for assuring individual immortality, Jewish thinkers were more able to perceive a spiritual afterlife,
perhaps because the Bible (particularly the Torah) spoke vaguely of
the afterlife and therefore did not emphasise a bodily resurrection, as
the Qur'an and New Testament did. Finally, we can infer from the different articles presented in this volume that medieval thinkers of all
three monotheistic traditions, while taking great interest in all aspects
of the Platonic tradition concerning human nature and fate, found the
question of the immortality of the individual human being the issue
of primary concern.

A. EARLY PERIOD

PHILO OF ALEXANDRIA AND PLATONIST PSYCHOLOGY

John Dillon*

The Jewish philosopher Philo of Alexandria (c. 25 B.C.E.–45 C.E.) is a remarkable literary and intellectual phenomenon. Imbued though he is with Greek culture, both literary and philosophical, by reason of the excellent education provided by his rich and thoroughly Hellenized father Alexander,[1] Philo also seems to have experienced, at some time in his early manhood, a 'conversion' to his ancestral Jewish religion and culture which leaves him determined, not to reject the Greek philosophical tradition as something alien, but rather to 'reclaim' it, by arguing that in fact Moses is the originator of philosophy, as can be demonstrated by the application of (Hellenic) methods of allegorizing to his writings (sc. the Pentateuch), and that he passed on this wisdom to the Greeks, in particular through the agency of Pythagoras, who will have communed with certain followers of Moses during his peregrinations in search of wisdom around the Eastern Mediterranean in the late sixth century B.C.E.[2]

This may appear to us a magnificently fantastic effort of oneupmanship on Philo's part—even if a fitting riposte to Greek cultural chauvinism—but it undeniably led to the production of a large corpus of creative and extremely interesting allegorical exegesis of the LXX version of the Pentateuch, which issues in much creative philosophizing. What is at issue in the present context is Philo's psychology, which is a particularly interesting aspect of his overall enterprise. In psychology, as in all other areas of philosophy, Philo is particularly indebted to the Platonic tradition, in the form in which he became acquainted with it. This is essentially the revived dogmatic Platonism propounded early in the first century B.C.E. by Antiochus of Ascalon, which involved

---

* Trinity College Dublin.

[1] Alexander held the position of 'Alabarch', which seems to have been the title of senior tax official in the imperial administration. Philo's nephew, Tiberius Julius Alexander also entered the imperial service, becoming Procurator of Judaea in A.D. 46, and later, under Nero, Prefect of Egypt.

[2] The full form of this theory only emerges, in extant literature, in Iamblichus' *Vita Pythagorica*, composed in the late third century C.E., but it is certainly much older than that, and some form of it must lie behind Philo's position.

18   JOHN DILLON

large-scale adoption of Stoic formulations (on the basis of Antiochus'
view that the Stoics were after all the truest heirs of the teaching of
Plato), overlaid by a Pythagoreanizing, transcendentalist turn from
Antiochus' rather immanentist and materialist take on the tradition
which we may associate with the position of Eudorus of Alexandria
(fl. c. 40 B.C.E.), who is nearer, both chronologically and geographi-
cally, to Philo himself. As we shall see, Philo permits himself a certain
degree of latitude in his accounts of the structure of the soul, since
he views the whole tradition descending from Pythagoras, including
not only Plato and the Old Academy, but Aristotle and the Stoics, as
valid, if slightly inadequate, heirs of Moses,[3] but basically his psychology is explicable as an interpretation of contemporary Platonism. I will
address in turn the topics of the nature and structure of the soul, and
of its immortality.

Nature and Structure of the Soul

Philo observes the basic Platonist bipartite division of the soul into
rational (*logikon*) and irrational (*alogon*) parts, as we can see from such
passages as *Leg. All.* II 6 and *Spec. Leg.* I 333. In the former, which is
an exegesis of Gen. 2:18 'Then the Lord God said: "It is not good that
man should be alone; I will make him a helper fit for him"'—in explaining in what sense Eve is 'later-born' and a 'helper', where Eve stands
for the irrational part of the soul, and Adam the rational, or 'leading'
part, Philo says:

> In just the same way,[4] it is thought, the leading element (*hégemonikon*)[5]
> of the soul is older than the soul as a whole, and the irrational element
> (*alogon*) younger. The irrational element is sense-perception (*aisthésis*)
> and its offspring, the passions (*pathé*), especially if they are not regarded
> as judgements of ours (*kriseis hémeterai*).[6] The 'helper', then, is later-born
> and, of course, created.

---

[3] Only the Atomists, Epicureans and (except for special purposes) the Sceptics are
excluded from this consensus, as not recognizing a providential divinity, or a purposeful universe.

[4] He has just described the heart as a sort of foundation for the body, a Stoic idea.

[5] Philo here employs the normal Stoic term for the rational part of the soul, which
he equates with *nous*, or the *logikon*. Cf., however, e.g. *Congr.* 26, where he uses simply
logikon.

[6] This is once again a Stoic reference. Zeno and Chrysippus had declared the passions to be *kriseis*, albeit distorted ones (*SVF* I 205–15; III 377–90).

PHILO OF ALEXANDRIA AND PLATONIST PSYCHOLOGY 19

In *Special Laws* I 333, a similar division is made between the rational (*logikon*) and the irrational elements, the former of which is identified with *nous*, while the latter is said to be divided into the five senses.

At *Special Laws* IV 92, however, we find the specifically Platonic tripartite division of the soul, specifically as set out in the *Timaeus* (69Eff.):[7]

> It was this (sc. disapproval of desire) which led those who had taken no mere sip of philosophy, but had feasted abundantly on its sound doctrines (sc. the Platonists), to the theory which they laid down. They had made researches into the nature of the soul and observed that its components were three-fold, reason (*logos*), spiritedness (*thymos*) and desire (*epithymia*). To reason, as sovereign, they assigned for its citadel the head as its most suitable residence, where are also set the stations of the senses, like bodyguards of their king, the intellect (*nous*). (trans. Colson, slightly adapted).

Philo also feels free, however, if it suits the scriptural passage with which he is dealing, to utilise the Stoic division into the *hégemonikon* ('ruling element') and the seven physical faculties, i.e. the five senses along with the faculties of speech and reproduction, e.g. at *On the Creation of the World* 117, where is engaged in extolling the Hebdomad, and a group of seven dependent on a monad is what suits his book:[8]

> Since things on earth are dependent on the heavenly realm through a natural affinity, the principle of the seven, which began on high, has also come down to us and made its presence felt among the mortal kinds. To start with, the part of our soul separate from the ruling element (*hége-monikon*) is divided into seven, into the five senses, the organ of speech, and finally the reproductive part. Just as in puppet shows, all these are manipulated by the ruling element through the nerves. Sometimes they are at rest, at other times they move, each producing its own appropriate disposition and movement. (trans. Runia, slightly adapted).

---

[7] Though of course the influence of *Republic* IV and of the myth of the *Phaedrus* are also present. The distribution of the parts of the soul about the body, however, is distinctive of the *Timaeus*. For a tripartite division, cf. also *Leg. All.* III 115–117, where the tendency to conflict between the three parts is stressed. At *Abr.* 29–30, however, we find a six-fold division of the irrational part, the procreative faculty being omitted, since his exegesis (of the six days of the working week contrasted with the Sabbath) calls for a total of seven rather than eight.

[8] Cf. also *Leg. All* I 11, *Heres* 232–3 (where he actually manages to relate the sevenfold division to the Circle of the Other at *Tim.* 36D) and *QG* II 12.

20   JOHN DILLON

We must note here that for the Stoics, the soul is actually, despite these
distinctions, a unitary essence, as it is not for Philo, and to this extent
he is subordinating the Stoic division to the Platonist one.

At *Questions on Genesis* II 59, on the other hand, we find a tripartite
division which is more Aristotelian than Platonic, distinguishing, as it
does, the three parts as the nutritive (*threptikon*), the sense-perceptive
(*aisthétikon*), and the rational (*logikon*). All this, however, need not
be seen as chaotic eclecticism on Philo's part. For him, each of these
divisions expresses some aspect of the truth, but the basic principle
remains the division into rational and irrational. When it comes down
to it, the spirited element and the passions are to be linked together in
opposition to the reason (as indeed they are in both Plato's *Phaedrus*—as
horses *versus* charioteer—and *Timaeus*). One of Philo's basic allegories,
after all, is that of Adam as the human *nous* and Eve as *aisthésis*,[9] the
union of which two is required for the human intellect in the body to
function.

A Doctrine of Two Souls?

A more substantial inconsistency in Philo's thinking, however, would
be a distinguishing, not of two or three, or even seven or eight, parts of
the soul, but of *two souls*. Such a distinction does indeed seem to occur
at places in his works, but even here the contradiction is more apparent than real. Philo becomes involved in this distinction, apparently,
in response to certain Biblical passages, notably Gen. 9:4, Lev. 17:11
and 14, and Deut. 12:23, where we find the statement that "the blood
is the life." As someone deeply affected by Platonism, Philo could not
accept this at face value. The rational soul is an immaterial entity, so
Moses must be referring to some kind of lower soul, or life-principle.
The essence of this may be agreed to be blood, even as the essence of
the rational soul is immaterial *pneuma*. At *QG* II 59 (on Gen. 9:4), we
find a strong distinction being made between the rational part (*meros*)
of the soul, whose substance is divine *pneuma*, and the nutritive and
sense-perceptive parts, whose substance is blood, and in this connection
a distinction is made between the veins and the arteries, the latter of
which contain a preponderance of *pneuma*, and only a small amount

---

[9] Besides the passage quoted above, cf. also *Leg. All.* II 24 and *Cher.* 58–60.

PHILO OF ALEXANDRIA AND PLATONIST PSYCHOLOGY   21

of blood, whereas the veins, having more blood than *pneuma*, are the seat of the lower parts.

What may be in the back of Philo's mind here is the theory of Aristotle, in *De Partibus Animalium* 736b27ff., concerning the function of what he calls the 'innate spirit' (*symphyton pneuma*), present in particular in the blood about the heart, which constitutes a sort of conduit between the passive intellect, itself an immaterial entity, and the nerves and sinews of the body, and initiates purposive action. Some such doctrine as this is behind the later Platonist doctrine of the 'vehicle' of the soul, of which we have evidence otherwise only from the second century C.E., but which may well have been already being bandied about in Platonist circles in Philo's day. Certainly there had been active speculation, ever since the period of the Old Academy, as to the precise mode of interaction between (immaterial) soul and (material) body—a problem that does not seem to have concerned Plato himself.[10]

Immortality of the Soul

At any rate, some such theory as this would seem to have been of assistance to Philo in resolving an awkwardness resulting from the Biblical assertion that 'the soul is the blood'. At *Det.* 82–3, again, we find what are initially called two *dynameis* or 'powers' of the soul, the vital (*zótiké*), or life-principle, and the rational, but they quickly begin to sound like separate entities, the life-principle being 'mortal', and the rational principle immortal:

> Each one of us, according to the most basic division, is two in number, an animal and a man. To either of these has been allotted an innate power (*syngenés dynamis*) akin to the qualities of their respective life-principles, to the one the power of vitality (*zótiké*), in virtue of which we are alive, to the other the power of reasoning (*logiké*), in virtue of which we are reasoning beings. Of the power of vitality the irrational creatures partake with us; of the power of reasoning God is, not indeed partaker, but originator, being the fount of archetypal reason (*logos*). To the faculty which we have in common with the irrational creatures blood has been given as the essence; but to the faculty which streams forth from the fount of reason spirit (*pneuma*) has been assigned; this not being just air in

---

[10] See my paper, 'How does the Soul direct the Body, after all? Traces of a Dispute on Mind-Body Relations in the Old Academy', in *Leib und Seele in der antiken Philosophie*, edd. Dorothea Frede & Burkhart Reis, (Berlin/New York, 2009).

motion,[11] but rather a sort of impression and stamp (*typon kai kharaktéra*) of the divine power, to which Moses gives the appropriate title of 'image' (*eikon*, Gen. 1: 26), thus indicating that God is the archetype of rational nature, while man is a copy and likeness—not the living creature of double nature, but the highest form in which life shows itself, which is termed intellect and reason. (trans. Colson, slightly emended)

Here, interestingly, even the rational soul is not presented as being immaterial, but rather as being composed of *pneuma;* but, as I have argued elsewhere,[12] for Philo the *pneuma* of which the Logos and the heavenly bodies also are composed is not to be regarded as 'material' in the sense proper to the other sublunary elements, but is to be assimilated to the *aithér* of Aristotle and the 'craftsmanly fire' (*pyr tekhnikon*) of the Stoics, as belonging to the active principle within the universe. As for the life-principle, at *On Flight and Finding* 67, it is seen as that part of the soul which God handed over to the 'helpers' to create, which, in imitation of Plato's *Timaeus*, 41E, is termed the 'mortal' part. The true man is to be identified with his mind in its purest state, of which God by himself is the creator (ibid. 71). For Philo, it is only this latter soul, or *part* of the soul, which is endowed with immortality, while the lower or 'mortal' soul disperses on the death of the individual. At *QG* III 11 (an exegesis of Gen. 15:15: "But thou shalt go to thy fathers with peace, nourished in a good old age"), we find a interesting statement of this doctrine:

Clearly this indicates the incorruptibility (*aphtharsia*) of the soul, which removes its habitation from this mortal body and returns as if to the motherland from which it originally removed its habitation to this place. For when it is said to a dying person, "Thou shalt go to thy fathers", what else is this than to represent another life without the body, which only the soul of the wise man ought to live?

It might be concluded from such a passage as this that the soul is fully immortal, in the Platonist sense, rather than being created by God for subsequent immortality, in the Judaeo-Christian sense; it is, after all, referred to as 'returning as if to the motherland'. Such in any case would be a natural conclusion from Philo's distinction between the creation of man 'in the image (of God)' at Gen. 1:26 and man 'formed of dust from the ground', at 2:7, since this would seem to imply the creation

---

[11] *Pneuma*, of course, could be taken to mean 'breath'.
[12] '*Asómatos:* Nuances of Incorporeality in Philo', in *Philon d'Alexandrie et le langage de la philosophie*, ed. Carlos Lévy, (Brepols, 1998), pp. 99–110.

PHILO OF ALEXANDRIA AND PLATONIST PSYCHOLOGY

(even though timelessly) of a pure human soul or intellect, prior to its embodiment; but it is not quite clear, in fact, from such a passage as *Opif.* 134, whether he is envisaging the creation of individual pure souls, or simply of a generic intelligible archetype of Man:

> He shows here (sc. at Gen. 2:7) that there is a vast difference between the man being fashioned now and the one that was created before 'in the image of God'. The one moulded now is perceptible by the senses, participates in quality, is a compound of body and soul, either male or female, by nature mortal. The one created 'in the image' is a sort of idea or genus or seal (*sphragis*), intelligible, immaterial, neither male nor female, by nature imperishable.

This certainly envisages, primarily, an archetypal Man as a Form among the thoughts of God. There is no need, however, to postulate a pre-incarnate existence for individual souls, and so no problem about re-incarnation, which is not a doctrine of which Philo would approve. One does, on the other hand, have, I think, to envisage individual *logoi* emanating from the Form of Man to join with the appropriate matter, to become individual men (and women). That is rather different, however, from postulating pre-existent individual souls.

A question may also be raised as to whether Philo envisages personal immortality for all embodied souls, or only for those of the wise. From such a text as *Questions on Genesis* I 16, one might conclude that he denied immortality to the souls of evil, or even ignorant, individuals:

> The death of good men (*spoudaioi*) is the beginning of another life. For life is twofold: one is with corruptible body, the other is without body and incorruptible. So that the evil man 'dies by death' (Gen. 2:17) even while he breathes, before he is buried, as though he preserved for himself no spark at all of the true life, which is excellence of character. The decent and good man, however, does not 'die by death', but, after living long, passes away to eternity, that is, he is borne to eternal life.

One might reasonably conclude from this that the soul of the evil man perishes on death, and enjoys no personal immortality. If this seems a harsh conclusion, one may perhaps take consolation from the fact that Philo seems to have no use for a concept of Hell. For him, indeed, as for many Platonists,[13] it is this sublunar realm that is actually the Hades

---

[13] Such as Xenocrates, for example, cf. Fr. 15 Heinze / 216 Isnardi Parente; and, later, Numenius, who attributes to Pythagoras the doctrine that Hades is the whole area between the earth and the moon (Frs. 32, 34–5 Des Places).

24   JOHN DILLON

of the poets. At *Heres* 45, for example, he refers to ordinary mortals as 'skulking in the caverns of Hades', and, a little later (78), as 'partaking in things earthly and nurtured on the things in Hades.'[14] It may be that he envisaged the souls of the great majority of the unenlightened as simply dissolving back into the atmosphere, without leaving any immortal trace, good or bad. Such a view would be very much in line with contemporary and later Platonism, though starkly opposed to that of later Christianity.

Conclusion

Philo, then, constitutes an interesting example of the creative appropriation of Platonist psychology in the service of a different theological system. Partly, at least, under the influence of the type of Platonism which he inherited, which was broadly, as I have said, that of Antiochus of Ascalon, as modified by Eudorus of Alexandria, he is hospitable to certain concepts of Stoicism, such as the Logos of God (which does away with the need for a World Soul), and the sevenfold division of the human soul (when the exigencies of exegesis demand it), while the awkward issue of reincarnation, which is an inseparable feature of the Platonist doctrine of an immortal soul, he simply elides (as does such a later Christian Platonist as Origen), while seeming to entertain the notion of some degree of pre-existence for the individual human soul. The troublesome scriptural assertion, on the other hand, that "the soul is the blood", he finesses into a postulation of something like the later Platonist 'pneumatic vehicle'. There is much in Philo, then, that we shall find replicated in later thinkers dealt with in this volume.

---

[14] Cf. also *Somn.* I 151; II 133.

ST PAUL ON SOUL, SPIRIT AND THE INNER MAN

George H. van Kooten*

Introduction

In this paper I shall address the issue of whether St Paul had a Jewish or a Greek understanding of the human soul, regardless of his views on the status of the body.[1] I shall argue that, despite some distinctively Jewish features—which Paul shares with his contemporary fellow-Jews Philo of Alexandria and Flavius Josephus—, his conceptuality of the soul is basically Greek, even to a greater extent than is commonly thought.

Until the present day, many biblical scholars continue to emphasize the distinctively Jewish or distinctively Pauline aspects of Paul's psychology and anthropology. To demonstrate the Jewish essence of his psychology, they point to the preponderance of allegedly Semitic concepts such as heart (καρδία) and flesh (σάρξ), often choosing to ignore the more 'noetic' language (e.g. νοῦς) which Paul also employs.[2] Similarly, they call attention to the Semitic expressions which have left their mark on the Greek translation of the Jewish bible, the Septuagint: the so-called Septuagintisms. Paul's use of the very word ψυχή, for instance, can be reduced to a mere Septuagintism if one focuses on such expressions as 'every soul' (πᾶσα ψυχή) which only function, it is

---

* University of Groningen.

[1] I wish to thank the participants in the seminar for their useful and stimulating suggestions and criticism, and in particular Prof. John Dillon. Sections 3–4 were first read at the 136th Annual Meeting of the American Philological Association in Boston, January 2005 (session 'Neoplatonism and Living the Good Life'), and likewise profited much from discussion. I am grateful also to Dr Robbert M. van den Berg (Leiden) for his careful comments on an earlier draft and to Dr Maria Sherwood-Smith for correcting the English in this paper. The present paper has now been incorporated into G. H. van Kooten, *Paul's Anthropology in Context: The Image of God, Assimilation to God, and Tripartite Man in Ancient Judaism, Ancient Philosophy and Early Christianity* (Wissenschaftliche Untersuchungen zum Neuen Testament 232), (Tübingen, 2008), esp. into chap. 5.2.1, pp. 298–302, and chap. 7.2.3, pp. 370–374.

[2] See, e.g., U. Schnelle, *The Human Condition: Anthropology in the Teachings of Jesus, Paul, and John* (trans. by O. C. Dean, Jr), (Edinburgh, 1996) (trans. of *Neutestamentliche Anthropologie: Jesus–Paulus–Johannes* [Biblisch-theologische Studien 18], Neukirchen-Vluyn, 1991), chap. 3 on Pauline anthropology, esp. chap. 3.7, pp. 59–63 on σάρξ and chap. 3.13, pp. 102–107, esp. pp. 102–104 on καρδία and pp. 104–105 on ψυχή.

26 GEORGE H. VAN KOOTEN

supposed, as a Semitic way of referring to each individual person. And to highlight the distinctiveness of Paul's own thoughts about the human soul, distinct from both Jewish and Greek thought, they highlight the antitheses which Paul forges between spirit (πνεῦμα) and flesh (σάρξ), for instance, and between spirit (πνεῦμα) and body (σῶμα).

My own position is that one should not be too quick to assume that Paul uses distinctively Jewish-Semitic concepts when writing Greek. Although σάρξ is an important concept in the Jewish scripture, in non-Jewish Greek, too, it can denote the flesh as the seat of the affections and lusts, the fleshly nature,[3] or man in his vulnerability (LSJ 1585 σάρξ II.1). The word is employed in this sense by Philo in a passage which otherwise develops a genuinely Greek psychology, as we shall see shortly. Seen in this light, there is nothing *distinctively* Jewish about Paul's use of σάρξ, nor anything *specifically* Pauline about his antithesis between σάρξ and πνεῦμα.

If this is true of the concept of flesh, the same applies to Paul's use of the term ψυχή. I will start with a discussion of the latter in §1, before focusing on the triadic expression πνεῦμα, ψυχή, and σῶμα in §2 and moving to the broader context of Paul's psychology, which is consistent with a Greek understanding of ψυχή, in §§3–4. In my discussion I hope to do justice both to Paul's Jewish colouring of his discourse of the soul, and to his own theological emphasis. Neither the Jewish nor the Pauline angle to this discourse should come as a surprise, as normally every thinker contextualizes 'general' topics within his or her own train of thought. In essence, however, Paul's discussion of the soul is inseparable from its larger setting in the Graeco-Roman period.

1. *The* ψυχή *in Paul*

There are certainly some instances of Septuagintisms in Paul's use of ψυχή. At the beginning of his *Letter to the Romans*, for example, Paul warns both Greek and Jews:

> for those who are self-seeking and who obey not the truth but wickedness, there will be wrath and fury. There will be anguish and distress *for*

---

[3] H. G. Liddell, R. Scott & H. S. Jones, *A Greek-English Lexicon*, (Oxford, 1996) (= LSJ), 1585 s.v. σάρξ II.1.

ST PAUL ON SOUL, SPIRIT AND THE INNER MAN 27

every soul of man (ἐπὶ πᾶσαν ψυχὴν ἀνθρώπου) who does evil, the Jew first and also the Greek (*Rom* 2.8–9 NRSV).[4]

The expression 'every soul of man' occurs only in the Septuagint (*Numbers* 19.11; *Isaiah* 13.7) and not in any other extant Greek literature.[5] In a periphrastic way, it refers to every individual human being, 'everyone'. Yet, one should not overemphasize the Semitic background of this Septuagintism, since in non-Jewish Greek, too, similar periphrastic descriptions of individual human beings do exist. Plato, for instance, in his *Laws*, speaks of 'every soul of all citizens' (πᾶσα ψυχὴ πολίτου παντός), clearly denoting each individual citizen, as the context makes clear:

> when *the soul of every citizen* (πᾶσα ψυχὴ πολίτου παντός) hangs upon this [i.e. upon his own private property], it is incapable of attending to matters other than daily gain. Whatsoever science or pursuit leads to this, every man individually (ἰδίᾳ πᾶς) is most ready to learn and to practise; but all else he laughs to scorn (*Laws* 831C).

The resemblance between Paul's use of ψυχή and general Greek usage is even closer when Paul just speaks about 'each soul' (πᾶσα ψυχή), without further qualification, in *Rom* 13.1; there are many parallels in the Septuagint, but at the same time the phrase frequently occurs in non-Jewish Greek literature, especially in Plato and Aristotle and in literature dependent upon them, and not always in a strictly technical sense. This should warn us against stressing the Semitic background of Paul's alleged Septuagintisms too much. At the very least, it is clear that these Septuagintisms were not incomprehensible in a non-Jewish Greek context and, more importantly, did not preclude Paul from developing a Greek understanding of the soul, as I hope to demonstrate.

There are some peculiar Septuagintisms, but their number is limited indeed. The most important example consists of a Septuagint quotation which entails the expression 'seek one's soul' (ζητεῖν τὴν ψυχήν τινος; *Rom* 11.3 quoting 1 *Kings* 19.10 LXX), which in the Septuagint stands for the intention of murdering someone. This particular meaning seems

---

[4] Translations from the Bible are normally taken from the New Revised Standard Version, with small alterations where necessary, and those from Classical authors are normally derived from the Loeb Classical Library, again with occasional changes.

[5] Observations with regard to the occurrence of particular linguistic terms in this section are based on consultation of the Online Thesaurus Linguae Graecae Digital Library (TLG®).

28 GEORGE H. VAN KOOTEN

to be absent from Classical Greek, where it means rather the opposite (see, e.g., Plato, *Phaedrus* 252E: 'The followers of Zeus *desire the soul* of him whom they love to be like Zeus'—οἱ μὲν δὴ οὖν Διὸς δῖόν τινα εἶναι ζητοῦσι τὴν ψυχὴν τὸν ὑφ᾽ αὐτῶν ἐρώμενον).

An interesting case is the expression 'risking one's soul' in Paul's *Letter to the Philippians* 2.30: παραβολευσάμενος τῇ ψυχῇ. This expression is not common in Greek, but is not found in the Septuagint either, so that its meaning seems rather to be dependent on the context, and to be a Pauline adaptation of the phrase's general Greek meaning of 'exposing oneself in one's soul', i.e. risking one's life.

Further instances of ψυχή in Paul can also be understood in the word's Greek meaning of ψυχή as 'life' (LSJ 2026 ψυχή I) or 'the conscious self or personality as centre of emotions, desires, and affections' (LSJ 2027 ψυχή IV), rather than in its philosophical meaning of 'the immaterial and immortal soul' (LSJ 2027 ψυχή III). Thus, particular fellow-workers of Paul's are said to have risked their own necks 'for my life' (ὑπὲρ τῆς ψυχῆς μου; *Rom* 16.4); Paul calls God for a witness 'to my own self' (ἐπὶ τὴν ἐμὴν ψυχήν; *2 Cor* 1.23); he tells the Corinthians that he will gladly spend and be spent 'for your lives' (ὑπὲρ τῶν ψυχῶν ὑμῶν; *2 Cor* 12.15) and, as he and his co-authors tell the Thessalonians, 'to impart their own soul and life to them' (μεταδοῦναι ὑμῖν... τὰς ἑαυτῶν ψυχάς; *1 Thess* 2.8).

In short, one should allow the possibility that various Greek meanings of ψυχή are present in Paul, including non-technical ones, rather than concluding that Paul employs this terminology in Septuagintist or idiosyncratic ways.

Paul also uses common Greek expressions which contain the word ψυχή or some cognate terms when he talks about (a) 'striving with one soul' (μιᾷ ψυχῇ; *Philipp* 1.27, from which he seems to develop the neologism σύμψυχοι in 2.2); (b) 'being of good courage' (εὐψυχεῖν; *Philipp* 2.19); (c) 'being of equal spirit, of like soul or mind' (ἰσόψυχος; *Philipp* 2.20); or about (d) τὰ ἄψυχα, the soulless, lifeless, material things (*1 Cor* 14.7), a term which, in the Septuagint, occurs only once in *The Wisdom of Solomon* (13.17; 14.29), a writing from the Hellenistic period. Later Pauline writings also speak of working, or of doing the will of God ἐκ ψυχῆς (*Col* 3.23; *Eph* 6.6), 'of one's own self', an expression which does not occur only in the Septuagint but is abundant in Greek literature. In 'Semiticizing' translations of these writings, this expression is wrongly translated as 'from the heart' or 'heartily'.

ST PAUL ON SOUL, SPIRIT AND THE INNER MAN 29

If we review all the ψυχ-passages in Paul, there are only a few examples of terms which are limited to the Septuagint and its subsequent Christian adaptation, probably the best example being the term ὀλιγόψυχος, faint-hearted or feeble-minded; this occurs in the Septuagint and is predominantly used in the Christian tradition and hardly at all in pagan Greek literature. Paul uses it in his exhortation to 'encourage *the faint-hearted*, support the weak, and be patient toward all' (*1 Thess* 5.14). These exceptions only serve to emphasize our findings that, as a rule, Paul's use of the term ψυχή reflects its broad application in Greek.

Paul is less idiosyncratic than is often assumed, as will become particularly clear from a few ψυχ-passages which will be discussed now. Although we shall see in these instances that the language is indeed coloured by specific Pauline and Jewish concerns and predilections, they also show that these are merely shades and tints in an otherwise Greek picture of man. In his discussion of the future resurrection of the body in *1 Cor* 15, for example, Paul argues that the future human body will be characterized as a σῶμα πνευματικόν, a pneumatic body, whereas the present body, which will be buried, is a 'psychical body', a σῶμα ψυχικόν. Although the latter expression seems to be a neologism, forged by Paul, the former expression, σῶμα πνευματικόν, is a term which is applied in Stoicism to characterize the abiding nature of God. Whereas God, insofar as he is material, is perishable and liable and subject to change, as becomes clear in the process of conflagration, the authoritative part of God's soul (τὸ ἡγεμονικὸν), the governing part of the universe, is a σῶμα πνευματικόν, a pneumatic and ether-like body (SVF 1054; = Origen, *Commentary on John* 13.21.128). As Origen puts it: the Stoics 'are not ashamed to say that since God is a body he is also subject to corruption, but they say his body is pneumatic and like ether, especially in the reasoning capacity of his soul'—οὐκ αἰδοῦνται λέγειν ὅτι καὶ φθαρτός ἐστιν σῶμα ὤν, σῶμα δὲ πνευματικὸν καὶ αἰθερῶδες, μάλιστα κατὰ τὸ ἡγεμονικὸν αὐτοῦ.[6] Although it is just possible that the terminology of σῶμα πνευματικόν is due to Origen, who preserved this passage, I regard it as an authentic Greek expression, as it is also

---

[6] Trans.: R. E. Heine, *Origen: Commentary on the Gospel according to John*, vol. 2: *Books 13–32* (The Fathers of the Church 89), (Washington, D.C., 1993, 94, with a small alteration.)

30   GEORGE H. VAN KOOTEN

attested elsewhere.[7] Paul regards this term as suitable to express the specific corporeality of the future, post-resurrection body.

This Stoic term is now placed in antithesis to σῶμα ψυχικόν, which combination Paul seems to have constructed himself. It is still possible to see where he derived his inspiration from, as his antithesis is followed by a quotation from *Gen* 2.7 LXX: 'So also it is written: "The first man, Adam, became a living soul"'—οὕτως καὶ γέγραπται, Ἐγένετο ὁ πρῶτος ἄνθρωπος Ἀδὰμ εἰς ψυχὴν ζῶσαν (*1 Cor* 15.45). As we shall see shortly, this text was also interpreted by fellow-Jews such as Philo and Josephus as a passage about the human soul. The contrast between a σῶμα πνευματικόν and a σῶμα ψυχικόν is developed by Paul to differentiate between (a) a life which is so dominated by the πνεῦμα that even the body becomes spiritual, and (b) a life dominated by the ψυχή, which is the entity—as we shall see in the next section—in the middle between body and spirit.

In the context of his discussion about the corporeality of the resurrection in *1 Cor* 15, Paul understandably focuses on the σῶμα and distinguishes between a pneumatic *body* and a psychic *body*. But the implied antithesis between πνεῦμα and ψυχή, which now manifests itself at the level of adjectives qualifying the sort of body involved, already comes to the fore in *1 Cor* 2 where, already in the present life, Paul distinguishes between two groups: on the one hand, there are the ψυχικοί (2.14)—whom we may assume to live only by their ψυχή and who are, therefore, effectively only σαρκίνοι (3.1) as their soul is lacking any guiding principle and gives in to the flesh; on the other hand, there are the πνευματικοί (2.15; 3.1; cf. *Gal* 6.1), who are able to receive and inquire into the things of God's πνεῦμα and possess the 'mind (νοῦς) of Christ' (2.16).

2. *The Trichotomy Between* πνεῦμα, ψυχή, *and* σῶμα

This differentiation between πνεῦμα and ψυχή is, I believe, already expressed in Paul's *First Letter to the Thessalonians*, where Paul exhorts his readers to preserve their entire πνεῦμα, ψυχή, and σῶμα so that they

---

[7] Comarius (1st cent. AD?), *De lapide philosophorum* 2.290; cf. also Zosimus (3rd/4th cent. AD), Ζωσίμου τοῦ Πανοπολίτου γνησία γραφὴ περὶ τῆς ἱερᾶς καὶ θείας τέχνης, τῆς του χρυσοῦ καὶ ἀργύρου ποιήσεως κατ' ἐπιτομὴν κεφαλαιώδη 2.146; and Damascius (5th/6th cent. AD), *In Phaedonem (versio 1)* 551.

ST PAUL ON SOUL, SPIRIT AND THE INNER MAN

may remain sound and perfect (5.23).[8] As I shall argue, this trichotomy seems to be the Jewish adaptation of the general Greek distinction between νοῦς, ψυχή, and σῶμα, which we find also in Greek philosophers contemporary with Paul, such as Plutarch.[9] As we have just seen at the end of §1, within *1 Cor* 2.14–16 Paul's wording switches easily from terms with πνεῦμα to the term νοῦς; they seem to be synonymous. I shall first demonstrate that in Jewish authors such as Philo and Josephus πνεῦμα is distinguished from ψυχή, and subsequently that, in Philo, the trichotomy between πνεῦμα, ψυχή, and σῶμα occurs alongside the differentiation between νοῦς, ψυχή, and σῶμα. Finally, it will be shown, in §§3–4, that the trichotomy Paul mentions in *1 Thess* is in line with his broader anthropological reflections, especially his views on God's image, the inner man, and the human νοῦς.

In Philo, the distinction between πνεῦμα and ψυχή is made clearly in his treatise *Quis rerum divinarum heres* 55–57. Because this entire passage is crucial, I give it first, signalling the relevant Greek key-terms between brackets:

> We use 'soul' (ψυχή) in two senses, both for the whole soul (ἥ τε ὅλη) and also for its dominant part (τὸ ἡγεμονικὸν), which properly speaking is the soul's soul (ψυχὴ ψυχῆς)... And therefore the lawgiver held that the substance of the soul is twofold, blood being that of the soul as a whole, and the divine breath or spirit (πνεῦμα) that of its most dominant part. Thus he says plainly 'the soul of every flesh is the blood': ψυχὴ πάσης σαρκὸς αἷμά ἐστιν (*Lev* 17.11 LXX). He does well in assigning the blood with its flowing stream to the riot of the manifold flesh (σάρξ), for each is akin to the other. On the other hand he did not make the substance of the mind (νοῦς) depend on anything created, but represented it as breathed upon by God (ὑπὸ θεοῦ καταπνευσθεῖσαν). For the Maker of all, he says, 'blew into his face the breath of life, and man became a living soul': ἐνεφύσησε...εἰς τὸ πρόσωπον αὐτοῦ πνοὴν ζωῆς, καὶ ἐγένετο ὁ ἄνθρωπος εἰς ψυχὴν ζῶσαν (*Gen* 2.7 LXX); just as we are also told that he was fashioned after the image (κατὰ τὴν εἰκόνα) of his Maker (*Gen* 1.27 LXX). So we have two kinds of men, one that of those who live by

---

[8] Cf. A. J. Festugière, *L'idéal religieux des grecs et l'évangile* (Études bibliques), 2nd ed. (Paris, 1932), Appendix B: 'La division *corps—âme—ésprit* de 1 Thessal. 5.23 et la philosophie grecque', pp. 196–220. For a detailed discussion of the trichotomy of πνεῦμα, ψυχή, and σῶμα in Philo and Paul, see van Kooten, *Paul's Anthropology in Context*, chap. 5: 'The Two Types of Man in Philo and Paul: The Anthropological Trichotomy of Spirit, Soul and Body', pp. 269–312.

[9] On the Greek philosophical trichotomy, see J. Dillon, 'Plutarch and the Separable Intellect', in: A. Pérez Jiménez & F. Casadesús (eds), *Estudios sobre Plutarco: Misticismo y Religiones Mistéricas en la Obra de Plutarco*, (Madrid-Málaga, 2001), pp. 35–44.

32   GEORGE H. VAN KOOTEN

reason, the divine inbreathing (τὸ μὲν θείῳ πνεύματι λογισμῷ βιούντων), the other of those who live by blood and the pleasure of the flesh (τὸ δὲ αἵματι καὶ σαρκὸς ἡδονῇ ζώντων). This last is a moulded clod of earth, the other is the faithful impress of the divine image (*Quis rerum divinarum heres* 55–57).

In this passage, Philo distinguishes the ψυχή from the soul proper, the ἡγεμονικὸν, whose substance he identifies with πνεῦμα. Whereas the soul, in the broad sense, is associated with the flesh (σάρξ) and with hedonistic pleasure (ἡδονή), the πνεῦμα is characterized as mind (νοῦς) and as an impress of the divine image, and is regarded as the direct result of God's breathing upon man. Even though the Septuagint text of *Gen* 2.7 does not state this explicitly, God's πνεῦμα is taken to be implied when it is says that God ἐνεφύσησε... πνοὴν ζωῆς, breathed a breath of life. In passing, I briefly note that Philo's antithesis between πνεῦμα and σάρξ resembles, or is in fact identical with, Paul's. The most important observation, however, is that Philo's antithesis between πνεῦμα and ψυχή is made on the basis of *Gen* 2.7, in which it is thought to be implied.

Elsewhere, too, Philo emphasizes this contrast between πνεῦμα and ψυχή on the basis of *Gen* 2.7 (*Quod deterius potiori insidiari soleat* 80–84). As in the previous passage, Philo sets out to reconcile two contradictory anthropological statements in the Pentateuch, one asserting that 'the life (ψυχή) of all flesh is the blood' (*Lev* 17.11), the other, that God 'breathed into his face the breath of life, and man became a living soul (ψυχή)' (*Gen* 2.7). According to Philo, Moses would not,

> having already said that the essence of life (ψυχή) is πνεῦμα (*Gen* 2.7 LXX), have said further on that it is some different substance, namely blood (*Lev* 17.11 LXX), had he not been bringing the matter under some most vital and essential principle. (...) Each of us (...) is two in number, an animal and a man. To either of these has been allotted an inner power akin to the qualities of their respective life-principles, to one the power of vitality, in virtue of which we are alive, to the other the power of reasoning, in virtue of which we are reasoning beings. Of the power of vitality the irrational creatures partake with us; of the power of reasoning God is, not indeed partaker, but originator, being the fountain of archetypal reason. To the faculty which we have in common with the irrational creatures blood has been given as its essence; but to the faculty which streams forth from the fountain of reason πνεῦμα has been assigned (...). This is why he says that the blood is the life (ψυχή) of the flesh, being aware that the fleshly nature has received no share of mind (νοῦς), but partakes of vitality just as the whole of our body (σῶμα) does; but man's life (ψυχή)

ST PAUL ON SOUL, SPIRIT AND THE INNER MAN 33

he names πνεῦμα, giving the title of 'man' not to the composite mass (...), but to that God-like creation with which we reason (*Quod deterius potiori insidiari soleat* 81–84).

The distinction between πνεῦμα and ψυχή is not only applied in the narrative of the creation of man, but also in narratives about virtuous men such as Abraham: 'the divine spirit (πνεῦμα) which was breathed upon him (καταπνευσθέν) from on high made its lodging in his soul (ψυχή), and invested his body (σῶμα) with singular beauty' (*De virtutibus* 217). This shows that the distinction between πνεῦμα, ψυχή, and σῶμα is considered to be of ongoing relevance.

Josephus also interprets *Gen* 2.7 in terms of the dichotomy of πνεῦμα and ψυχή. In the retelling of the Pentateuch in his *Jewish Antiquities*, Josephus even explicitly inserts the term πνεῦμα in his alleged quotation of *Gen* 2.7: 'Moses begins to interpret nature, writing on the formation of man in these terms: "God fashioned man by taking dust from the earth and instilled into him πνεῦμα and ψυχή." Now this man was called Adam' (1.34; cf. 3.260).

Against this background of Jewish-Hellenistic interpretations of *Gen* 2.7, it becomes clear that Paul, in distinguishing between πνεῦμα, ψυχή, and σῶμα in *1 Thess* 5.23, is following Jewish practice, as attested in Philo and Josephus. Yet, at the same time, Philo renders it clear that this trichotomy is simply the Jewish adaptation of the general Greek differentiation between νοῦς, ψυχή, and σῶμα. As I shall now show, in Philo's writings many passages indicate that he uses *both* trichotomies and equates the God-inbreathed human spirit (πνεῦμα) with the mind (νοῦς).

According to Philo, the νοῦς is the ruler of the entire ψυχή (*De opificio mundi* 30); it is the sovereign element of the ψυχή (69); 'what the νοῦς is in the ψυχή, this the eye is in the body; for each of them sees, one the things of the mind (τὰ νοητά), the other the things of sense' (53). Or, using a different metaphor, the νοῦς is said to be 'the ruler of the flock, taking the flock of the ψυχή in hand' (*De agricultura* 66). As he describes it clearly in *Legum allegoriarum* 1.39:

> the νοῦς (is) the dominant element of the ψυχή: into this only does God breathe, whereas He does not see fit to do so with the other parts (...); for these are secondary in capacity. By what, then were these also inspired? By the νοῦς, evidently. For the νοῦς imparts to the portion of the ψυχή that is devoid of reason a share of that which it has received from God, so that the νοῦς was be-souled by God, but the unreasoning part by the

34   GEORGE H. VAN KOOTEN

νοῦς. For the νοῦς is, so to speak, God of the unreasoning part. (...) The νοῦς that was made after the image and original might be said to partake of πνεῦμα (*Legum allegoriarum* 1.39).

It is 'the wholly purified νοῦς which disregards not only the σῶμα, but that other section of the ψυχή which is devoid of reason and steeped in blood, aflame with seething passions and burning lusts' (*Quis rerum divinarum heres sit* 64). This differentiation between νοῦς, ψυχή, and σῶμα also clearly comes to the fore when the wise man is called 'the first of the human race (...), as a ψυχή in a σῶμα and a νοῦς in a ψυχή, or once more heaven in the world or God in heaven' (*De Abrahamo* 272).

These examples will suffice to show that in Philo both trichotomies occur, the triad πνεῦμα, ψυχή, and σῶμα as well as the triad νοῦς, ψυχή, and σῶμα, and that in fact the former is the specifically Jewish adaptation (inspired by *Gen* 2.7 LXX) of the latter, general ancient philosophical trichotomy. I shall not discuss the Greek background of the differentiation between νοῦς, ψυχή, and σῶμα any further here. The point I want to emphasize now is that Paul clearly resembles Philo and Josephus in distinguishing between πνεῦμα, ψυχή, and σῶμα, and that he, too, will have understood this in a Greek way.

My analysis differs notably from the interpretation of *1 Thess* 5.23 offered in one of the most recent, rare comprehensive treatments of Paul's anthropology, that of Udo Schnelle:

> The trichotomous sounding phrase τὸ πνεῦμα καὶ ἡ ψυχὴ καὶ τὸ σῶμα reflects *no* Hellenistic anthropology according to which a person is divided into body, soul, and spirit. Paul is *merely* emphasizing that the sanctifying work of God concerns the whole person. This interpretation is suggested (...) by the observation that in 1 Thessalonians πνεῦμα is for Paul not a component of the human essence but the expression and sign of the new creative activity of God in humankind. With ψυχή and σῶμα Paul is *only* adding what constitutes each person as an individual. What is actually new and determinative is the Spirit of God. With his use of ψυχή Paul stands in Old Testament tradition, where *nèphèsh* designates the whole person.[10]

This interpretation ignores the similarities between Paul and his contemporaries Philo and Josephus, who show incontrovertibly that they are acquainted with trichotomous Hellenistic anthropology.

---

[10] Schnelle, *The Human Condition*, pp. 104–5 (italics mine).

ST PAUL ON SOUL, SPIRIT AND THE INNER MAN

As further support of my interpretation of Paul, I wish to point to the broader context of his anthropology, in which terms such as *metamorphosis* into God's image and within one's νοῦς, and the notion of the 'inner man' (ὁ ἔσω or ὁ ἐντὸς ἄνθρωπος) play an important role. In Paul, the 'inner man' (*2 Cor* 4.16; *Rom* 7.22) is synonymous with the νοῦς (*Rom* 12.2), which—as in Philo—is in turn identical with the Jewish notion of the God-inbreathed human πνεῦμα.[11] I shall now demonstrate the importance of such anthropological notions in Paul's Corinthian correspondence (§3) and in his *Letter to the Romans* (§4).

3. *Paul's* Second Letter to the Corinthians (2 Cor)

Paul's *2 Cor* has been transmitted as a composite letter; the part I am currently interested in runs from *2 Cor* 2.14 to 7.4 and constitutes a clearly distinguishable text fragment within *2 Cor*. It is clear from the outset that Paul is involved in a philosophical discussion with his Corinthian public. According to Paul, he himself is intent on spreading the knowledge of God throughout the Eastern Mediterranean (2.14), but he flatly denies that his working methods are comparable with the practices of those 'who sell the word of God by retail': οὐ γάρ ἐσμεν ὡς οἱ πολλοὶ καπηλεύοντες τὸν λόγον τοῦ θεοῦ (2.17).

Paul's language clearly echoes the warnings of Socrates in Plato's *Protagoras* against buying knowledge from the sophist Protagoras. Socrates urges Hippocrates:

> we must see that the sophist in commending his wares does not deceive us, like the wholesaler and the retailer who deal in food for the body. (...) So too those who take the various subjects of knowledge from city to city, and sell them by retail (οἱ τὰ μαθήματα περιάγοντες κατὰ τὰς πόλεις καὶ πωλοῦντες καὶ καπηλεύοντες) to whoever wants them, commend everything that they have for sale (*Protagoras* 313D–E).

In his letter, Paul has to face accusations that he himself behaves like itinerant sophists who demand money for their instruction, though he falls short of their standards of rhetoric and performance.

As Bruce Winter has shown, in his Corinthian community Paul is confronted with a sophistic movement among Jewish Christians, who

---

[11] For πνεῦμα, see *1 Cor* 2.11; for νοῦς, see *1 Cor* 1.10; 14.14–15, 14.19.

36   GEORGE H. VAN KOOTEN

are critical of Paul as orator and debater.[12] Apparently, Paul deliberately distances himself from the sophist movement by drawing on Platonic criticism of the sophists and characterizing their activity as καπηλεύειν. This shows that the setting of Paul's text under discussion is philosophical from the very beginning. He himself claims to speak not for financial gain, but with sincerity (εἰλικρινεία). Paul stresses that he is not interested in using letters of recommendation (3.1). Rather than using an outward, rhetorical *modus operandi* in communicating with his public, he is bent on their inner transformation. 'We all', Paul says, 'who, with uncovered faces, behold as in a mirror the glory of the Lord, are being transformed into the very one image': ἡμεῖς δὲ πάντες ἀνακεκαλυμμένῳ προσώπῳ τὴν δόξαν κυρίου κατοπτριζόμενοι τὴν αὐτὴν εἰκόνα μεταμορφούμεθα ἀπὸ δόξης εἰς δόξαν, καθάπερ ἀπὸ κυρίου πνεύματος (3.18)—the image, that is, of Christ, who is the image of God: εἰκὼν τοῦ θεοῦ (4.4).[13]

Soon Paul underpins this line of thought by drawing on the notion of the 'inner man', and it is there that the closest parallels between Paul and Platonist philosophers are found. According to Paul, rather than being occupied with shallow rhetoric, man should experience *metamorphosis* towards God, and acquire a new form within.

In a similar passage in his *Letter to the Romans*, Paul points out that this transformation takes place by renewing one's νοῦς, one's mind: μεταμορφοῦσθε τῇ ἀνακαινώσει τοῦ νοός (*Rom* 12.2). According to Paul, this renders Christian religion into a λογικὴ λατρεία, an intellectual, non-cultic, ethical worship of God (*Rom* 12.1–2). In *2 Cor*, this transformation of one's mind is said to take place when it is modelled on God's image. The underlying thought is, of course, that by being transformed into God's image, man starts to partake of God himself.

Having pointed to the need to experience inner transformation, Paul concludes that, on account of this ontological change, and because of his involvement in spreading this message, he will not lose heart, despite

---

[12] B. W. Winter, *Philo and Paul among the Sophists: Alexandrian and Corinthian Responses to a Julio-Claudian Movement*, 2nd ed. (Grand Rapids, Michigan, 2002), esp. p. 91 and pp. 167–8 with reference to Plato, *Protagoras* 313. Whereas Winter focuses predominantly on *1 Cor* 1–4 and *2 Cor* 10–13, my exploration takes its starting point in *2 Cor* 2.14–7.4 and, accepting Winter's reconstruction of Paul's critique of his sophistic opponents, deals less with this critique and more explicitly with Paul's alternative to sophism, i.e. with his view on the 'inner man' and man's transformation into God's image.

[13] Cf. van Kooten, *Paul's Anthropology in Context*, chap. 6, pp. 313–339.

ST PAUL ON SOUL, SPIRIT AND THE INNER MAN   37

the controversy which he faces (4.1). He once again emphasizes that he does not disguise God's message (4.2), like the Jewish-Christian sophists, by selling the word of God by retail (2.17). He claims to reveal the truth and not to make use of letters of recommendation, recommending himself instead to the consciousness or conscience (συνείδησις) of all men (4.2)—quite the opposite of mere sophistic rhetorical strategies. Despite his circumstances, Paul indeed does not lose heart, since if the 'outer man' is destroyed, he says, 'the inner man (ὁ ἔσω ἄνθρωπος) is renewed day by day' (4.16). Paul now uses the Platonic notion of the 'inner man' (Plato, *Republic* IX 589A–B) to support his line of thought.[14]

The same antithesis between the outer and inner man is present in Plotinus. My choosing to compare Paul with Plotinus, who flourished about two hundred years later, may be justified by the vast corpus of Plotinus' writings, which facilitates a careful analysis between philosophical-Platonic and Pauline anthropology. Of course, Plotinus himself contributed to the further development of Platonic thought, yet the significant terminological similarities between Paul and Plotinus must be due, in no small part, to a shared philosophical heritage. This heritage includes their extensive reflections on the Platonic 'inner man'. In Plotinus' view,

> it is not the soul within (ἡ ἔνδον ψυχή) but the outside shadow of man (ἡ ἔξω ἀνθρώπου σκιά) which cries and moans and carries on in every sort of way on a stage which is the whole earth where men have in many places set up their stages. Doings like these belong to a man who knows how to live only the lower and external life (τὰ κάτω καὶ τὰ ἔξω μόνα ζῆν; III.2.15).

'And even if Socrates, too,' Plotinus adds, 'may play sometimes, it is by the outer Socrates (ὁ ἔξω Σωκράτης) that he plays' (III.2.15). Paul seems

---

[14] On this notion, see Th. K. Heckel, *Der Innere Mensch: Die paulinische Verarbeitung eines platonischen Motivs* (Wissenschaftliche Untersuchungen zum Neuen Testament II.53), (Tübingen, 1993); C. Markschies, 'Die platonische Metapher vom "inneren Menschen": Eine Brücke zwischen antiker Philosophie und altchristlicher Theologie', *Zeitschrift für Kirchengeschichte* 105 (1994), pp. 1–17 (also published in: *International Journal of the Classical Tradition* 1.3 [1995], pp. 3–18); cf. also 'Innerer Mensch', in: *Reallexikon für Antike und Christentum*, vol. 18, (Stuttgart, 1998), pp. 266–312; W. Burkert, 'Towards Plato and Paul: The "Inner" Human Being', in: A. Y. Collins (ed.), *Ancient and Modern Perspectives on the Bible and Culture. Essays in Honor of Hans Dieter Betz*, (Atlanta, GA, 1998), pp. 59–82; and H. D. Betz, 'The Concept of the "Inner Human Being" (ὁ ἔσω ἄνθρωπος) in the Anthropology of Paul', *New Testament Studies* 46.3 (2000), pp. 315–341. See also van Kooten, *Paul's Anthropology in Context*, chap. 7.2.2: 'The inner man—the history of a concept', pp. 358–370.

38   GEORGE H. VAN KOOTEN

to employ this notion of the 'inner man' because it is very suitable as a supplement to his criticism of the sophists' outer modus operandi; as a matter of fact, it substantiates his criticism of their position. For him it expresses, in a positive, emphatic, and constructive way, what the Christian message is about.

4. *The Inner Man and His Vices—Paul's* Letter to the Romans

Comparison with Plotinus shows very clearly that Paul has a genuine command of the notion of the inner man and does not use this terminology only superficially. Both Paul and Plotinus appear to dwell on the question of how the inner man relates to virtues and sin. I shall first focus on Plotinus' view on this relation, in order to provide a context in which Paul's reflections on the inner man can be appreciated more clearly. To this end, we shall now first address the question of what Plotinus thinks of the vices which, despite the process of becoming god-like, remain in man. Plotinus devotes much discussion to this specific topic, and his deliberations help us to understand the ins and outs of the notion of the 'inner man'. As we shall see subsequently, it is highly remarkable that this topic is also discussed in Paul, in an extensive passage in the *Letter to the Romans*, which Paul wrote during his final stay in Corinth.

(a) *Plotinus on the Inner Man, Virtues and Sin*

According to Plotinus, the real, proper virtues, which belong to the sphere of intellect, have their seat in the 'true man' (ὁ ἀληθὴς ἄνθρωπος), the 'inner man'/the 'man within' (ὁ ἔνδον ἄνθρωπος), or the 'separate soul', as he also calls it—that which transcends the human life and is different from the body and its affections. The other, lesser virtues, however, which result from habit and training, are located in what Plotinus calls 'the joint entity'; this entity is also the seat of the vices (I.1.10). The proper virtues are those which effect the purification of the soul and make it similar to God (I.2.3). Plotinus is interested in the question of how this purification deals with 'passion and desire and all the rest (...), and how far separation from the body is possible'. In his view, the soul 'gets rid of passion as completely as possible, altogether if it can', but the reason why it cannot lies in 'the involuntary impulse' (τὸ ἀπροαίρετον). This impulse, which is not under the

ST PAUL ON SOUL, SPIRIT AND THE INNER MAN

control of will, belongs to something other than the soul, and is small and weak (I.2.5).

On the one hand, Plotinus is optimistic about the soul's possibility to be pure and to achieve its aim of making the irrational part, too, pure. This part profits from the soul's purification,

> just as a man living next door to a sage would profit by the sage's neighbourhood, either by becoming like him or by regarding him with such respect as not to dare to do anything of which the good man would not approve (I.2.5).

Insofar as this is the case, the soul is sinless. Yet Plotinus stresses that he is not obsessed, in a negative way, by trying to avoid sin. Rather, his concern, in a positive way, is to become god-like, to be a god. Nevertheless, although Plotinus is optimistic about the soul's potential, he does have to concede that there may still be an element of involuntary impulse in man, which causes him to be not *simply god* (θεὸς μόνον), but 'a god or spirit who is *double*' (διπλοῦς)[15] (I.2.6).

As Plotinus says elsewhere, one can argue that the soul is sinless if one assumes the soul to be 'a single completely simple thing and identifies soul and essential soulness'. Yet, the soul is regarded to be sinful if one 'interweaves with it and adds to it another form of soul (…): so the soul itself becomes compound (…) and is affected as a whole, and it is the compound which sins'. This 'other form of soul' is also called the soul's image (εἴδωλον). In order to illustrate his views on the compound soul, Plotinus uses two metaphors, one drawn from Plato, the other from Homer.

The first image relates to the sea-god Glaucus, who is likened to the soul because its real nature is only seen if one knocks off its encrustations (Plato, *Republic* X 611D–612A). Similarly, the soul's image—the other, added, encrusted form of soul—is abandoned and 'no longer exists when the whole soul is looking to the intelligible world'.

The other image, taken from Homer, concerns the figure of Heracles: 'The poet seems to be separating the image with regard to Heracles when he says that his *shade* is in Hades, but he *himself* among the gods' (Homer, *Odyssey* 11.601–602). Heracles is above inasmuch as he is a contemplative person, but, insofar he is an active person, 'there is

---

[15] Cf. also 'the other form of soul' in I.1.12 and 'the two souls' in IV.3. Perhaps the notion of a 'double soul' also occurs in *The Letter of James*, which speaks of δίψυχος in 1.8 and 4.8.

40 GEORGE H. VAN KOOTEN

also still a part of him below' (I.1.12; cf. IV.3.27 and VI.4.16). In this respect, Plotinus also speaks of 'the two souls' (IV.3.27).[16]

(b) *St Paul on the Inner Man and Sin*

It is highly remarkable that this specific discussion in Plotinus about the relation between the 'inner man' and his vices, which do not belong to the 'inner man' but to something else, and about the 'involuntary impulse' which causes these vices, also seems to occur in Paul's *Letter to the Romans*.[17] According to Paul, man is 'fleshly', exported for sale under sin (7.14). The word 'exported for sale' (πεπραμένος) is usually used of deporting captives to foreign parts for sale as slaves (LSJ 1394 πέρνημι) and it is difficult to neglect the overtones of deportation from the heavenly fatherland.

Being deported, Paul does not acknowledge his actions as his own, because what he does is not what he wants to do, but what he detests (7.15). He acts against his will, and for this reason, Paul does not regard himself as the one who performs the action, but rather the sin that dwells in him (7.16–17):

---

[16] For a bibliography on this interpretation of Heracles, see A. H. Armstrong, *Plotinus: Ennead IV* (Loeb Classical Library), Cambridge, Mass./London, p. 121 note 2. Cf. also R. Lamberton, *Homer the Theologian: Neoplatonist Allegorical Reading and the Growth of the Epic Tradition* (The Transformation of the Classical Heritage 9), (Berkeley, Calif, 1986), pp. 100–103.

[17] For an analysis of *Rom* 7 against the background of Graeco-Roman culture and philosophy, see also T. Engberg-Pedersen, 'The Reception of Graeco-Roman Culture in the New Testament: The Case of Romans 7.7–25', in: M. Müller & H. Tronier (eds), *The New Testament as Reception* (Journal for the Study of the New Testament Supplement Series 230; Copenhagen International Seminar 11), (London, 2002), pp. 32–57; and R. von Bendemann, 'Die kritische Diastase von Wissen, Wollen und Handeln: Traditionsgeschichtliche Spurensuche eines hellenistischen Topos in Römer 7', *Zeitschrift für die Neutestamentliche Wissenschaft und die Kunde der Älteren Kirche* 95 (2004), pp. 35–63, esp. pp. 55–61 on Epictetus. Von Bendemann, however, scarcely mentions the 'inner man' (see briefly pp. 52, 59, 61–62) and does not refer to Plotinus' discussion of the inner man and the involuntary impulse within man. An excellent approach is undertaken by E. Wasserman, 'The Death of the Soul in Romans 7: Revisiting Paul's Anthropology in Light of Hellenistic Moral Psychology', *Journal of Biblical Literature* 126 (2007), pp. 793–816. Wasserman argues that 'Romans 7 appropriates a Platonic discourse about the nature of the soul and describes what happens to its reasoning part when the bad passions and appetites get the upper hand' (Wasserman, 'The Death of the Soul', 800). See also E. Wasserman, *The Death of the Soul in Romans 7: Sin, Death, and the Law in Light of Hellenistic Moral Psychology* (Wissenschaftliche Untersuchungen zum Neuen Testament II.256), (Tübingen, 2008).

ST PAUL ON SOUL, SPIRIT AND THE INNER MAN
41

For I know that nothing good dwells within me, that is, in my flesh. I can will what is right, but I cannot do it. For I do not do the good I want, but the evil I do not want is what I do. Now if I do what I do not want, it is no longer I that do it, but sin that dwells within me (7.18–20).

These ideas clearly share Plotinus' insistence that it is the compound soul which sins, and not the inner man; if this compound soul does sin, it does so involuntarily. Like Plotinus, Paul contrasts the 'flesh', his 'unspiritual self', with the 'inner man', which is regarded as sinless:

In the inner man (κατὰ τὸν ἔσω ἄνθρωπον), I delight in the law of God (συνήδομαι γὰρ τῷ νόμῳ τοῦ θεοῦ), but I see in my members another law at war with the law of my mind (νοῦς), making me captive to the law of sin that dwells in my members. (…) (…) So then, with my mind (νοῦς) I am a slave to the law of God, but with my flesh I am a slave to the law of sin (7.22–23, 25b).

Although Paul puts it in a more dramatic fashion, he and Plotinus basically seem to agree that the true self, the inner man, is sinless and rejoices in God's law. This compliance with divine law is also brought out in Plotinus. According to him,

when a man (…) comes to the divine, it stands over him and sees to it that he is man; that is, that he lives by the law (νόμος) of providence, which means doing everything that its law says (ὃ δή ἐστι πράττοντα ὅσα ὁ νόμος αὐτῆς λέγει). But it says that those who have become good shall have a good life, now, and laid up for them hereafter as well, and the wicked the opposite (III.2.9).

There is fundamental agreement between Plotinus and Paul about the ethical purpose of the notion of the 'inner man', and of the real possibility that man rejoices in God's law, the law of providence. To acknowledge that there is still an involuntary impulse operative in man is, for them, not to justify unethical conduct. Quite the opposite, since the driving force behind the notion of 'inner man' is the idea that man should be transformed into God's image and become as god-like as possible: Plato's notion of the ὁμοίωσις θεῷ κατὰ τὸ δυνατόν (*Theaetetus* 176B).[18] The Lutheran interpretation of Paul's view on man as 'simul

---

[18] On this notion, see D. Sedley, 'The Ideal of Godlikeness', in: G. Fine (ed.), *Plato*, vol. 2: *Ethics, Politics, Religion, and the Soul* (Oxford Readings in Philosophy), (Oxford, 1999), chap. 14, pp. 309–328; J. Annas, *Platonic Ethics, Old and New* (Cornell Studies in Classical Philology 57), (Ithaca, N.Y., 1999), chap. 3: 'Becoming Like Gods: Ethics, Human Nature, and the Divine', pp. 52–71; and van Kooten, *Paul's Anthropology in Context*, chap. 2.2: 'The "image of God" and "being made like God": The traditions of *homoiōsis*

42   GEORGE H. VAN KOOTEN

iustus et peccator', as if this were a steady, static mixture, leads to a severe misunderstanding of Paul's anthropology.[19] Paul and Plotinus regard the 'inner man' as progressive in nature: 'The soul gets rid of passions *as completely as possible*, altogether if it can, but if it cannot, at least it does not share its emotional excitement' (I.2.5); 'we are being transformed into God's image *with ever-increasing glory*' (*2 Cor* 3.18), and 'the inner man is renewed *day by day*' (4.16).

Paul's deliberations in chapter 7 of his *Letter to the Romans* about the relation between the 'inner man' and the vices which involuntarily remain in man show that he is indeed very well acquainted with the Platonic notion of the 'inner man'. Later on in this letter, Paul's line of thought again closely resembles the ideas already expressed in *2 Cor*. Man is destined to acquire the same form as the image of God's Son, so that he becomes σύμμορφος τῆς εἰκόνος τοῦ υἱοῦ αὐτοῦ (*Rom* 8.29). As is the case in *2 Cor*, this form (μορφή) is the result of his transformation. This transformation is effected by the renewing of one's mind, Paul explains in *Rom* 12. There, Paul exhorts his readers to be transformed by the renewing of the mind (μεταμορφοῦσθε τῇ ἀνακαινώσει τοῦ νοός), so that they can examine the will of God, which—as in Plato's *Euthyphro*—is not arbitrary, but is characterized as that which is good, pleasant and perfect: μεταμορφοῦσθε τῇ ἀνακαινώσει τοῦ νοός, εἰς τὸ δοκιμάζειν ὑμᾶς τί τὸ θέλημα τοῦ θεοῦ, τὸ ἀγαθὸν καὶ εὐάρεστον καὶ τέλειον (12.2).

According to Paul, this inward transformation is in fact—as we have already seen—a λογικὴ λατρεία, a 'logical', intellectual, i.e. non-cultic worship of God (12.1).[20] That this transformation is effected within

---

theōi in Greek philosophy from Plato to Plotinus', pp. 124–181. On its importance in Middle Platonism, contemporarily with Paul, see J. Dillon, *The Middle Platonists: A Study of Platonism 80 B.C. to A.D. 220—Revised edition with new afterword*, London, 1996 (1977[1]), Index, s.v. 'Likeness to God'.

[19] For this Lutheran interpretation, see H. Lichtenberger, *Das Ich Adams und das Ich der Menschheit: Studien zum Menschenbild in Römer 7* (Wissenschaftliche Untersuchungen zum Neuen Testament 164), (Tübingen, 2004), chap. 3.3, pp. 24–28, esp. 27.

[20] For Paul's polemical purpose behind this passage, and behind the beginning of his letter in *Rom* 1, see G. H. van Kooten, 'Pagan and Jewish Monotheism according to Varro, Plutarch and St Paul: The Aniconic, Monotheistic Beginnings of Rome's Pagan Cult—Romans 1:19–25 in a Roman Context', in: A. Hilhorst, É. Puech & E. Tigchelaar (eds), *Flores Florentino: Dead Sea Scrolls and Other Early Jewish Studies in Honour of Florentino García Martínez* (Supplements to the Journal for the Study of Judaism 122), (Leiden/Boston, 2007), pp. 633–651 (= van Kooten, *Paul's Anthropology in Context*, chap. 7.1, pp. 343–356).

ST PAUL ON SOUL, SPIRIT AND THE INNER MAN   43

the mind (νοῦς) is consistent with Paul's view, expressed earlier in the letter, that the 'inner man' is located within the mind. This follows from Paul's saying that he rejoices in the law of God κατὰ τὸν ἔσω ἄνθρωπον, in the inner man (7.22), and serves God's law τῷ μὲν νοΐ, with the mind (7.25).

5. *Concluding Observations*

The passages from the Pauline epistles adduced above seem to demonstrate that in Paul, as in Philo, πνεῦμα—in the trichotomy πνεῦμα, ψυχή, and σῶμα—is identified with νοῦς. Philo's and Paul's anthropology of tripartite man is very similar. One might ask whether there is in fact any difference between their anthropology and pagan trichotomous counterparts. Inasmuch as Philo and Paul refer to the highest part of man not only as νοῦς but preferably (on account of their exegesis of *Gen* 2.7) as πνεῦμα, one might also suggest that they stress the identical, pneumatic nature of God and man in a far more egalitarian and accessible way than is the case in the Greek equivalent anthropology. In order to experience fellowship with God, man does not have to improve the intellectual abilities of his νοῦς but is connected through the πνεῦμα. In Plutarch, as John Dillon explains, the highest class of people, who possess νοῦς, is rather restricted: 'Intellect [νοῦς] thus becomes something rather special, not readily accessible to the mass of humankind.'[21] Both Philo and Paul make transition from νοῦς to πνεῦμα. According to Festugière: 'Du νοῦς au πνεῦμα, voilà toute la différence, ce qui (…) distingue spécifiquement le christianisme.'[22] More than in pagan philosophy, participation in God himself is open to all:

> Notre âme est déjà son πνεῦμα. Tout naturellement, dès lors, elle devient siège de la grâce, Ἡ χάρις μετὰ τοῦ πνεύματος ὑμῶν,—ainsi s'achèvent les lettres aux Galates, VI, 18, aux Philippiens IV, 23, à Philémon 25,—habitacle de l' ἅγιον πνεῦμα, du saint-Esprit. (…) Ainsi, grâce à Paul, grâce au christianisme, ce qu'il y eut de meilleur dans l'âme païenne trouve enfin son vrai sens. (…) L'intelligence devient esprit.[23]

---

[21] Dillon, 'Plutarch and the Separable Intellect', p. 44.
[22] Festugière, *L'idéal religieux des grecs et l'évangile*, p. 217.
[23] Festugière, *L'idéal religieux des grecs et l'évangile*, pp. 219–220.

44   GEORGE H. VAN KOOTEN

The free accessibility of this pneumatic identity is an aspect of Paul's 'Adam Christology', as James Dunn calls it.[24] By participating in Christ's death and resurrection in baptism (*Rom* 6.3–11), the human identity starts to fuse with that of Christ, the second Adam, the second man who, in contrast to the first man, is from heaven. Whereas man still bears the image of the first, earthly Adam (*1 Cor* 15.49), Christians increasingly bear the image of the heavenly man and are increasingly transformed into his likeness (*2 Cor* 3.18). In this way their πνεῦμα is restored and they again turn into trichotomous human beings, *pneumatikoi*. For this reason, they can boldly claim to possess the νοῦς of Christ (*1 Cor* 2.15–16), the νοῦς of the heavenly, archetypal man. Whereas for Plutarch the highest class of human beings, the possessors of νοῦς, is sparsely populated, for Paul, this possession is within reach for all Christians. The more they share in the πνεῦμα and νοῦς, the more their outer man decreases and their inner man, the ἔσω ἄνθρωπος, develops. Despite this significant difference in emphasis, at the same time Paul's anthropology appears to be highly Greek-philosophical in nature; it entails the trichotomous differentiation between πνεῦμα / νοῦς, ψυχή, and σῶμα / σάρξ, and builds upon reflections on the inner man.

---

[24] See J. D. G. Dunn, *The Theology of Paul the Apostle*, (Edinburgh, 1998), chaps 4, 8.6, 10.2. The principle passages containing Adam Christology are *Rom* 5.12–6.11; *1 Cor* 15.20–28; *1 Cor* 15.45–49.

B. CHRISTIAN TRADITION

FAITH AND REASON IN LATE ANTIQUITY: THE PERISHABILITY AXIOM AND ITS IMPACT ON CHRISTIAN VIEWS ABOUT THE ORIGIN AND NATURE OF THE SOUL

Dirk Krausmüller*

In recent years the question of whether Christian belief is reconcilable with scientific fact or whether the two spheres are not rather mutually exclusive has been the subject of vivid discussion. This is without doubt a consequence of the great advances of science in the last two centuries. However, it would be wrong to believe that the tension between faith and reason is a modern phenomenon. When Christianity became a mainstream religion in Late Antiquity it was already confronted with a set of concepts that were considered to be incontrovertible scientific facts. One of these concepts was the so-called perishability axiom, derived from the teachings of Plato and Aristotle, which stated that whatever comes into existence in time must also perish in time. In this article I will investigate how Christian authors dealt with this axiom when they set out their views on created being and in particular how they applied it to the human soul, which according to Scripture had been infused into Adam on the sixth day of creation. I will first define the parameters within which the discussion took place through analysis of selected passages by authors from the late fourth and early fifth centuries, and will then devote the bulk of the article to a study of the writings of two authors from the late fifth and early sixth centuries, Aeneas of Gaza and John of Scythopolis, where the question is given greater prominence than in most other Christian texts of the time.

When in the second half of the fourth century Basil of Caesarea in his *Homilies on the Hexameron* made an attempt at developing a coherent Christian cosmology that could satisfy the expectations of an educated audience he included among his topics the question about the status of created being.[1] Quoting Genesis 1:1 "At the beginning God made..."

---

* Cardiff University.
[1] Basil of Caesarea, *Homiliae in Hexaemeron*, ed. S. Giet (Paris, 1968). Cf. Y. Courtonne, *Saint Basile et l'Hellénisme* (Paris, 1934), p. 26.

48   DIRK KRAUSMÜLLER

he added the observation that "what has begun in time must indeed also come to an end in time" (τὰ ἀπὸ χρόνου ἀρξάμενα πᾶσα ἀνάγκη καὶ ἐν χρόνῳ συντελεσθῆναι),[2] in order to draw the conclusion that the material world must therefore be perishable.[3] Shortly afterwards he then complemented this point with the assertion that "there was a condition more ancient than the coming-to-be of the world, which befits the supra-cosmic powers, and which is supra-temporal, eternal and ever-lasting" (ἦν τις πρεσβυτέρα τῆς τοῦ κόσμου γενέσεως κατάστασις ταῖς ὑπερκοσμίοις δυνάμεσι πρέπουσα ἡ ὑπερχρόνιος ἡ αἰωνία ἡ ἀΐδιος).[4] The two-fold nexus between existence in time and perishability on the one hand and existence beyond time and imperishability on the other was not derived from Scripture, but had a philosophical pedigree and was considered to have been first formulated by Plato and Aristotle.[5] In Late Antiquity this nexus had gained the status of a scientific fact and was accepted as such by members of the elite who usually had at least a smattering of philosophical knowledge.[6] This explains why Basil could base his argument on it without feeling the need to give a justification for its use.

At first sight this conceptual framework seems to support Basil's project of giving a rational basis to the Christian understanding of the world: it explains why this world will come to an end and thus confirms the belief that matter is not co-eternal with God, and at the same time it provides a reason why angels despite being creatures are nevertheless considered to be immortal. However, one class of beings is conspicuously absent from Basil's discussion, namely the souls of human beings, which were also regarded as immortal. Since most Christians conceived of souls as immaterial entities similar to the angels and since Basil creates a close link between creation in time and materiality only one answer seems possible, namely that the souls must also have been created before the visible world and thus must have pre-existed the coming-to-be of their bodies, and this is indeed what some later

---

[2] Basil of Caesarea, *Homiliae in Hexaemeron*, 1.3, ed. Giet, p. 98, and note 6 on p. 99.

[3] Basil of Caesarea, *Homiliae in Hexaemeron*, 1.3, p. 100.

[4] Basil of Caesarea, *Homiliae in Hexaemeron*, 1.5, p. 104.

[5] Cf. e.g. John Philoponus, *De aeternitate mundi et contra Proclum*, 17, ed. H. Rabe (Leipzig, 1899), p. 589, ll. 8–9, with references to Plato, *Respublica*, p. 546A, and Plato, *Phaedrus*, p. 245D.

[6] Gregory of Nyssa even gave it Scriptural authority by seeing it expressed in Wisdom 7:1–18, cf. e.g. *PG*, 45, col. 796BC.

FAITH AND REASON IN LATE ANTIQUITY

readers inferred from Basil's text.[7] Basil never dealt with this question since he gave up his project before he had reached the sixth day of creation. However, his brother Gregory of Nyssa wrote a treatise *De opificio hominis* that was intended to fill this gap.[8] In this text he avers that the soul is created at the same time as the body but he does not mention the perishability axiom in this context although he employs it in another part of his text in order to make the point that the world will come to an end.[9] This suggests that Gregory uses philosophical concepts selectively: he refers to them when he feels that they can shore up Christian beliefs but chooses to disregard them when they appear to contradict these beliefs.

Not all Christian authors, however, dealt in such a cavalier fashion with what the Late Antique elites considered to be scientific fact. Towards the end of the fourth century Nemesius, the bishop of Emesa in Syria, composed the treatise *De natura hominis*, which is heavily influenced by contemporary Neoplatonic philosophy.[10] In the section of his work that sets out different views on the nature of human souls he takes issue with the definition of the soul as "an incorporeal substance created in a body" (οὐσίαν ἀσώματον ἐν σώματι κτιζομένην) that had been proposed by Eunomius, the bishop of Cyzicus.[11] Nemesius accepts the first half of this definition as correct but rejects the second half, which Eunomius had evidently derived from Genesis, because it violates the axiom that "all that has corporeal and at the same time temporal generation is corruptible and mortal" (πᾶν γὰρ τὸ γένεσιν

---

[7] Anastasius of Sinai, *Viae Dux*, 22.3.49–54, ed. K.-H. Uthemann (Turnhout, 1981), p. 299: πάλιν γὰρ εἴρηται τῷ μακαρίῳ Βασιλείῳ ἐν τῷ λόγῳ τῆς Ἐξαημέρου ὅτι πᾶν τὸ ἀρχὴν ἔχον πάντως καὶ τέλος ἔχει· ἐὰν γὰρ ἀρχήν μοι εἴπῃς περὶ τοῦ τέλους, φησί, μὴ ἀμφιβάλῃς· ὅπερ δὴ πάλιν προφέρουσιν ἡμῖν οἱ ματαιόφρονες Ὠριγενιασταὶ βουλόμενοι δεῖξαι τὴν προΰπαρξιν τῶν ψυχῶν ἐν οὐρανοῖς πρὸ τῶν σωμάτων <ὑπαρχουσῶν>.

[8] Gregory of Nyssa, *De hominis opificio*, PG 44, coll. 123–256.

[9] Gregory of Nyssa, *De hominis opificio*, 23, PG 44, coll. 209B–212C. One must be careful not to take Gregory's statements to their logical conclusions. Cf. R. A. Norris, *Manhood and Christ. A Study in the Christology of Theodore of Mopsuestia* (Oxford, 1963), p. 28: 'Nyssen rejects not only the doctrine that the soul is everlasting, but also the view that the individual soul comes into existence apart from its body.' Here Norris no doubt bases his claim on Gregory's acceptance of the perishability axiom. However, there is plenty of evidence that Gregory held no such view.

[10] Nemesius of Emesa, *De natura hominis*, ed. M. Morani (Leipzig, 1987). For a more detailed discussion cf. Norris, *Manhood and Christ*, pp. 21–41.

[11] Nemesius of Emesa, *De natura hominis*, 2.104–108, ed. Morani, p. 30, l. 18– p. 32, l. 2.

50 DIRK KRAUSMÜLLER

ἔχον σωματικὴν ὁμοῦ καὶ χρονικὴν φθαρτόν ἐστι καὶ θνητόν).[12] Here Nemesius makes reference to the same conceptual framework as Basil in his *Homilies* and Gregory of Nyssa in *De opificio hominis* but unlike Basil and Gregory, he spells out the consequences: a being cannot be at the same time incorporeal and temporal. Accordingly he challenges Eunomius' interpretation of Genesis and claims that it is based on a misunderstanding of Moses' statement that God infused the soul into Adam's already existing body "for Moses does not say that the soul was created at that moment *nor is it reasonable*" (οὔτε γὰρ ὁ Μωϋσῆς τότε αὐτὴν ἐκτίσθαι λέγει ὅτε τῷ σώματι ἐνεβάλλετο οὔτε κατὰ λόγον οὕτως ἔχει).[13] Nemesius is of the opinion that Moses' account of the creation only deals with the sensible world. We have already come across this view in Basil's *Homilies on the Hexameron* but there it is mentioned only in the context of the creation of angels. By contrast, Nemesius states explicitly that the immaterial souls must pre-exist their bodies and must have come into being before the creation of the visible world.

We do not know how Eunomius would have responded to Nemesius' position because we no longer have the work that contained his definition of the soul. However, other texts of the time reveal that there existed a radically different conceptual framework. It is set out, for example, in Cyril of Alexandria's *Thesaurus de sancta consubstantiali trinitate*.[14] There Cyril states:

> Everything that appears to be originate in its substance will also once end in non-being when the creator wills it. And whatever has a nature that is capable of suffering would suffer even if it has not yet suffered. By contrast, that which cannot suffer by its nature would never suffer and is something other than the former. And what is always the same has neither begun to be nor indeed does it know a course towards an end.
>
> πᾶν ὅπερ ἂν φαίνηται γεγονὸς κατ᾽ οὐσίαν καὶ εἰς τὸ μὴ εἶναι καταλήξει ποτὲ θελήσαντος τοῦ δημιουργοῦ· καὶ ὅπερ ἂν ἔχοι φύσιν τοῦ παθεῖν δεκτικὴν πάθοι ἂν εἰ καὶ μήπω πέπονθε· τὸ δὲ πάσχειν οὐ πεφυκὸς οὐκ ἄν τι πάθοι ποτὲ καὶ ἕτερον παρ᾽ ἐκεῖνό ἐστι· καὶ τὸ ἀεὶ ὡσαύτως ὂν οὔτε τοῦ εἶναι ἤρξατο οὔτε μὴν οἶδε τὸν ἐπὶ τέλει δρόμον.[15]

---

[12] Nemesius of Emesa, *De natura hominis*, 2.104, p. 30, ll. 22–23.

[13] Nemesius of Emesa, *De natura hominis*, 2.105, p. 31, ll. 3–4.

[14] Cyril of Alexandria, *Thesaurus de sancta consubstantiali trinitate*, PG 75, coll. 9–656.

[15] Cyril of Alexandria, *Thesaurus*, PG 75, col. 345C.

FAITH AND REASON IN LATE ANTIQUITY   51

Like the authors we have been discussing so far Cyril bases his argument on the perishability axiom.[16] However, there is no reference to the distinction between temporal and material on the one hand and supra-temporal and immaterial on the other. Instead we are presented with a stark opposition: whatever has a beginning has an end and whatever has no beginning has no end. It is clear that the first category now also encompasses invisible beings, and indeed the class of beings that Cyril has in mind here are the angels.[17] Of course, Cyril also believed that angels and human souls are immortal. However, this immortality is not grounded in their natural make-up but rather in the will of God, which overrides natural restrictions. In his *Thesaurus* Cyril argues exclusively within a Christian framework but in other writings he seeks additional justification in Greek philosophy. In his apologetic treatise *Contra Julianum* he adduces a passage from Plato's *Timaeus* where the demiurge addresses the naturally perishable Gods, which are kept alive through his will.[18] However, there can be no doubt that Plato is only brought into the discussion because references to Greek philosophy were one of the staples of Christian apologetic literature, which had by then become more or less fossilised.[19] There is certainly no sign of an engagement with or even an awareness of the problems inherent in Plato's position.[20] This is not surprising because Cyril's interest in the issue was not prompted by philosophical considerations but rather caused by the specifically Christian concern for a proper distinction between God and creation: he evidently considered it to

---

[16] Like Gregory, he gives it a Scriptural pedigree by quoting Ps. 101:27–28.

[17] Cyril of Alexandria, *Thesaurus, PG* 75, col. 345D, is a proof that the Son of God is not consubstantial with the angels: εἰ γὰρ καὶ ἀθάνατόν τι χρῆμα ὁ ἄγγελός ἐστι διὰ τὴν οὕτω κειμένην ἐπ' αὐτῷ τοῦ ποιήσαντος βούλησίν τε καὶ χάριν ἀλλ' ἐπείπερ ἀρχὴν τοῦ εἶναι ἔχει δύναιτ' ἂν καὶ εἰς τέλος ἐλθεῖν.

[18] Cyril of Alexandria, *Contra Julianum*, II, *PG* 76, coll. 557–612, esp. col. 597AB. Cf. *Timaeus*, p. 41B.

[19] Cyril was not the first Christian author to appeal to the speech of the demiurge from the *Timaeus*: it had already been quoted in the second century AD by Justin the Martyr. Cf. e.g. J. C. M. van Winden, *An early Christian philosopher. Justin Martyr's Dialogue with Trypho. Chapters one to nine. Introduction, Text and Commentary* (Leiden, 1971), pp. 84–110.

[20] Such problems were only highlighted by Christian authors when they wished to question the value of Greek philosophy. Zacharias of Mitylene, for example, criticises Plato for contradicting himself when he claims on the one hand that everything that comes into being will also pass away and states on the other hand that the divine will overrides this axiom. Cf. Zacharias of Mitylene, *Ammonius*, ed. M. Minniti Colonna (Napoli, 1973), p. 118, ll. 695–701.

52   DIRK KRAUSMÜLLER

be a dangerous blurring of boundaries if angels and human souls were somehow to be regarded 'naturally' immortal.[21] As a consequence the very concept of nature is completely eroded as can be seen from the conclusion that Cyril draws from his quotation of the *Timaeus*: "For as I have said nothing is immortal or insoluble; but what God has willed for each of his creatures, that is its nature" (ἀθάνατον μὲν γὰρ ὡς ἔφην ἢ ἄλυτον οὐδέν· ἡ δὲ ἐφ' ἑκάστῳ τῶν πεποιημένων τοῦ θεοῦ βούλησις τοῦτο φύσις αὐτῷ).[22]

There can be little doubt that Cyril is representative of the views of the majority of Christians whereas theologians like Nemesius would always have been few and far between, in particular since the notion of pre-existence was regarded with increasing suspicion and since Christians who accepted it such as the Origenists were considered to be little better than pagans.[23] To judge by the surviving texts the issue seems to have been of minor importance in the fourth and early fifth centuries: it is usually treated in passing in texts that have quite different objectives.[24] This situation, however, changed a hundred years later when the perishability axiom began to be discussed more frequently and in greater depth. This development must be seen in the context of the astonishing revival of Neoplatonic philosophy under the aegis of Proclus. This revival prompted a vivid Christian response, which took two forms: Christian intellectuals attempted to refute explicit criticisms that Neoplatonic philosophers directed against basic tenets of their belief system—a typical example is John Philoponus' *De aeternitate mundi contra Proclum*—or they strove to Christianise the Neoplatonic system—a development that led to the creation of the so-called Pseudo-Dionysian corpus. John Philoponus, in particular, discusses the perishability axiom frequently both in his theological and in his

---

[21] Cyril composed his *Thesaurus* in order to refute the Arians who did not accept the divine status of the Son of God and therefore had to emphasise the difference between creator and creation.

[22] Cyril of Alexandria, *Contra Julianum*, 2, *PG* 76, col. 597C.

[23] Cf. E. A. Clark, *The Origenist Controversy: the cultural construction of an early Christian debate* (Princeton, N.J., 1992), which focuses on the late fourth and early fifth centuries. On Origenism in the sixth century cf. B. Daley, "What Did Origenism Mean in the Sixth Century?", in *Origeniana Sexta. Origène et la Bible. Actes du Colloquium Origenianum Sextum, Chantilly, 30 août–3 septembre 1993*, ed. G. Dorival and A. Le Boulluec (Leuven, 1995), pp. 627–638.

[24] Gregory of Nyssa and Gregory of Nazianzus, for example, employ it to score cheap points in their polemics against the Arians, cf. e.g. Gregory of Nazianzus, *Oratio*, 29.13, ed. P. Gallay (Paris, 1978), p. 202, l. 10.

FAITH AND REASON IN LATE ANTIQUITY   53

philosophical writings.[25] However, proper study of these texts go would well beyond the scope of this article.[26] I have therefore chosen to focus on two further authors who contributed to the debate, the Christian sophist Aeneas of Gaza, a renowned teacher of rhetoric who lived in the late fifth and early sixth century,[27] and the bishop John of Scythopolis in Palestine, a writer of theological treatises who in the first half of the sixth century made a name for himself as a defender of Chalcedonian Christology against Monophysite attacks.[28] Aeneas dealt with the question in a dialogue called *Theophrastus*, which ostensibly sets itself the task to win over pagan philosophers through philosophical arguments to the Christian view that human souls were created together with their bodies.[29] By contrast, John tackled the issue in his *scholia* on the Pseudo-Dionysian corpus, which show strong philosophical influences that are by no means always mediated through the text he is setting out to explain.[30]

---

[25] For general introductions to these authors, cf. R. R. K. Sorabji, "John Philoponus," *TRE* 17 (1987), pp. 144–150, and A. Louth, *Dionysius the Areopagite* (London, 1989).

[26] Philoponus' views have repeatedly been discussed in secondary literature, cf. e.g. L. Judson, "God or Nature? Philoponus on Generability and Perishability," in *Philoponus and the Rejection of Aristotelian Science*, ed. R. Sorabji (Leiden, 1987), pp. 179–196, and L. P. Schrenk, "John Philoponus on the Immortal Soul", *Proceedings of the American Catholic Philosophical Association* 64 (1990), pp. 151–160. However, none of these studies is based on in-depth study of both his philosophical and his Christian writings. For Pseudo-Denys, cf. e.g. *Corpus Dionysiacum*, I: *De divinis nominibus*, 4.25, ed. B. R. Suchla (Berlin, New York, 1990), p. 173, ll. 6–7, and the discussion in the last part of this article.

[27] On Aeneas' biography see M. Wacht, *Aeneas von Gaza als Apologist. Seine Kosmologie im Verhältnis zum Platonismus* (Bonn, 1969), pp. 15–17. Aeneas is attested between 484 and 492.

[28] On John's biography see most recently R. Aubert, "Jean, évêque de Scythopolis, dit Jean le Scolastique (première moitié du VIe s.)," *Dictionnaire d'Histoire et de Géographie Ecclésiastiques* 27, pp. 617–619. John is attested between the years 536 and 548.

[29] Aeneas of Gaza, *Theophrastus*, ed. M. E. Colonna (Napoli, 1958).

[30] The following discussion will be based on the *Scholia in Dionysii Areopagitae librum de Divinis Nominibus*, PG 4, coll. 158–432. In Migne's *Patrologia Graeca* these *scholia* are published under the name of Maximus Confessor. However, a substantial proportion of these scholia have been attributed to John of Scythopolis, based on a comparison with the Syriac translation, cf. H. U. von Balthasar, "Das Scholienwerk des Johannes von Scythopolis," *Scholastik* 5 (1940), pp. 16–38. Unfortunately, the critical edition of John's *scholia* on *De divinis nominibus* by B. R. Suchla has not yet appeared. A list of the *scholia* that also appear in the Syriac translation can be found in B. R. Suchla, "Die sogenannten Maximus-Scholien des Corpus Dionysiacum Areopagiticum," *Nachrichten der Akademie der Wissenschaften in Göttingen, Philosophisch-historische Klasse*, 1980, fasc. 3 (Göttingen, 1980), pp. 31–66. In the following only *scholia* found in this list will be considered. For an English translation of a selection of John's *scholia*

54 DIRK KRAUSMÜLLER

Aeneas of Gaza's *Theophrastus* is a philosophical dialogue in the Platonic tradition. The scene is set at the beginning of the text where the Platonic overtones are particularly strong. Having embarked on a journey to Athens, the Christian Euxitheus is forced off his course by adverse winds and has to go ashore in Alexandria where he had once studied under the Neoplatonic philosopher Hierocles. There he is introduced by a former fellow-pupil to the pagan philosopher Theophrastus from Athens who happens to be on a visit to Alexandria.[31] From the manner in which these figures 'talk shop' readers may well draw the conclusion that the ensuing discussion will be based on commonly accepted philosophical premises, including the perishability axiom, and will therefore be curious to see how Aeneas will manage to reconcile the two parts of his project, namely "that there is no pre-existence of human beings *and* that the soul is immortal" (ὅτι οὐκ ἔστιν ἀνθρώπων προβιοτὴ καὶ ὅτι ἀθάνατος ἡ ψυχή).[32]

The discussion about this topic starts in earnest when the pagan interlocutor Theophrastus raises the question about the origin of the souls. His Christian counterpart Euxitheus replies that such a question is inadmissible. Instead, one should simply accept that the existence and specific nature of each being, whether it be an angel or a star, is the direct consequence of an act of divine will.[33] This is a stark expression of Christian voluntarism, quite similar to what we have already found in Cyril of Alexandria. However, this does not prevent Theophrastus from asking further questions: he wishes to be informed why God created all the other rational powers beforehand whereas he continues to bring forth human souls.[34] Euxitheus responds that creation of the souls before their bodies would entail a long period of idleness and thus contradict the purposeful character of creation. This is a traditional argument that may well have passed muster in a discussion with pagans.[35] However, the main focus is on a radically different explanation:

---

cf. P. Rorem and J. C. Lamoreaux, *John of Scythopolis and the Dionysian Corpus. Annotating the Areopagite* (Oxford, 1998).

[31] Aeneas of Gaza, *Theophrastus*, ed. Colonna, p. 2, l. 1–p. 4, l. 17. The first words of the dialogue, 'where to and where from?' are a literal quotation from *Phaedrus*, p. 227A.

[32] Aeneas of Gaza, *Theophrastus*, ed. Colonna, p. 1, ll. 2–3.

[33] Aeneas of Gaza, *Theophrastus*, p. 36, l. 18–p. 37, l. 6.

[34] Aeneas of Gaza, *Theophrastus*, p. 37, ll. 16–18.

[35] Aeneas of Gaza, *Theophrastus*, p. 38, l. 18–p. 39, l. 10.

FAITH AND REASON IN LATE ANTIQUITY

God knew beforehand that human beings would admire the rational powers and consider them to be without beginning and ingenerate and that they would fashion many principles and countless gods and thus introduce a chaotic democracy instead of an orderly monarchy.... Therefore he even now brings forth our souls, which are also rational, as an example of his power and as an instruction of those who pre-exist (i.e. of the angels), that all things and all rational and intellectual powers and substances have come forth and are still coming forth from one creator and one cause.

προεῖδεν ὁ θεὸς ὅτι τὰς λογικὰς δυνάμεις θαυμάσαντες ἄνθρωποι, ἀνάρχους τε καὶ ἀγενήτους νομίσαντες καὶ πολλὰς ἀρχὰς καὶ μυρίους θεοὺς ποιοῦντες, δημοκρατίαν ἄτακτον ἀντὶ τῆς τεταγμένης μοναρχίας εἰσοίσουσιν...διά τοι τοῦτο τὰς ἡμετέρας ψυχὰς λογικὰς οὔσας ἔτι καὶ νῦν προβάλλεται, παράδειγμα τῆς αὐτοῦ δυνάμεως καὶ διδασκαλίαν τῶν προϋφεστώτων, ὡς ἐξ ἑνὸς δημιουργοῦ πάντα καὶ ἐκ μιᾶς ἀρχῆς πᾶσα λογικὴ καὶ νοερὰ δύναμις καὶ οὐσία προῆλθε καὶ ἔτι πρόεισι.[36]

With this reasoning the common ground between Christians and pagans has clearly been left behind: Euxitheus sketches a world that is not based on rational rules but rather is the result of 'free' divine decisions that have as their sole purpose the shepherding of angels and human beings towards a proper understanding of their status as created beings.

It is at this point that the pagan Theophrastus brings the perishability axiom into the discussion: "If the soul comes into existence in time, how can it be immortal?" (ἀλλ᾽ εἰ ἐν χρόνῳ προέρχεται, πῶς ἀθάνατος).[37] This query evidently follows on from his previous question about angels and human souls: the former are not mentioned again because their creation before time means that in their case the problem does not arise. By contrast, the immortality of the soul seems to hang in the air and therefore requires an explanation. However, as the previous responses by Euxitheus show, Theophrastus is by now hopelessly out of step with the reasoning of his Christian counterpart who does not even seem capable of conceiving what a 'natural law' is. This is glaringly obvious from the way in which Euxitheus then deals with the perishability axiom:

There are not two different creators of the heavenly powers and of the human soul but one and the same brings forth both the former and the

---

[36] Aeneas of Gaza, *Theophrastus*, p. 37, l. 24–p. 38, l. 7. This 'educational' argument is then further supported with examples taken from nature: God creates the moon as waxing and waning so that the other stars are not believed to be ingenerate. Cf. Aeneas of Gaza, *Theophrastus*, p. 38, ll. 7–13.
[37] Aeneas of Gaza, *Theophrastus*, p. 39, l. 12.

56 DIRK KRAUSMÜLLER

latter. And if it is the same, then it is not odd if one power and one knowledge, then as now, creates it (sc. the soul): for the power of the creator does not wane over time nor does his knowledge come to an end at a certain point; accordingly we must either admit that not even the former are immortal or we must necessarily be persuaded that it, too, is such a one.

οὐκ ἄλλος τὰς ἄνω δυνάμεις ἄλλος δὲ τὴν τοῦ ἀνθρώπου ψυχὴν δημιουργεῖ ἀλλ᾽ ὁ αὐτὸς ἐκείνας τε καὶ ταύτην προβάλλεται· εἰ δὲ ὁ αὐτὸς καινὸν οὐδὲν εἰ μία δύναμις καὶ ἐπιστήμη τότε καὶ νῦν ταύτην ἐργάζεται· οὐ γὰρ χρόνῳ ἡ τοῦ δημιουργοῦ δύναμις ἐναπομαραίνεται οὐδὲ ἐπιστήμη μέχρι τοῦ διορίζεται· ἢ τοίνυν μηδ᾽ ἐκείνας ἀθανάτους εἶναι συγχωρήσομεν ἢ καὶ ταύτην ἀνάγκη τοιαύτην εἶναι πείσεσθαι.[38]

From this passage it is clear that for Euxitheus God's will and power are the only factors worth considering. God decides to endow certain classes of his creatures with eternal life and puts this decision into practice by making them immune against the ravages of time. In such a framework the distinction between 'supra-temporal' and 'temporal' has become meaningless, if it is indeed still understood by Aeneas for one rather gets the sense that he sees eternity simply as a never-ending time-span.

It is evident that such an argument can be made without considering the specific characteristics of the creatures on which immortality is conferred. Nevertheless, Euxitheus also refers to the rational nature of human souls, which they share with angels, and which according to him shows that they are likewise immortal. Yet this supposed link between rationality and immortality is not supported by a logical proof. Instead, Euxitheus develops an argument based on God's stated intention in Genesis to make man in his image and likeness: he argues that God would have gone against his own word if he had made human souls mortal because he himself is immortal and the soul would not be like him if it could die.[39]

Euxitheus then returns to his main argument with a direct challenge to Plato's perishability axiom, based on a lengthy quotation from the speech of the demiurge in the *Timaeus*.[40] This quotation is followed by references to several Platonic concepts such as the ever-movement and self-movement of the soul, which Euxitheus presents as sure

---

[38] Aeneas of Gaza, *Theophrastus*, p. 39, ll. 14–19. The supporting argument of direct creation is hardly conclusive since God also created heaven and earth 'directly'.

[39] Aeneas of Gaza, *Theophrastus*, p. 39, ll. 20–25. Aeneas is careful to distinguish the divine likeness of angels and souls from consubstantiality with God.

[40] Aeneas of Gaza, *Theophrastus*, p. 40, ll. 1–5. Cf. *Timaeus*, p. 41B.

FAITH AND REASON IN LATE ANTIQUITY

57

indicators for the immortality of the soul.[41] It is evident that these notions are dear to the speaker. However, it is also clear that they are ensconced by two statements that deny Plato's fundamental premise of the soul's ingeneracy, firstly the reference to the demiurge's decision in the *Timaeus* to confer immortality on generate beings, and secondly Aeneas' own conclusion that "he who has given being has also given ever-being as a gift to our souls: and the gift was nature" (ὁ γὰρ τὸ εἶναι δοὺς καὶ τὸ ἀεὶ τὰς ἡμετέρας ψυχὰς εἶναι δῶρον παρέσχε· καὶ τὸ δῶρον φύσις ἦν).[42]

Taken together, the quotation from the *Timaeus* and Aeneas' own statement seem to imply that mortality is the 'normal state' for created being and that immortality is something that needs to be bestowed in addition. However, this is not as clear as it might seem because as we have seen Euxitheus no longer subscribes to the perishability axiom but rather focuses on God's limitless power as the reason for the immortality of beings, regardless of whether they are created before time or in time. This makes one wonder whether it is not perishability rather than imperishability that requires an explanation, and this is indeed borne out in the following section in which the discussion turns to the material world. There Euxitheus argues that the world is composite and will therefore dissolve. However, at the same time he affirms that this dissolution will not result in non-being but in a change to imperishability, which is clearly regarded as the result of a full and unchecked exercise of divine power.

At this point Theophrastus raises the question why God did then not create the world incorruptible right from the beginning.[43] In his answer to Theophrastus Euxitheus attempts to make sure that God cannot be accused of powerlessness by pointing to parts of nature that are already now incorruptible.[44] The reason why this incorruptibility has not been extended to all creation is again explained through secondary considerations: according to Euxitheus God wishes to give the ideas ample opportunity to impress themselves on matter,[45] and he wishes

---

[41] Aeneas of Gaza, *Theophrastus*, p. 40, ll. 7–12.

[42] Aeneas of Gaza, *Theophrastus*, p. 40, ll. 14–16.

[43] Aeneas of Gaza, *Theophrastus*, p. 48, ll. 19–20.

[44] Aeneas of Gaza, *Theophrastus*, p. 49, l. 19–p. 50, l. 3. Aeneas refers to the pagan Olympus and the Islands of the Blessed but mention of the *logia* suggests that this is a veiled reference to the Christian Heaven and Paradise. On the Platonic background for some of this argument cf. Wacht, *Aeneas von Gaza*, p. 109.

[45] Aeneas of Gaza, *Theophrastus*, p. 50, ll. 5–13.

58 DIRK KRAUSMÜLLER

to teach rational creatures that their immortality is not a necessity but a gift and that they are not made immortal because the option to make them mortal did not exist.[46]

It is evident that for Aeneas the perishability axiom has lost all meaning. He simply cannot conceive of perishability as something that is of necessity inherent in the structure of temporal beings. For him it can only be grounded in acts of divine self-limitation, which are in turn rationalised as 'providential' measures intended to keep angels and human beings from getting above themselves.[47] While he still pays lipservice to distinctions such as material and immaterial, composite and simple, or supra-temporal and temporal, these distinctions have now become irrelevant since the rationally organised world of the philosophers has been replaced by the world of faith where everything is explained through the interplay between divine will and divine power.[48]

Despite the Platonic trappings of the *Theophrastus* we must therefore conclude that Aeneas had little interest in engaging with pagan philosophers on their own terms. However, not all Christian intellectuals were equally unconcerned about the scientific knowledge of their time. A much more sophisticated contributor to the discourse was the second author whom I have chosen to focus on, John Scholasticus, the bishop of Scythopolis and first scholiast of the *Corpus Areopagiticum*. In the remainder of this article I will try to glean from John's *scholia* on Pseudo-Denys' treatise *De divinis nominibus* what views he holds about the immortality of angels and of human souls and what argu-

---

[46] Aeneas of Gaza, *Theophrastus*, p. 50, l. 13–p. 51, l. 12.

[47] The concept of divine self-limitation would later be developed by Leontius of Jerusalem in his treatise *Contra Nestorianos*, 7.11, *PG* 86, col. 1768hi. For a discussion cf. D. Krausmüller, "Divine self-invention: Leontius of Jerusalem's reinterpretation of the Patristic model of the Christian God," *Journal of Theological Studies* 57 (2006), pp. 526–545.

[48] I am well aware that Wacht is much more prepared to see Aeneas in conventional Neoplatonic terms, However, Wacht tends to focus on the different arguments in isolation and to pay much more attention to similarities than to discrepancies and as a consequence he tends to lose sight of the fundamental differences between Aeneas' approach and that of traditional philosophers. Cf. esp. Wacht, *Aeneas von Gaza*, pp. 38–50, where Aeneas' contention that all beings are created by God is compared with the Neoplatonic concept of emanation, without any consideration for context or implications! Significantly, the only Christian aspects mentioned in this section are obvious features such as the agency of Jesus Christ.

FAITH AND REASON IN LATE ANTIQUITY 59

ments he puts forward in order to support these views.[49] Like all his contemporaries John of Scythopolis believes in the immortality of incorporeal beings,[50] angels as well as human souls: in a doxographical passage he denounces those Greek philosophers that regarded the soul as perishable and praises Plato's position whom he only faults for not having considered a future resurrection of the body.[51] At the same time he accepts the nexus between generation and corruption.[52] Like Nemesius before him, he maintains that the axiom is conditional on the framework in which generation takes place. Commenting on *De divinis nominibus* V.4 where Pseudo-Denys characterises God both as "the eternity of the entities that are" (αἰὼν τῶν ὄντων) and as "the time of the entities that come to be" (χρόνος τῶν γινομένων),[53] John first defines the αἰών as the *nunc stans* and then clarifies its relationship to God on the one hand and to the ὄντα on the other:

> Accordingly, eternity is not the substrate, but that which shines forth from the substrate itself: what is intelligible and what is invisible is according to the apostle eternal entities, and eternal entities are not eternity itself but that which participates in eternity, that is in the non-dimensional and boundless life.

> αἰὼν τοίνυν ἐστὶ οὐ τὸ ὑποκείμενον ἀλλὰ τὸ ἐξ αὐτοῦ τοῦ ὑποκειμένου ἐκλάμπον· τὰ οὖν νοητὰ καὶ τὰ μὴ ὁρώμενα κατὰ τὸν ἀπόστολον αἰώνια· αἰώνιον δὲ οὐκ αὐτός ἐστι ὁ αἰὼν ἀλλὰ τὸ αἰῶνος μετέχον τουτέστι τῆς ἀδιαστάτου καὶ ἀπείρου ζωῆς.[54]

---

[49] The *scholia* have repeatedly been studied but without focus on the perishability axiom. Cf. B. R. Suchla, "Verteidigung eines platonischen Denkmodells einer christlichen Welt," *Nachrichten der Akademie der Wissenschaften in Göttingen, Philosophisch-historische Klasse*, 1995, 1 (Göttingen, 1995), pp. 1–28; P. Rorem, "The doctrinal concerns of the first dyonisian [sic] scholiast, John of Scythopolis," in *Denys l'Aréopagite et sa postérité en Orient et en Occident. Actes du Colloque International Paris, 21–24 Septembre 1994*, ed. Y. De Andia, (Paris, 1997), pp. 187–200; B. R. Suchla, "Das Scholienwerk des Johannes von Scythopolis zu den areopagitischen Traktaten in seiner philosophie- und theologiegeschichtlichen Bedeutung," in *Denys l'Aréopagite et sa postérité*, ed. De Andia, pp. 155–165.

[50] Cf. e.g. John of Scythopolis, *Scholia in De Divinis Nominibus*, PG 4, col. 336B10–12.

[51] John of Scythopolis, *Scholia in Ecclesiasticam Hierarchiam*, PG 4, col. 123D5–126A13.

[52] John of Scythopolis, *Scholia in De Divinis Nominibus*, PG 4, col. 217C6–7: ὡμολόγηται τὰ ἐν γενέσει πάντως καὶ φθείρεσθαι. The context of this statement will be discussed in detail further down.

[53] Pseudo-Denys, *De Divinis Nominibus*, 5.4, ed. Suchla, p. 182, l. 21–p. 183, l. 1.

[54] John of Scythopolis, *Scholia in De Divinis Nominibus*, PG 4, col. 313D5–10. [In the following abbreviated to *Scholia*.]

60　　　　　　　　　　DIRK KRAUSMÜLLER

Here John explains eternity as an emanation of the divine in which the entities that are called eternal then participate.[55] Despite the reference to II Corinthians 4:18, "what is not seen is eternal" (τὰ μὴ βλεπόμενα αἰώνια), it has long been noticed that this passage is a literal borrowing from *Enneads* III.7.[56] However, John does not adopt Plotinus' conceptual framework without change for he continues:

> As maker of the entities that participate in eternity (that is, in ever-being), which are called eternities according to a relation based on likeness, God is said to have made the eternities (that is, the intelligibles), since he is their eternity and conserver.
>
> τῶν αἰῶνος τουτέστι τοῦ ἀεὶ ὄντος μετεχόντων καθ' ὁμοιότητα αἰώνων λεγομένων ποιητὴς ὁ θεὸς πεποιηκέναι τοὺς αἰῶνας λέγεται ἀντὶ τοῦ τὰ νοητὰ αἰὼν αὐτῶν ὢν καὶ συνοχεύς.[57]

This sentence is evidently based on Hebrews 1:1-2, "God...made the eternities" (ὁ θεός...ἐποίησεν τοὺς αἰῶνας), which is then rephrased by John in such a way that the Biblical term αἰῶνες becomes synonymous with Plotinus' αἰώνια.[58] This time the Biblical reference is not merely cosmetic but has an important function within the argument: it complements the Neoplatonic framework of emanation and participation with the specifically Christian notion of creation. This combination results in a highly ambiguous statement, which establishes a precarious balance between philosophical and religious concerns: through his borrowings from Plotinus John is able to interpret Scriptural data in a way that safeguards a rational explanation for the imperishability of the νοητά because their creation is now firmly located in the eternal realm, and through the explicit mention of creation he can allay Christian fears that recourse to Plotinian concepts might blur the boundaries between the νοητά and God.

---

[55] God himself is defined as 'supra-substantial' (ὑπερουσίως) and 'supra-eternal' (ὑπεραιωνίως).

[56] W. Beierwaltes and R. Kannicht, "Plotin-Testimonia bei Johannes von Skythopolis," *Hermes* 96 (1968), pp. 247–251, who refer to Plotinus, *Enneads*, 3.3.23–24: ὥστε εἶναι τὸν αἰῶνα οὐ τὸ ὑποκείμενον ἀλλὰ τὸ ἐξ αὐτοῦ τοῦ ὑποκειμένου οἷον ἐκλάμπον, and *Enneads*, 3.2.25–26: ὥσπερ οὐδὲ τὸν αἰῶνα ἐροῦμεν αἰώνιον· τὸ γὰρ αἰώνιον τὸ μετέχον αἰῶνος. Cf. R.M. Frank, "The use of the Enneads by John of Skythopolis," *Le Muséon* 100 (1988), pp. 101–108. On Plotinus' views on eternity and time in general cf. W. Beierwaltes, *Plotin, Über Ewigkeit und Zeit* (Frankfurt, 1967), and also S. Sambursky and S. Pines, *The Concept of Time in Late Neoplatonism* (Jerusalem, 1971).

[57] John of Scythopolis, *Scholia*, PG 4, coll. 313D10–316A2.

[58] Cf. Hebrews 1:1-2: ὁ θεός...ἐλάλησεν ἡμῖν ἐν υἱῷ...δι' οὗ καὶ ἐποίησεν τοὺς αἰῶνας.

FAITH AND REASON IN LATE ANTIQUITY   61

Several references to this passage in other *scholia* leave no doubt that it was intended by John as a definite presentation of his position on the issue.[59] In one respect, however, it remains curiously vague. We are never informed about the identity of the intelligibles that are eternal through participation in and creation by the divine as eternity. What are the most likely candidates? One clue we are given is the identification of the αἰώνια with the Biblical αἰῶνες. In Patristic interpretations such references can be taken to refer to angels,[60] and this is also the case in John's *scholia*: later on he paraphrases 'maker of the αἰῶνες' as 'maker of angels'.[61] John's earlier reference to II Corinthians as a Scriptural justification for the equation of νοητά and αἰώνια points into the same direction. When he quotes the same verse elsewhere in his *scholia* he creates a straightforward identification of Paul's 'invisible things' with angels and the upper heaven.[62]

This raises the question: how does John support his belief in the imperishability of human souls? As a first step to finding an answer we need to return to John's exegesis of *De divinis nominibus* V.4 and explore the complementary statement that God is 'the time of those entities that come to be':

> We say that time once reposed in ever-being and that it shone forth in decreasing degree when later it was necessary for the visible nature to come forth. Accordingly we call time the procession to the sensibles of the goodness of God in order to create these.
>
> τὸν χρόνον (sc. λέγομεν) τότε μὲν ἐν τῷ ἀεὶ ὄντι ἀναπαύεσθαι, ἐκφανῆναι δὲ καθ᾽ ὑπόβασιν ὅτε καὶ ὕστερον φύσιν ὁρατὴν ἐχρῆν προελθεῖν· τὴν οὖν

---

[59] John of Scythopolis, *Scholia*, PG 4, col. 208B9–12 (Syr: Suchla, 48): αἰώνιον μέν φασι τὸν τῶν αἰώνων ποιητὴν καὶ τῷ ὄντι αἰῶνα εἴγε ὁ ἀεὶ ὢν αὐτός ἐστιν ὅθεν καὶ αἰὼν λέγεται· αἰώνιον δέ ἐστιν οὐκ αὐτὸς ὁ αἰὼν ἀλλὰ τὸ αἰῶνος μετέχον. John of Scythopolis, *Scholia*, 336A3–9 (not in Syr, but in HA, MA, FA, cf. Suchla 51): εἴρηται καὶ ἀνωτέρω αἰώνιον λέγεσθαι κυρίως οὐκ αὐτὸν τὸν αἰῶνα ἀλλὰ τὸ αἰῶνος μετέχον.

[60] Cf. e.g. Pseudo-Athanasius, *Sermo maior de fide*, PG 26, col. 1284A8–10: ὁ πατὴρ γὰρ διὰ τοῦ υἱοῦ ἐποίησεν τοὺς αἰῶνας—ἀρχάς τε καὶ ἐξουσίας—καὶ πᾶσαν κτίσιν.

[61] John of Scythopolis, *Scholia*, PG 4, col. 229B3–4 (Syr: Suchla, 48): ποιητὴς τῶν αἰώνων ἅτε τῶν ἀγγέλων ποιητὴς ὤν. Cf. also *Scholia*, PG 4, col. 336A11–B2 (Syr: Suchla, 51): μέτρα τῶν ὄντων εἰσὶν οἱ αἰῶνες τῶν νοητῶν… τὰ γὰρ νοητὰ ὡς ὑπὸ μέτρου μετρεῖται τοῦ αἰῶνος εἰ καὶ ὁμωνύμως τῷ μετροῦντι αἰῶνι καὶ τὰ μετρούμενα λέγονται· αἰῶνες γὰρ λέγονται καὶ οἱ ἄγγελοι.

[62] John of Scythopolis, *Scholia*, PG 4, col. 324C10–13 (Syr: Suchla, 50): σημειωτέον δὲ ὅτι τὰς νοητὰς δυνάμεις αἰωνίας ἐκάλεσεν ὡς αἰῶνος μετεχούσας· ἡ δὲ τοῦτο λέγουσα γραφή ἐστι· τὰ γὰρ βλεπόμενα πρόσκαιρα· τὰ δὲ μὴ βλεπόμενα αἰώνια. Cf. also col. 385D5–8: εἴτε ἀγγέλους εἴτε ἀνώτερον οὐρανόν.

62 DIRK KRAUSMÜLLER

εἰς τὰ αἰσθητὰ πρόοδον τῆς εἰς τὸ ταῦτα δημιουργεῖν ἀγαθότητος τοῦ θεοῦ καλοῦμεν χρόνον.[63]

This passage, which defines time as a further emanation of the divine, is also adapted from *Enneads* III.7, although again not without introducing the Christian corrective of creation. It contains Plotinus' famous explanation of time as the life of the soul, which is discursive and sequential; and the concomitant rejection of a physical explanation is then duly reproduced in the remainder of the *scholion*.[64] Thus one might think that John links the human soul to this mode of existence of the divine. It would certainly fit in with what he says about the operations of souls. Whereas he states that angels operate 'supra-cosmically' (ὑπερκοσμίως) and 'in a unified manner' (ἑνιαίως), which locates them in the timeless realm, he speaks about the 'descent' and 'division' of the 'simple' human νοῦς into discursive and sequential time-bound thought, in very much the same language that he uses for the divine processus into the world.[65] It is evident that this model would safeguard the imperishability of human souls: while participating in time they would nevertheless not be subjected to corruption in the way of sensible beings because like time itself they would have their ground of being in eternity. However, there is no sign that John intended such an explanation: while he explicitly speaks about the participation of the αἰώνια in eternity he creates no such link between time and the souls but instead focuses exclusively on the sensible world.[66]

This negative conclusion can be corroborated when we look at other passages where John presents a static picture of the hierarchy of being. These passages invariably juxtapose the ὄντα and νοητά with the γινόμενα and αἰσθητά (further characterised as μεριστά and μετάβλητα), which

---

[63] John of Scythopolis, *Scholia*, PG 4, col. 316A8–13. Cf. Beierwaltes and Kannicht, "Plotin-Testimonia", pp. 247–251, with reference to Plotinus, *Enneads*, 3.11.3: περὶ ἓν ἑστῶσαν· χρόνος δὲ οὔπω ἦν ἢ ἐκείνοις γε οὐκ ἦν, γεννήσομεν δὲ χρόνον λόγῳ καὶ φύσει τοῦ ὑστέρου...ἐκφανείς...πρότερον...ἐν τῷ ὄντι ἀνεπαύετο.

[64] John of Scythopolis, *Scholia*, PG 4, col. 316A13–B7. Cf. Sh. Sambursky, "The Concept of Time in Later Neoplatonism," *Proceedings of the Israel Academy of Science and Humanities* II.8 (1966), pp. 153–167.

[65] Cf. e.g. John of Scythopolis, *Scholia*, PG 4, col. 193D3–B1, and col. 256B1–C3.

[66] Interestingly John gives discursive thought a material substrate and thus at least implies that it may be mortal, cf. *Scholia*, PG 4, coll. 193D9–196A4. By contrast, the human νοῦς belongs to the ὄντα in the strict sense: it is separable from the body and can reach up to the supra-cosmic realm.

FAITH AND REASON IN LATE ANTIQUITY 63

are located respectively in eternity and in time.[67] This leaves no doubt that the human νοῦς must be classed with the former.[68] Indeed, John is much more insistent than Pseudo-Denys on linking angelic and human νόες and distinguishing them from other beings. This is most obvious in a passage where Pseudo-Denys' text has a simple sequence of angels, human souls and animal souls whereas John in his *scholion* introduces the distinction between ὄντα and γινόμενα, which then permits him to group the human νόες together with the angels, albeit at a lower level, and to juxtapose them with the lower forms of life.[69]

In passages containing statements about the created order there can thus be no doubt that the human νόες belong to the νοητά. Why then is John so reticent in his discussions about the origins of this order where as we have seen he appears to focus exclusively on the angels without indicating that human souls might be included among the νοητά?[70] The answer is not difficult to find: as I have already pointed out earlier, the pre-existence of the soul was increasingly considered to be a non-Christian concept and voicing it might well have left an author open to accusations of heresy: after all, we know that John was accused of being a Manichaean, a sect that did indeed subscribe to a belief in the pre-existence of souls.[71]

---

[67] John of Scythopolis, *Scholia*, PG 4, col. 316A3–4: ὅπερ γὰρ ἐν τοῖς νοητοῖς αἰών, τοῦτό ἐστιν ἐν τοῖς αἰσθητοῖς χρόνος. Cf. also col. 376D2–4: τὴν εἰς τὰ μεριστὰ καὶ μεταβλητὰ καὶ αἰσθητὰ καὶ τὴν εἰς τὰ ὄντα δὲ ἤτοι νοητὰ δημιουργικὴν πρόνοιαν.

[68] It is true that John usually reserves the term νοητά to the angelic νόες and calls the human νοῦς instead with the term νοερός, cf. *Scholia*, PG 4, col. 309B10–12: ἐπισημήνασθαι χρὴ πῶς ὅταν μὲν περὶ ἀγγέλων φησὶ καὶ ἀνθρώπων τοὺς ἀγγέλους νοητά φησιν τὰς δὲ ἡμετέρας ψυχὰς νοεράς. However, the two terms are not mutually exclusive: a being can be νοητός insofar as it is contemplated by beings of a lower order and at the same time νοερός insofar as it contemplates beings of a higher order. The distinction rests on the fact that human souls occupy the lowest rank in the invisible realm, having only sensible beings beneath them, and are therefore only νοερός but not νοητός, Cf. John of Scythopolis, *Scholia*, PG 4, col. 396A6–11.

[69] In a discussion about 'power' Pseudo-Denys simply presents the list νοερά, λογική, αἰσθητική, cf. Pseudo-Denys, *De divinis nominibus*, 8.3, p. 201, l. 19. By contrast, John introduces the general category ὄντα, which according to him includes not only the νοητά and ἀσώματα but also the λογικά as ψυχικά because the human soul is to a lower degree also νοερά, and only then speaks about the other powers, cf. *Scholia*, PG 4, col. 357B8–C1 (Syr: Suchla, 51).

[70] It is clear that John has not simply 'forgotten' them: they are mentioned in the next *scholion*; cf. PG 4, col. 316D: περὶ τῶν ἐξ αὐτοῦ δημιουργικῶς ὑποστάντων νοητῶν τε καὶ νοερῶν καὶ αἰσθητῶν καὶ λοιπῶν.

[71] Cf. Basil the Cilician, *Contra Johannem Scythopolitanum*, in Photius, *Bibliotheca*, cod. 107, ed. R. Henry, Photius, 9 vols. (Paris, 1959–1991), 2:74: ὅτι τε ἐν ὑπονοίᾳ γέγονε Μανιχαϊσμοῦ. For a discussion cf. Rorem and Lamoreaux, *John of Scythopolis*, pp.

64   DIRK KRAUSMÜLLER

On the whole John seems to be very careful not to come out in favour of such a belief. However, there is one passage where he breaks his silence. Commenting on Pseudo-Denys' statement that God is "above all that is ingenerate" (ὑπὲρ πᾶν ἀγένητον).[72] John observes that the use of such a formula implies the existence of other ingenerate entities after the Trinity and then proceeds to clarify what the author might have had in mind here. He argues that Pseudo-Denys responded to the 'Ionian' philosophers of his time who used the term 'ingenerate' rather freely, applying it both to the intelligible and the sensible world, and that he wished to remind them that 'ingenerate' in this sense presupposes an external cause whereas God is utterly without cause and should therefore be referred to as 'supra-ingenerate'.[73] For our purposes it is sufficient to discuss the first part of the passage:

> He knew that it was the doctrine of some of them to say that all intelligible beings and immortal and intellectual beings are all generate and ingenerate, generate insofar as they have come into existence from God as cause through procession of enlightenment, and ingenerate insofar as they have come forth not in time but eternally, that is, in the eternities, for we have said earlier that the sensible beings have time whereas the intelligible ones have eternity for which reason they are also called eternal. Since, then, these shone forth through procession, they also called them ingenerate.

> ᾔδει οὖν εἶναι δόγμα τινῶν αὐτῶν λεγόντων τὰ νοητὰ πάντα καὶ ἀθάνατα καὶ νοερὰ γενητὰ πάντα καὶ ἀγένητα· γενητὰ μὲν ὡς ἐξ αἰτίου τοῦ θεοῦ ὑποστάντα κατὰ πρόοδον ἐλλάμψεως· ἀγένητα δὲ καθ' ὃ μὴ ἐν χρόνῳ ἀλλ' αἰωνίως τουτέστιν ἐν τοῖς αἰῶσι προῆλθον—καὶ γὰρ ἔφημεν ἄνω τὰ αἰσθητὰ τὸν χρόνον ἔχειν· τὰ δὲ νοητὰ τὸν αἰῶνα ὅθεν καὶ αἰώνια λέγονται—ὡς οὖν ἐκ προόδου λαμψάντα καὶ ἀγένητα αὐτὰ εἶπον.[74]

This statement applies to all invisible beings, both νοητά and νοερά, which leaves no doubt that the human souls are included. At first sight John does not appear to present his own beliefs but simply to set out the views of a group of pagan philosophers who lived in the distant past, and indeed the choice of words at first seems to point to a pagan source: Proclus, for example, in his interpretation of the *Timaeus* called

---

30–36, who refer to E. Honigmann, *Évêques et évêchés monophysites d'Asie antérieure au VI siècle* (Leuven, 1951). That the Manichaeans of the time did indeed appeal to the perishability axiom to support their views is evident from Paul the Persian's discussion with the Manichaeans Photinus, *Dialectus I, PG* 88, col. 532B.

[72] Pseudo-Denys, *De divinis nominibus*, 9.4, p. 209, l. 15–p. 210, l. 1.

[73] Cf. John of Scythopolis, *Scholia, PG* 4, col. 373C4–9.

[74] John of Scythopolis, *Scholia, PG* 4, col. 373B1–8.

FAITH AND REASON IN LATE ANTIQUITY 65

the soul both ingenerate and generate, albeit for different reasons.[75] However, John clearly does not take issue with the concept as such but only with its possible and mistaken application to God. Moreover, he includes a reference to the passage we have discussed at the beginning, which gives a clear impression that he personally approves of this theory. In any case, every single statement has a parallel in *scholia* where John states his own position.[76] Discrepancies are confined to the terminological level: when he speaks in his own name, John replaces the philosophical term ἀγένητα with αἰώνια, which is its synonym but has a Scriptural pedigree. This suggests that John hid behind the mask of the 'Ionian' philosophers in order to be able to state more explicitly how he conceived of the origin and status of the human soul.

In the passages that we have discussed so far John attempts to establish the 'natural' immortality of intelligible beings within a Christian framework. Given the effort he expends to achieve his aim we would expect him to be dismissive of voluntaristic models. Surprisingly, however, this is not the case. Commenting on Pseudo-Denys' statement that the αἰώνια are not co-eternal with the pre-eternal God,[77] John first refers back to his earlier discussion of the αἰώνια as not being identical with the αἰών but rather participating in it. However, the next sentence introduces a new theme:

> Therefore one must call the intelligible entities in the true sense both 'being' as having come into being as immortal, and 'eternal' as remaining unending through the will of God, because they were also produced by God, not being before.
>
> οὐκοῦν τὰ νοητὰ κυρίως καὶ ὄντα ὡς ἀθάνατα γενόμενα καὶ αἰώνια ὡς ἀτελεύτητα βουλήσει θεοῦ διαμένοντα χρὴ λέγειν ἅτε καὶ παραχθέντα ὑπὸ θεοῦ οὐ πρότερον ὄντα.[78]

Here the permanence of intelligible beings is explained through recourse to divine will and supported by a stark reference to their creation from nothing. The carefully constructed distinction between αἰών and χρόνος

---

[75] Proclus Diadochus, *In Platonis Timaeum Commentaria*, ed. E. Diehl, 3 vols. (Leipzig, 1904), 2:124–125: καὶ ἀγένητός (ἐστι) καὶ γενητή.

[76] Cf. e.g. John of Scythopolis, *Scholia*, PG 4, col. 389A11–12: ὁ μὲν οὖν ἀνώτερος οὐρανὸς ἐν τοῖς αἰῶσι γέγονε.

[77] Pseudo-Denys, *De divinis nominibus*, 10.3, p. 216, ll. 16–17: χρὴ τοιγαροῦν οὐχ ἁπλῶς συναΐδια θεῷ τῷ πρὸ αἰῶνος οἴεσθαι τὰ αἰώνια λεγόμενα.

[78] John of Scythopolis, *Scholia*, PG 4, col. 388C11–D1.

66   DIRK KRAUSMÜLLER

is completely swept away: participation is now grounded in an act of divine will.

In order to understand why John brings in God's will as an alternative cause we need to look at the remainder of the passage in which he tries to make sense of Pseudo-Denys' introduction of an intermediate category of entities that participate partly in eternity and partly in time.[79] John identifies this intermediate category with the firmament and the stars, which came into existence in time and thus are not properly eternal like the 'upper heaven', which originated in the αἰών,[80] but have subtle bodies, made up of the most limpid matter,[81] unlike the bodies of the sub-lunar sphere, which are made up of crass and earthly matter and which suffer a rapid succession of generation and corruption.[82] Given this emphasis on the changeability of crass bodies, which implies a causal link between quality of matter and permanence, one would therefore expect John to conclude this passage with the statement that because of their limpidity the firmament and the stars, while being corporeal and temporal, are nevertheless not subjected to corruption. However, this is not what happens. Instead of stating that they will forever persevere in this mode of existence he claims that they will at some point in the future also become αἰώνια in the strict sense.[83] This shift find its explanation in the following statement where John establishes a parallel with the refashioning of the human bodies that are at present of a crass and earthly nature but will become more subtle as a consequence of the resurrection.[84] In the next sentence John seems to

---

[79] Pseudo-Denys, De divinis nominibus, 10.3, p. 216, l. 16–20: χρὴ τοιγαροῦν οὐχ ἁπλῶς συναΐδια θεῷ τῷ πρὸ αἰῶνος οἴεσθαι τὰ αἰώνια λεγόμενα, τοῖς σεπτοτάτοις δὲ λογίοις ἀπαρατρέπτως συνεπομένους αἰώνια μὲν καὶ ἔγχρονα κατὰ τοὺς συνεγνωσμένους τρόπους, μέσα δὲ ὄντων καὶ γιγνομένων ὅσα πῇ μὲν αἰῶνος πῇ δὲ χρόνου μετέχει.

[80] John of Scythopolis, Scholia, PG 4, col. 389A11–15: ὁ μὲν οὖν ἀνώτερος οὐρανὸς ἐν τοῖς αἰῶσι γέγονε... ἐν τοῖς χρονικοῖς διαστήμασι τὸ στερέωμα καὶ οἱ ἀστέρες.

[81] John of Scythopolis, Scholia, PG 4, col. 389A6–8: σώματα γὰρ καὶ ταῦτα εἰ καὶ λεπτομερέστερα καὶ τῆς ὕλης τὸ εἰλικρινέστατον.

[82] John of Scythopolis, Scholia, PG 4, col. 388D6–9: εἰσὶ δὲ καὶ τὰ γινόμενα ταῦτα φησὶ τὰ πρόσγεια σώματα ἃ καὶ γένεσιν καὶ φθορὰν ὀνομάζουσιν, ὡς τῆς ὑποστάθμης ὄντα τῆς ὕλης, καὶ παχύτερα πάντα τὰ μετὰ τὴν σελήνην, and col. 389A1–3: παχυτέρων καὶ προσγείων σωμάτων τῶν γινομένων τε καὶ ἀπογινομένων πυκνῶς εἰς γένεσιν καὶ φθοράν.

[83] John of Scythopolis, Scholia, PG 4, col. 389B1–3: κἂν σώματα καὶ ἔγχρονα—εἰσὶ γὰρ καὶ ἁπτὰ καὶ ὁρατά—ὅμως αἰώνια ἔσονται, μεθέξοντα... τοῦ αἰῶνος.

[84] John of Scythopolis, Scholia, PG 4, col. 389B3–4: μεθέξοντα καὶ αὐτὰ (τὰ οὐράνια σώματα) τοῦ αἰῶνος ὡς καὶ τὰ σώματα ἡμῶν μεταχηματιζόμενα εἰς ἀφθαρσίαν. This shift is probably caused by Pseudo-Denys, De divinis nominibus, 10.3, p. 216, ll. 11–13.

FAITH AND REASON IN LATE ANTIQUITY

backtrack again for he asserts the permanence of the firmament and the stars from the moment of their creation. However, whereas before he had developed a rational argument and Scriptural passages had done little more than add a Christian varnish,[85] he now takes Scripture as his starting point, quoting Psalm 149:6, which links back the 'eternal' permanence of the heavenly bodies to a divine decision: "he has set down a command, and it will not pass away" (πρόσταγμα ἔθετο, καὶ οὐ παρελεύσεται). The reason for these shifts is without doubt the parallel with the resurrection body, which can only be explained through a direct divine intervention into the created order. The nexus is evident in the final passage:

> Note then that the stars and the sun and the moon and the sky are subtler bodies but they have become immortal through the will of God, just as our bodies, too, become after the resurrection.
>
> σημείωσαι οὖν ὅτι οἱ ἀστέρες καὶ ὁ ἥλιος καὶ ἡ σελήνη καὶ ὁ οὐρανὸς σώματα μέν εἰσι λεπτομερέστερα ἀθάνατα δὲ θεοῦ βουλήσει ἐγένοντο ὡς καὶ τὰ σώματα ἡμῶν γίνονται μετὰ τὴν ἀνάστασιν.[86]

In this sentence John creates a stark juxtaposition between corporality and eternity, and subtlety while mentioned is not given any function within the argument. The result of these transformations is a new coherence but it is coherence of a different sort: on all levels it is God's will that guarantees permanence.

The previous discussion has shown that the need to integrate the concept of a resurrection of the body is most likely responsible for the erosion of any kind of rational, logically coherent explanation of the world. It is debatable whether this was John's intention. Indeed, one might argue that John identified the μέσα with the heavens and the stars so as to have a precedent that would allow him to create a rational context for the doctrine of the resurrection of the material body,[87] but if this was his plan it is clear that it did not succeed: the inclusion of the resurrection results in a collapse of his original framework and leaves only the divine will as a possible cause.

---

[85] The distinction between earthly and heavenly bodies is based on I Cor. 15:40–41.

[86] John of Scythopolis, *Scholia, PG* 4, col. 389B9–13.

[87] Cf. John of Scythopolis, *Scholia, PG* 4, col. 396B8–11, where he defines the μέσα as the link that binds together the ἄκρα, i.e. the angels on the one hand and the earthly beings on the other.

68   DIRK KRAUSMÜLLER

Other passages within John's text are even further removed from traditional philosophical concepts. Commenting on a passage where Pseudo-Denys characterises God as 'position' and 'abstraction', he presents the following argument:

> The philosophers, too, call 'position' the forms that have been imposed on matter and 'abstraction' when the qualities are abstracted from the forms, as being heavy from earth and being wet from water. God then who changes the shape of these, too, is the 'position' and 'abstraction' of all; the 'position' of all as having posited everything and having made it and having caused it to be firmly fixed—for in him all things exist—and the 'abstraction' of all as changing even the very 'position' of the beings and reordering and refashioning the creation and abstracting from what has been posited that which it is according to nature. For if it is agreed that whatever comes to be is also corruptible, he himself in the wealth of his goodness has removed from some beings this very corruption as is the case with the angels and the souls whereas as regards 'others beings' he leads what is corrupt to incorruptibility and what is mortal to immortality, as is the case with our bodies in the resurrection.

> λέγουσι δὲ καὶ οἱ φιλόσοφοι θέσιν τὰ ἐπιτιθέμενα εἴδη τῇ ὕλῃ ἀφαίρεσιν δὲ ὅταν αἱ ποιότητες ἀφαιρεθῶσι τῶν εἰδῶν· οἷον γῆς τὸ βαρὺ ὕδατος τὸ ὑγρόν· ὁ οὖν θεὸς ὁ καὶ ταῦτα μετασχηματίζων ἡ πάντων θέσις καὶ ἀφαίρεσίς ἐστι· θέσις μὲν πάντων ὡς τὰ πάντα θεὶς καὶ ποιήσας καὶ ἱδρῦσθαι παρασκευάζων—ἐν αὐτῷ γὰρ τὰ ἅπαντα συνέστηκεν—ἀφαίρεσις δὲ πάντων ἐστὶν ὡς καὶ τὴν θέσιν αὐτὴν τῶν ὄντων καὶ τὴν ποίησιν μεταρρυθμίζων καὶ μετασκευάζων καὶ ἀφαιρῶν ἐκ τῶν τεθειμένων τὰ κατὰ φύσιν· εἰ γὰρ ὡμολόγηται τὰ ἐν γενέσει πάντως καὶ φθείρεσθαι αὐτὸς δὲ πλούτῳ ἀγαθότητος τῶν μὲν ἀνεῖλε καὶ τὸ φθαρτὸν ὡς ἀγγέλων καὶ ψυχῶν· τῶν δὲ τὸ φθαρτὸν εἰς ἀφθαρσίαν καὶ τὸ θνητὸν εἰς ἀθανασίαν μετάγει ὡς τὰ σώματα ἡμῶν ἐν τῇ ἀναστάσει.[88]

In this passage John not only accepts the perishability axiom but also concedes that it applies both to angels and to souls. However, he then argues that their perishability has been removed through divine *fiat* at the moment of their coming-to-be. This can only mean that here John has again relinquished the distinction between being and becoming, between origination in eternity and origination in time, and has instead subjected all created being to the perishability axiom. At the same time he accepts the divine will as sovereign player in all parts of creation, which then allows him without problems to extend this model to the resurrection of the flesh. It is clear that under these circumstances the

---

[88] John of Scythopolis, *Scholia, PG* 4, Col. 217B9–C11.

FAITH AND REASON IN LATE ANTIQUITY 69

immortality of angels and human souls takes on the character of a permanent miracle. This explanation is not completely without precedent because already Pseudo-Denys had averred that the resurrection and immortalisation of the human body was not 'against nature' but 'above nature', although Pseudo-Denys had obscured the voluntaristic aspect by identifying God with a 'superior nature' and claiming that this 'superior nature' is not intelligible to human beings.[89] John's contribution then consists in the application of this model to angels and human souls, a step that Pseudo-Denys had not yet taken.

It must be said, however, that at this point John displays a rather odd understanding of the perishability axiom: instead of presenting perishability as consequence of temporal existence he seems to regard it here as a separable quality. There can be little doubt that his argument is based on the traditional Christian explanation of the resurrection, which located the change from a corruptible to an incorruptible state at the level of quality. Such a conceptual framework evidently creates serious problems because either the quality of corruptibility is a mere accident, which would mean that all created beings are intrinsically incorruptible, or the quality of corruptibility is constitutive of souls, angels and human bodies, as is indeed suggested by John's reference to the heaviness of earth and the wetness of water, in which case God would destroy their natures, a point of view that John Philoponus opposed with great vigour at the very time that John of Scythopolis was composing his *scholia*.[90]

We must conclude that John of Scythopolis does not succeed in creating a coherent system: philosophical and Christian concepts are either imperfectly integrated or stand side by side, and when in doubt John tends to opt for the Christian position even if in doing so he is forced to sacrifice the premises on which his arguments rest. However, in one point John is quite firm. Regardless of what explanation he puts forward, the immortality of angels and souls is always understood by

---

[89] Pseudo-Denys, *De divinis nominibus*, 6.2, p. 192, ll. 6–8: ὑπὲρ φύσιν δὲ τὴν καθ᾽ ἡμᾶς φημι τὴν ὁρωμένην, οὐ τὴν πανσθενῆ τῆς θείας ζωῆς, αὐτῇ γὰρ ὡς πασῶν οὔσῃ τῶν ζωῶν φύσει καὶ μάλιστα τῶν θειοτέρων οὐδεμία ζωὴ παρὰ φύσιν ἢ ὑπὲρ φύσιν.

[90] Cf. A. Grillmeier and Th. Hainthaler (tr. O. C. Dean), *Christ in Christian Tradition*, 2: *From the Council of Chalcedon (451) to Gregory the Great (590–604)*, 4: *The Church of Alexandria with Nubia and Ethiopia after 451* (London, 1996), pp. 138–141, and A. Van Roey, "Un traité cononite contre la doctrine de Jean Philopon sur la résurrection," *ANTIΔΩPON. Festschrift M. Geerard* (Wetteren, 1984), 1:123–139.

70 DIRK KRAUSMÜLLER

him as both intrinsic and continuous.[91] Usually, he simply states his views without engaging in polemics. However, there is one exception in John's exegesis of Pseudo-Denys' speculations about God as 'life' where we find the following paragraph:

> From it (sc. the divine life) the souls, too, have imperishability and all animals and plants have life according to the most distant echo of life. And when it (sc. the divine life) is taken away, all life wastes away, according to Scripture, and towards it, too, those who have expired return again through their weakness regarding participation and again become living beings.

> ἐξ αὐτῆς (sc. τῆς θείας ζωῆς) καὶ αἱ ψυχαὶ τὸ ἀνώλεθρον ἔχουσι καὶ ζῷα πάντα καὶ φυτὰ κατ' ἔσχατον ἀπήχημα τῆς ζωῆς ἔχουσι τὸ ζῆν ἧς ἀνταναιρουμένης κατὰ τὸ λόγιον ἐκλείπει πᾶσα ζωή, καὶ πρὸς ἢν καὶ τὰ ἐκλελοιπότα τῇ πρὸς τὸ μετέχειν αὐτῆς ἀσθενείᾳ πάλιν ἐπιστρεφόμενα πάλιν ζῷα γίγνεται.[92]

Here Pseudo-Denys starts with his usual list of classes of beings that participate in aspects of the divine. However, he then continues with a rather odd statement. He avers that 'all life' (πᾶσα ζωή) will expire because of its inability to participate permanently in 'divine life' (θεία ζωή) and that it will then return to it in order again to be revivified. This statement, which is evidently based on the imperishability axiom,[93] has so far attracted little interest in contemporary scholarship.[94] Judging by the phrase 'they again become living beings' (πάλιν ζῷα γίγνεται), it seems to point back to 'all living beings' (ζῷα πάντα) and by extension also to plants. Accordingly the formula 'all life' (πᾶσα ζωή) most likely refers to 'nature' (φύσις) and to the Aristotelian concept of 'forms-in-matter' (ἔνυλα εἴδη), which were usually regarded to be inseparable from their substrate and thus to be perishable but which here seem to be translated into the Neo-Platonic framework of procession and return: having expired, the forms-in-matter return to their origin and are then 'energised', which permits them to proceed and shape matter

---

[91] Cf. especially John of Scythopolis, *Scholia*, PG 4, col. 244A3, and col. 244B5–6.

[92] Pseudo-Denys, *De divinis nominibus*, 6.1, p. 191, ll. 4–8.

[93] Cf. Pseudo-Denys, *De divinis nominibus*, 4.25, p. 173, ll. 6–7: φθορὰ δὲ φύσεως ἀσθένεια καὶ ἔλλειψις τῶν φυσικῶν ἕξεων καὶ ἐνεργειῶν καὶ δυνάμεων.

[94] It is not mentioned in J. M. Rist, "Pseudo-Dionysius, Neoplatonism and the weakness of the soul," in *From Athens to Chartres. Neoplatonism and medieval thought. Studies in honour of E. Jeauneau*, ed. H. J. Westra (Leipzig, 1992), pp. 135–161; P. Rorem, *Pseudo-Dionysius: a commentary on the texts and an introduction to their influence* (New York, Oxford, 1993); or Louth, *Dionysius the Areopagite*.

FAITH AND REASON IN LATE ANTIQUITY 71

once again.[95] However, the passage is not without ambiguities. Apart from the references to Greek philosophy on which we have focused so far Pseudo-Denys also appeals to Scripture, paraphrasing Psalm 103:29–30: "You will take away their spirit and they will expire and return to their dust; you will send your spirit and they will be created, and you will renew the face of the earth" (ἀντανελεῖς τὸ πνεῦμα αὐτῶν καὶ ἐκλείψουσιν καὶ εἰς τὸν χοῦν αὐτῶν ἐπιστρέψουσιν· ἐξαποστελεῖς τὸ πνεῦμά σου καὶ κτισθήσονται καὶ ἀνακαινιεῖς τὸ πρόσωπον τῆς γῆς). In earlier Christian exegesis these psalm verses had been interpreted as referring to the resurrection of the human body,[96] and such an interpretation also seems to be implied by Pseudo-Denys: the phrase 'they again become living beings' (πάλιν ζῷα γίγνεται) is evidently a wordplay on 'rebirth' (παλινζῳΐα), which is synonymous with the more common παλιγγενεσία. This interpretation can be supported through further exploration of allusions to Scripture. The notion of a return to God is not derived from Psalm 103:28, which speaks of a return to the dust, but from another Biblical passage, namely Lamentations 5:21: "Make us turn back to you, Lord, and we will return, and renew our days as before!" (ἐπίστρεψον ἡμᾶς, κύριε, πρὸς σέ, καὶ ἐπιστραφησόμεθα καὶ ἀνακαίνισον ἡμέρας ἡμῶν ὡς ἔμπροσθεν). It is evident that this creates ambiguity, especially since the human soul was considered to be not only 'essential life' (οὐσία ζωῆς) but also 'principle of life' (ἀρχὴ ζωῆς) as the 'form' of the human body.[97]

In his explanation of this passage John is evidently concerned about possible misunderstandings. Having replaced Pseudo-Denys' Aristotelian framework with the Stoic concept of the 'spirit-in-matter (ἔνυλον πνεῦμα),[98] John quotes Psalm 103:29–30 in full and then insists that this

---

[95] For a possible parallel cf. Damascius Successor, *Dubitationes et solutiones de primis principiis, in Platonis Parmenidem*, ed. C. E. Ruelle, 2 vols. (Paris, 1889; repr. Amsterdam, 1966), 2:144, ll. 20–27, about Kronos and the πρόοδος and ἐπιστροφή of the ἔνυλον εἶδος.

[96] In earlier Christian exegesis these verses are taken to refer to life and death of the human compound as in Athanasius of Alexandria, *Expositiones in Psalmos*, PG 27, col. 441A, and in Theodoret of Cyrus, *Interpretatio in Psalmos*, PG 80, col. 1705AB, where the first part is interpreted as individual death and the second as resurrection.

[97] John of Scythopolis, *Scholia*, PG 4, col. 340AA9–B5.

[98] John of Scythopolis, *Scholia*, PG 4, col. 336C3–4: αἱ δὲ ζωαὶ τῶν ἀλόγων καὶ τῶν φυτῶν οὔκ εἰσι θεῖαι ἀλλὰ τοῦ ἐνύλου πυρός τε καὶ πνεύματος. The important role of this concept and its Stoic provenance was first stressed by von Balthasar, *Kosmische Liturgie*, pp. 658–659. On the survival of these Stoicizing concepts in the West cf. M. L. Colish, *The Stoic Tradition. From Antiquity to the Early Middle Ages. 2: Stoicism in Christian Latin thought through the sixth century* (Leiden, 1985), esp. pp. 236–237.

72   DIRK KRAUSMÜLLER

last statement cannot possibly refer to angels and human souls but must be limited to animals and plants.[99] In order to support his claim, he produces two arguments: firstly he contends that God made their life a part of their substance and that its withdrawal would therefore amount to their destruction,[100] and secondly he appeals to the steadfastness of the divine will through a quotation of Romans 11:29,[101] thus supporting his claim with both ontological and voluntaristic arguments.

Why did John expend so much effort to refute the view that this passage might indeed refer to angels and human souls as well? The following *scholion*, which is not by John, gives us an insight into the contemporary discussion. It acknowledges the fact that Psalm 103:29–30 was traditionally taken to refer to the resurrection of the body,[102] but then continues to state that Pseudo-Denys uses it in a different sense here and that he speaks "about all entities that have life in any manner whatsoever" (περὶ πάντων τῶν ὁπωσοῦν ζῆν ἐχόντων) because he wishes to show that all living beings have their life from God.[103] Within this framework Pseudo-Denys' phrase 'weakness regarding participation' is explained as meaning that "they do not have life intrinsically and from themselves but brought in from God" (διὰ τὸ μὴ οἴκοθεν καὶ παρ' ἑαυτῶν ἔχειν τὴν ζωὴν ἀλλ' ἐπακτὴν ἐκ θεοῦ).[104] The author of

---

[99] John of Scythopolis, *Scholia*, PG 4, col. 336C4–13: περὶ τούτων οὖν μόνων τῶν ἐσχάτων ὡς εἴρηται ζωῶν φησι τὸ τοῦ Δαβὶδ εἰρῆσθαι· ἀντανελεῖς τὸ πνεῦμά σου (instead of αὐτῶν) καὶ ἐκλείψουσιν καὶ εἰς τὸν χοῦν αὐτῶν ἐπιστρέψουσιν· ἐξαποστελεῖς τὸ πνεῦμά σου καὶ κτισθήσονται καὶ ἀνακαινιεῖς τὸ πρόσωπον τῆς γῆς· ἐπὶ γὰρ αἰσθητικῆς μόνης ψυχῆς καὶ τῆς φυτικῆς ζωῆς ταῦτα δέχεται τὰ θεῖα λόγια ὁ μέγας Διονύσιος· περὶ γὰρ τῆς τῶν νοητῶν ζωῆς ἢ τῆς καθ' ἡμᾶς οὐ νοεῖ ταῦτα, tr. Rorem and Lamoreaux, *John of Scythopolis*, p. 224. Cf. also col. 355C13–D3.

[100] John of Scythopolis, *Scholia*, PG 4, col. 336C13–D1: τὴν γὰρ ζωὴν ταύτην οὐσιωδῶς δημιουργήσας εἰς ἀθανασίαν ὁ θεὸς τοῖς νοητοῖς καὶ ταῖς ψυχαῖς ἡμῶν οὐκ ἂν ἀφείλοι αὐτῶν τὸ ζῆν ἐπεὶ οὐδὲ οὐσίαι ἔσονται, tr. Rorem and Lamoreaux, *John of Scythopolis*, p. 224. A similar argument is already found in Augustine, cf. G. Watson, *Augustine, Soliloquies and Immortality of the Soul* (Warminster, 1990), p. 208.

[101] John of Scythopolis, *Scholia*, PG 4, col. 336D3–8: καὶ περὶ τῆς ζωῆς δὲ τῶν ἑκουσίως ἀποβάντων δαιμόνων ἐπάγει ὅτι καὶ αὐτὴ διαμένει ἀνώλεθρος τοῦ κτίσαντος αὐτοὺς θεοῦ τοῦτο βουλομένου κἂν αὐτοὶ ἀπέστησαν τοῦ θεοῦ· ἀμεταμέλητα γὰρ χαρίσματα τοῦ θεοῦ· τοῦ ἐξ ἀρχῆς ποιήσαντος αὐτοὺς ἀθανάτους, tr. Rorem and Lamoreaux, *John of Scythopolis*, p. 224.

[102] *Scholia*, PG 4, col. 377A1–2: τὸ μὲν ψαλμικὸν ῥητὸν περὶ ἀνθρώπων καὶ τῆς τελευταίας καὶ κοινῆς ἀναστάσεως λέγει.

[103] *Scholia*, PG 4, col. 377A4–7: ἐνταῦθα δὲ τὸ ῥητὸν παρήγαγε τὸν λόγον ποιούμενος περὶ πάντων τῶν ὁπωσοῦν ζῆν ἐχόντων δεικνὺς μὴ ἄλλως ταῦτα ἢ ἐκ θεοῦ τὸ ζῆν θεωρεῖσθαι ἐν αὐτοῖς.

[104] *Scholia*, PG 4, col. 337A9–12: ἀσθενεῖν δὲ ταῦτα πρὸς τὸ μετέχειν φησὶ διὰ τὸ μὴ οἴκοθεν καὶ παρ' ἑαυτῶν ἔχειν τὴν ζωὴν ἀλλ' ἐπακτὴν ἐκ θεοῦ.

FAITH AND REASON IN LATE ANTIQUITY   73

the *scholion* does not distinguish between mortal and immortal living beings but this is not necessary for his argument because he only takes into view the time during which beings are alive, which in the case of souls would, of course, be forever.

At first sight it seems that John reacted against such a position. We have seen that in his exegesis of the passage he insists that angels and human souls are 'substantially created lives' (κτισθεῖσαι οὐσιώδεις ζωαί) and elsewhere he makes it clear that this excludes an interpretation of this condition as something brought in 'from the outside' (ἔξωθεν).[105] However, it needs to be emphasised that the author of the second *scholion* never questions the actual continuous immortality of angels and human souls. By equating ἀνταναιρεῖσθαι with κεχωρίσθαι and ἐπιστρεφόμενα with μετέχοντα, he replaces Pseudo-Denys' dynamic framework with a juxtaposition of two states of which the former is merely hypothetical since living beings always participate in God.[106] Accordingly, the term 'revivification' is explained as a manner of speech, which denotes nothing more than a permanent dependence on God.[107]

In order to find a more likely candidate for the position that so incensed John of Scythopolis we need to turn to a considerably later author, the eighth-century theologian John of Damascus.[108] John of Damascus discusses the immortality of angels and human souls in his *Expositio fidei*, where he stresses its gratuitous and supernatural character with reference to the perishability principle but nevertheless presents their existence as continuous and everlasting.[109] However, in another of his writings, the treatise *Contra Manichaeos*, he takes a radically different position.[110] This text is best known for John's discussion of the

---

[105] John of Scythopolis, *Scholia*, PG 4, col. 244C1–3.

[106] *Scholia*, PG 4, col. 377A7–9: τὸ δὲ ἀνταναιρεῖσθαι ἀντὶ τοῦ κεχωρίσθαι τέθεικεν ὥσπερ καὶ τὸ ἐπιστρεφόμενα ἀντὶ τοῦ μετέχοντα.

[107] *Scholia*, PG 4, col. 337A12–15: τὰ γὰρ ὅσον ἐφ' ἑαυτῶν οὐκ ἐν τῷ ζῆν θεωρούμενα τῇ δὲ πρὸς θεὸν ἀναθέσει τοῦτο ἔχοντα, τρόπον τινὰ ἀναζῇ, καὶ ὡς αὐτός φησι, πάλιν ζῷα γίνεται.

[108] On John of Damascus, cf. A. Louth, *St John Damascene* (Oxford, 2002).

[109] Cf. e.g. John of Damascus, *Expositio fidei*, 17, ed. B. Kotter, *Die Schriften des Johannes von Damaskos*, 2: *Expositio Fidei* (Berlin, New York, 1973), p. 45, ll. 21–23: ἄγγελος...ἀθάνατος οὐ φύσει ἀλλὰ χάριτι· πᾶν γὰρ τὸ ἀρξάμενον καὶ τελευτᾷ κατὰ φύσιν· μόνος δὲ ὁ θεὸς ἀεὶ ὢν μᾶλλον δὲ καὶ ὑπὲρ τὸ ἀεί· οὐχ ὑπὸ χρόνον γὰρ ἀλλ' ὑπὲρ χρόνον ὁ τῶν χρόνων ποιητής.

[110] John of Damascus, *Contra Manichaeos* (CPG 8048), ed. B. Kotter, *Die Schriften des Johannes von Damaskos*, 4: *Liber de haeresibus. Opera Polemica*, (Berlin, New York, 1981), 351–398. On the authorship of John of Damascus cf. Kotter, *Schriften*, 4:334.

74 DIRK KRAUSMÜLLER

concepts of divine foreknowledge and predetermination, which takes up the second half of the text.[111] By comparison, the earlier section has so far received little attention from scholars. This section is devoted to the refutation of the Manichaean myth and of the dualistic cosmology that underpins it. At one point John lets the Manichean ask whether God is without beginning in all respects or only in some.[112] The Christian affirms that God must be without beginning in every respect if he is to be without beginning 'by nature',[113] and then continues:

> What is without beginning is also without end because the end is also a form of beginning. Now everything that has a beginning also has an end according to its own nature and everything that has an end also has a beginning. And the angels who have a beginning also have an end according to their own nature even if through divine grace they begin to be again and are renewed.

> τὸ δὲ ἄναρχον καὶ ἀπέραντον· ἐν γὰρ ἀρχῆς εἶδος καὶ τὸ τέλος· πᾶν οὖν ἔχον ἀρχὴν καὶ τέλος ἔχει κατὰ τὴν ἑαυτοῦ φύσιν καὶ πᾶν τέλος ἔχον καὶ ἀρχὴν ἔχει· καὶ οἱ ἄγγελοι γοῦν ἀρχὴν ἔχοντες καὶ τέλος ἔχουσι κατὰ τὴν ἑαυτῶν φύσιν εἰ καὶ τῇ θείᾳ χάριτι πάλιν ἄρχονται τοῦ εἶναι καὶ ἀνακαινίζονται.[114]

Here John of Damascus insists on the difference between God and created being against opponents who consider angels and human souls to be parts of the divine. Accordingly he focuses on angels as the highest form of created being, just as Cyril of Alexandria had done in his *Thesaurus* several centuries earlier. Both texts share the strong emphasis on divine grace as the source of everlasting created being but there is one clear difference: whereas Cyril sees the discontinuity of angelic life only as a possibility, John of Damascus insists on a real break followed by a re-creation.[115] On the face of it this passage seems to imply that John accepts an autonomous natural sphere besides God. However, from the

---

[111] Cf. H. Beck, *Vorsehung und Vorherbestimmung in der theologischen Literatur der Byzantiner* (Rome, 1937).

[112] John of Damascus, *Contra Manichaeos*, 21, ed. Kotter, 4:362, ll. 1–2: ὁ θεὸς κατὰ πάντα ἐστὶν ἄναρχος ἢ κατὰ τὶ μὲν κατὰ τὶ δὲ οὔ.

[113] John of Damascus, *Contra Manichaeos*, 21, ed. Kotter, 4:362, ll. 2–4: εἰ οὐ κατὰ πάντα ἄναρχος καὶ ἄναρχος καὶ οὐκ ἄναρχος· εἰ δὲ κατὰ πάντα ἄναρχος ὄντως ἄναρχος καὶ φύσει ἄναρχος.

[114] John of Damascus, *Contra Manichaeos*, 21, ed. Kotter, 4:362, ll. 4–8.

[115] For the voluntarism of John of Damascus cf. D. Krausmüller, "Murder is good if God wills it. Nicetas Byzantius' polemic against Islam and the Christian tradition of divinely sanctioned murder," *Al-Masaq (Islam and the Medieval Mediterranean)* 16 (2004), pp. 163–176.

FAITH AND REASON IN LATE ANTIQUITY 75

remainder of the passage it is clear that he was a radical 'voluntarist' and that he made use of the perishability axiom not because he wished to limit divine intervention to certain points in time but because it gave him an effective means to demonstrate God's absolute control over his creatures.[116] By asserting real discontinuity he could make sure that this control was not endangered by an however vestigial autonomy of angels and human souls. Although it cannot be shown beyond doubt, the argument put forward by John of Damascus may well have been the position against which John of Scythopolis argued in his *scholia*, in particular because the passage in *Contra Manichaeos* contains the verb 'to renew' (ἀνακαινίζειν), which points to the same Psalm verses to which Pseudo-Denys had made reference.

Since we have by now completely left behind the philosophical discourse it may be fitting to end the discussion with a hagiographical text. In the *Life* of Symeon of the Wondrous Mountain, a Christian wonderworker of the sixth century, we are told that when overwhelmed by the demands of his visitors the saint blessed wooden staffs, which he then gave to his disciples in order effect cures. However, the hagiographer then hastens to add:

> Each staff was active for up to three men and if the saint did not touch them again and bless them the staff was no longer active. This happened according to a divine dispensation lest the brothers be seized by thoughts of arrogance.
>
> ἑκάστη δὲ ῥάβδος ἐνήργει ἕως τριῶν ἀνδρῶν καὶ εἰ μὴ πάλιν ἥψατο αὐτῶν ὁ μακάριος καὶ ηὐλόγησεν οὐκέτι ἐνήργει ἡ ῥάβδος· τοῦτο δὲ κατ' οἰκονομίαν θείαν ἐγένετο διὰ τὸ μὴ κατασχεθῆναι τοὺς ἀδελφοὺς ἐπάρσεως λογισμῷ.[117]

---

[116] John of Damascus, *Contra Manichaeos*, 21, ed. Kotter, 4:362, l. 8–p. 363, l. 15, esp. ἕως ἂν ὁ κελεύων αὐτὸ κινεῖσθαι θέλῃ. John's repeated reference to the circular movement of the soul implies that he argued against opponents who considered circular movement to be potentially eternal, cf. Simplicius' comment about the Aristotelians, cf. *In Aristotelis de caelo commentaria*, ed. I. L. Heiberg (Commentaria in Aristotelem graeca, 8) (Berlin, 1894), pp. 43, ll. 8–10: ἀΐδιον τὴν ἐγκύκλιον ὑποτίθενται κίνησιν μήτε ἀρχὴν μήτε πέρας ἔχουσαν. John's comparison of God's agency with a potter who gives a push to his wheel that makes it go round for a while, could be understood as a crude form of the impetus theory, cf. M. Wolff, "Philoponus and the Rise of Preclassical Dynamics," in *Philoponus and the Rejection of Aristotelian Science*, ed. Sorabji, pp. 84–120, esp. p. 86.

[117] *Vita Symeonis Stylitae Junioris*, 50, ed. P. van den Ven (Brussels, 1962), 1:46.

Some Christians evidently thought that God needed to assert his control over creation in a similar fashion and drew the conclusion that he did so by endowing angels, and presumably also human souls, with a life force that would expire at some point and would then require to be renewed. At this point one may wonder what prompted this radical deviation from a long-standing consensus. It is notoriously problematic to explain religious changes through political and social developments but one might at least venture the opinion that the growing concern about divine omnipotence was related to the disintegration of the Roman Empire when the emperors as God's image on earth were experiencing ever greater difficulties to maintain their hold over the state.

In conclusion, it can be said that Late Antique Christians were divided into two camps. Those belonging to the first camp regarded nature as an autonomous realm based on rational rules even if its ultimate cause was the Christian God. When they made reference to the perishability axiom in their writings they therefore presented it as an inevitable corollary of God's decision to create the material world. By comparison, representatives of the second camp believed that God could do with his creation whatever he liked. They also made use of the perishability axiom, but they did so selectively and only if it allowed them to reinforce the Christian belief that creatures are radically different from and completely dependent on God. Moreover, they understood perishability not as a 'structural' limitation of created being but rather as the result of a refusal of God, for reasons best known to himself, to bring to bear on his creatures the full potential of his powers. However, it would be wrong to regard this as a simple clash between reason and faith for it is quite clear that for the former camp the existence of fixed rules provided reassurance and limited anxiety in the face of an all-powerful and—just possibly—capricious God. For this reason John of Scythopolis could live with a voluntaristic explanation of the immortality of angels and human souls as long as it guaranteed some measure of stability and predictability. However, when those concerned about divine sovereignty took the extreme step of denying the continuous existence of angels and souls and even adduced the perishability axiom in support of their position, the possibility for a compromise had clearly disappeared.

THE NATURE OF THE SOUL ACCORDING TO ERIUGENA

Catherine Kavanagh[*]

Introduction

Eriugena's treatment of the soul depends in many ways on his predecessors, which consist of (i) a limited selection of ancient philosophical texts and (ii) the Patristic tradition, which preserves and develops
a good deal of ancient metaphysics in its theology.[1] However, strong
tendencies in his own thought lead him to a difference of emphasis
from many of the Fathers which make his presentation of the soul very
distinctive. As I. P. Sheldon-Williams observed, Eriugena is working
his way back by sheer ratiocination to pure Hellenistic Neoplatonism,
(having strong similarities with the thought of Plotinus in particular),
whereas Augustine is working away from it; they pass in mid-stream,
so to speak.[2] The doctrine of the soul, then, as Eriugena encountered it
in the philosophers available to him—Augustine, the *Timaeus*, Boethius
and the Western Fathers generally[3]—is as follows: it is an intermediate

---

[*] Mary Immaculate College Limerick.
[1] There is an extensive bibliography dealing with the issue of ancient metaphysics
in the writings of the Fathers: see, for example, the works of Pierre Hadot, *Marius
Victorinus. Recherches sur sa vie et ses œuvres* (Paris, 1971), Pierre Courcelle, *Connais-
toi toi-même, de Socrate à saint Bernard* (Paris: Études Augustiniennes, 1974–5), idem,
Recherches sur saint Ambroise: "vies" anciennes, culture, iconographie (Paris, 1973), idem,
Recherches sur les Confessions de saint Augustin (Paris, 1968), idem, *La consolation de
philosophie dans la tradition littéraire* (Paris, 1967), Werner Beierwaltes, *Platonismus im
Christentum* (Frankfurt am Main, 1998), idem, *Denken des Einen. Studien zur neupla-
tonischen Philosophie und ihrer Wirkungsgeschichte* (Frankfurt am Main, 1985), idem,
Identität und Differenz (Frankfurt am Main, 1980), René Roques, *Structures théologiques,
de la gnose à Richard de Saint-Victor. Essais et analyses critiques* (Paris, 1962), and
Stephen Gersh, *From Iamblichus to Eriugena: an Investigation of the Prehistory and
Evolution of the Pseudo-Dionysian Tradition* (Leiden, 1978), all of which deal, in one
way or another, with the question of Neoplatonic influence on the Fathers.
[2] See I. P. Sheldon-Williams, "Eriugena's Greek Sources", in *The Mind of Eriugena.
Papers of a Colloquium. Dublin, 14–18 July 1970*, (Dublin, 1973), pp. 1–15.
[3] In the Latin West of the ninth century, the main source of philosophical doctrines
were the Latin Fathers of the Church rather than the philosophers themselves, with one
or two exceptions. The most important Fathers are St. Ambrose, St. Jerome, St. Gregory
the Great, and, of course, St. Augustine. Of these, Jerome and Gregory are significant

78 CATHERINE KAVANAGH

principle between God and matter; it is spiritual and therefore immortal; it is that which gives life to matter, and when it departs, matter is said to be lifeless. This was variously expressed by calling the soul the "life-principle" or the "form" of the body. In Christian writers, the term "soul" normally refers to the soul of the individual human being, but the notion of the world-soul, so strong in the *Timaeus*, had not been dismissed—in fact, it is quite important to Eriugena, and in the twelfth century a vigorous debate arose as to whether it was to be identified with the Holy Spirit of Christian theology.[4] These basic ideas about the soul are fundamentally philosophical rather than Biblical but they fit into the Biblical context easily enough.

---

mainly for their work on Biblical texts and hermeneutics, although Jerome is extremely well formed in the Pagan tradition also, and Gregory wrote one of the most important of medieval saint's lives in his *Life of St. Benedict*. Augustine is by far the most important from the point of view of philosophy, and displays a notable metaphysical originality; it has been said that Augustine distorted the whole Platonic tradition for those who came after him. Ambrose is not as philosophically original as Augustine, but in some points he represents an earlier Greek tradition from which Augustine had departed, a characteristic which was to be important for Eriugena in places. In addition, the work of Boethius was well known, and his systematisation of the rhetorical tradition inherited from Aristotle and Cicero seems to have been important for Eriugena. The *Timeaus* of Plato, along with Calcidius' commentary on it was also available. An important influence on Eriugena's doctrine of the soul also comes from certain Greek Fathers: pseudo-Dionysius, Maximus the Confessor and Gregory of Nyssa; above all, from Maximus the Confessor. See: Jeauneau, É. "Pseudo-Dionysius, Gregory of Nyssa, and Maximus the Confessor in the Works of John Scottus Eriugena", in U.-R. Blumenthal ed. *Carolingian Essays. Andrew W. Mellon Lectures in Early Christian Studies* (Washington D.C., 1983), pp. 138–49; idem, "L'heritage de la philosophie antique durant le Haut Moyen Age," in *La cultura antica nell Occidente Latino del VII al XI secolo: 18–24 Aprile 1974* (Spoleto, 1975), pp. 19–54. Also: McKitterick Rosamond, "Knowledge of Plato's *Timaeus* in the ninth century: the implications of Valenciennes, B. M., Ms 293" in Westra, H. J. *From Athens to Chartres. Neoplatonism and Medieval Thought. Studies in Honour of Edouard Jeauneau.* (Leiden, New York, Koln, 1992), pp. 85–97; Armstrong A. H. ed., *The Cambridge History of Later Greek and Early Medieval Philosophy* (London, 1967), pp. 518–643; Riché, P. *Éducation et Culture dans l'Occident barbare, VIe–VIIIe siècles.* (Paris, 1962), pp. 27–92, 140–220, 353–530, transl. Contreni, J. *Education and Culture in the Barbarian West, Sixth through Eighth Centuries* (Columbia, 1975); idem. *Écoles et enseignement dans le Haut Moyen Age. Fin du Ve siècle-milieu du XIe siècle.* (Paris, 1989), pp. 8–111; Manitius, M., *Geschichte der lateinischen Literatur des Mittelalters.* 3 vols., Munich 1911–1931, Vol. I, pp. 22–153.

[4] This is associated in particular with the Cathedral School of Chartres in the twelfth century: see Bernard of Chartres, *The Glosae super Platonem of Bernard of Chartres*, ed. P. E. Dutton (Toronto, 1991), and William of Conches, *Glosae super Platonem. Editionem novam trium codicum super repertarum testimonio ceffultom* ed. É. Jeauneau, (Turnhout, 2006).

THE NATURE OF THE SOUL ACCORDING TO ERIUGENA 79

Other philosophical doctrines regarding the soul were eventually to be rejected, however. Following Plato, Plotinus had systematized the Platonic universe into the different hypostases of One, Intellect, Soul and Matter, and it was this cosmology which informed the developing theology of Christianity as it emerged from the close exegesis of the Biblical texts. According to the Neoplatonic scheme, the soul is eternal, and has fallen into matter; therefore, it pre-exists its manifestation in the material world, and matter is no more than an encumbrance to it. Events in this world are of no importance to it, since its final goal is to escape matter altogether, and return to the world of the Forms from which it has come. In spite of the influence of Origen of Alexandria, (whose doctrine of the soul is very strongly Platonic in that for him it is eternal),[5] Christianity ultimately came to teach that the human soul was immortal, but not eternal, that it was created along with the body, and was ultimately to be reunited with the body in the resurrection at the *Parousia*. In the Greek-speaking Eastern Church, the theology of the cosmic significance of the Resurrection was also very highly developed, so the whole material world acquired a new, deeper significance. The Christian attitude to matter is deeply ambivalent: on the one hand, body and soul together form the human being; on the other, the world is still a dangerous place, and the passions are to be fought at all costs. However, the Christian understanding of these matters left room for a wide diversity of interpretation: the crucial term "body" means very different things to different people. It could be argued also that the Christian positing of the *logos* of a human being (along with other seminal reasons) in the mind of God, which is eternal, represents, if not pre-existence, then a closer approach to the Origenist position than one might suppose.[6]

What made the Christians introduce all these modifications of the Platonic scheme was, of course, the pressure of the Biblical text. It introduced a different understanding of time, as linear rather than cyclic, moving towards some moment of definitive crisis, after which

---

[5] See Origen. *De principiis. Traité des principes: (Peri archon) Origène; traduction de la version latine de Rufin, avec un dossier annexe d'autres témoins du texte*, par M. Harl, G. Dorival, A. Le Boulluec. (Paris, 1976).

[6] On the seminal reasons, see Augustine, *De Genesi ad litteram*. J. Zycha ed. CSEL 28/1. Wien 1894 *passim*. Also: *The Cambridge History of Later Greek and Early Medieval Philosophy*, ed. A. H. Armstrong, Part V, pp. 331–406.

80 CATHERINE KAVANAGH

the universe would be totally different. Historical events mattered a great deal to the Biblical writers, as contributing to or obstructing this progress, and therefore took on a new urgency. Genesis also says that God created the world *ex nihilo*, that "he saw what he had made and found it very good", which, on the one hand, is reminiscent of the goodness of the world made by the Demiurge in the *Timaeus*, but on the other differs, in that in the *Timaeus* the Demiurge has to struggle with the recalcitrance of pre-existing matter of some kind, which seems to have a certain chaotic motion already, whereas in Genesis everything is created out of nothing, including matter which, because of this, is not refractory in the same way. This neutralizes the Neoplatonic tendency to view matter as the source of evil. However, the Bible is a difficult text to interpret, and several different traditions existed.[7] The Platonism of Christian theologians emerges in their Biblical hermeneutics: the more strongly figurative the interpretation, the more Platonic it tends to be. For Eriugena, the most compelling interpretations, of Scripture are allegorical and eschatological; what he calls spiritual. The literal reading of Scripture, on the other hand, relates only to the material "surface" of the text, and is less important—it is the hermeneutical equivalent of the shadows in the myth of the cave in the *Republic*—and this intensely spiritual understanding of reality also affects his psychology and anthropology.

The Eriugenian Definition of the Soul

Eriugena introduces a general discussion of the nature of soul in Book III of the *Periphyseon*, at 728A, where he is presenting a kind of commentary on the Hexaemeron, the first six days of creation. On the fifth day, Genesis tells us, *dixit etiam deus producant aquae reptile animae uiuentis et uolatile super terram sub firmamento caeli*. Eriugena fastens on the word *anima*—soul—here, and begins to discuss why it is that we have heard no mention of it in Genesis up to this. He remarks that it may be that the things created up to this have no life and no soul, but he goes on to observe:

> But Plato, the greatest of philosophers, and his sectaries not only affirm a general life of the world, but also declare that there is no form attached

---

[7] See de Lubac, Henri. *Exégèse médiévale: Les quatres sens de l'Écriture.* (Paris, 1959–64); also, Riché, P. *Éducation et Culture dans l'Occident barbare, VIᵉ–VIIIᵉ siècles.*

THE NATURE OF THE SOUL ACCORDING TO ERIUGENA   81

to bodies nor any body that is deprived of life; and that life, whether general or special, they dare to call soul, and the great commentators of…Scripture affirm their opinion, affirming that plants and trees and all things that grow out of the earth are alive. Nor does the nature of things permit it to be otherwise. For if there is no matter which without form [*sine specie*] produces body, and no form subsists without its proper substance, and no substance can be without the vital motion which contains it and causes its subsistence—for everything which is naturally moved receives the source of its motion from some life, it necessarily follows that every creature is either Life-through-itself or participates in life and is somehow alive….[8]

Eriugena agrees here with Plato that soul is life, and, more significantly, that life need not be sentient life, but is rather a kind of motion, producing substance, which produces form, which imposes itself on matter to produce bodies. It follows then that matter cannot produce body without species, or form, i.e. that in order to exist intelligibly, matter must be specified or formed. Since being as such, which is the continual unfolding of the *Logos*, is intelligible, then pure, unformed or unspecified, matter does not, in effect, exist. Therefore a body—any body, not merely a living one—is informed matter. Form, in turn, relies on substance; it is the expression of substance in matter, and so a body is an embodied substance—i.e., formed matter. But substance itself cannot be without "the vital motion which contains it": that is to say, the creative force bringing the universe into being is a motive force, which penetrates, surpasses and encompasses the individual substances, and without which they cannot be. This motion is intelligible; in fact, it is the unfolding of the *Logos*, and can be identified with the *spiritus dei* "moving over the waters" in the first few lines of Genesis. The *Logos* produces it as it proceeds from the Godhead into matter, but it is not itself to be identified with the *Logos*, giving us a third element, soul. Soul,

---

[8] Plato vero philosophorum summus et qui circa eum sunt non solum generalem mundi uitam asserunt, verum etiam nullam speciem corporibus adhaerentem neque ullum corpus uita priuari fatentur, ipsamque uitam seu generalem seu specialem uocare animam fiducialiter ausi sunt. Quorum sententiae summi expositores divinae Scripturae fauent, herbas et ligna, cunctaque de terra orientia uiuere affirmantes. Neque aliter rerum natura sinit. Si enim nulla materia est, quae sine specie corpus efficiat, et nulla species sine substantia propria subsistit, nulla autem substantia uitali motu, qui eam contineat, et subsistere faciat, expers esse potest—omne enim quod naturaliter mouetur ex uita quadam motus sui principium sumit—necessario sequitur ut omnis creatura aut per seipsam uita sit aut uitae particeps, et quodammodo uiuens….*Periphyseon*, Books I–V Édouard Jeauneau ed. CCCM 161–5. (Turnhout, 1996–2001) (Translation: I. P. Sheldon-Williams, Books IV–V revised by J. J. O'Meara. *Periphyseon*, (Montréal, 1987), Book III, 728A–B, pp. 156–57.

82 CATHERINE KAVANAGH

therefore, is the intelligible motion of the *Logos*, proceeding from the Godhead, producing substance which in turn produces the species with which matter is informed to produce certain types of beings—bodies. So any embodied being at all, from the highest to the lowest, even the most insensate, has soul in some measure: it must have specified matter to produce the body, and this species or form is itself ultimately the product of soul, which is the operation of the *Logos*.

At this point the influence of Augustinian trinitarianism on the one hand and Byzantine cosmology on the other becomes evident. According to Augustine anything that exists must in some respect have a three-fold structure, since it is produced by a God who is trinitarian.[9] Augustine credited the "Platonists" with this insight into the nature of God, and he is thinking in particular of Plotinus, whom he had read in Marius Victorinus' translation. What marks the division between "Platonism" and Christianity for Augustine is the Incarnation.[10] According to Byzantine cosmology, on the other hand (which is, of course, an inheritance from Stoicism and Neoplatonism), any life or being at all will ultimately relate back to the *Logos*.[11] Life, then, is not merely sentience, and is not confined to rational creatures, or to sentient creatures, but is found in any kind of coherent existing creature, either in itself or by participation. To a certain extent, this is simply to say that the universe is intelligible, that even things which do not directly enjoy sentient life do, one way or another, reveal the purposes of the creator, and in that sense, possess soul—although each body does not necessarily possess an individual soul. Soul, then, is understood here to mean the intelligible motion in any creature, whether voluntary or involuntary, form to its matter.

It is not clear from the passage thus far whether soul, in this context, is simply the form of a given individual, or of a group of materially individuated instances, or whether it is to be understood as intelligible motion in the universe as a whole—in other words, is the individual

---

[9] See Augustine, *De Trinitate*. François Glorie and William J. Mountain eds. CCSL 32. (Turnhout, 1968).

[10] See *Confessions*, Bk VII: also, Armstrong, A. H., In fact, he is adapting Plotinus quite radically; whereas for Plotinus the One was absolute and simple, overflowing into Intellect and then into Soul, for Augustine, the first three hypostases of Plotinus are equal, as Father (One), Son (*Logos*) and Spirit (Soul), and all found in the One; he also confuses *Nous* and *Logos*, making them one hypostasis and then making that an aspect of the One. See *Cambridge History*, Part III "Plotinus," pp. 195–264.

[11] See, for example, Balthasar, H. U. von, *Kosmische Liturgie; das Weltbild Maximus' des Bekenners* (Einsiedeln, Switzerland, 1961).

THE NATURE OF THE SOUL ACCORDING TO ERIUGENA 83

soul an aspect of the world soul? It would appear that it is; Eriugena continues:

> For as there is no body which is not contained within its proper species, so there is no species which is not controlled by the power of some life. Therefore if all bodies which are naturally constituted are governed by some species of life, and every species seeks its own genus while every genus takes its origin from universal substance, it must be that every species of life which contains the numerousness of the various bodies returns to an universal life by participation in which it is a species.
>
> Now, this universal life is called by the natural philosophers the Universal Soul.... while those who contemplate the Divine Sophia call it the common life, which, while it participates in that one Life which is substantial in itself and the fountain and creator of all life, by its division into things visible and invisible distributes lives in accordance with the Divine ordinance.[12]

The great theological question here is whether the World Soul is to be identified with the Holy Spirit of the Christian Trinity. On the one hand, it seems to be a creature—which had led Augustine to reject the identification[13]—whereas on the other, by virtue of the fact that it is, in effect, the creator of the world, it would seem to be divine. One can see why identifying the World Soul with the Holy Spirit could cause problems: it would seem to identify God with His creation, and therefore to subject Him to the laws of place and time, in which case He ceases to be all-powerful and all-knowing, which would limit His capacity as the Good. As far as Eriugena is concerned, the solution is rather complex. His identification of God the Father with the One of Plotinus, and God the Son with the *Logos* in Whom the world was created was perfectly Augustinian, of course, but as regards the identification of the third person of the Trinity, the Holy Spirit with the World Soul, there are two other very powerful ideas which Eriugena brings

---

[12] Ut enim nullum corpus est, quod propria specie non continetur, ita nulla species est, quae cuiuspiam uitae uirtute non regitur. Proinde si omnia corpora naturaliter constituta quadam specie uitae administrantur, omnisque species genus suum appetit, omne autem genus a generalissima substantia originem ducit, omnem speciem uitae, quae diversorum corporum numerositatem continet, ad generalissimam quandam uitam recurrere necesse est, cuius participatione specificatur. Haec autem generalissima uita a sapientibus mundi uniuersalissima anima,.... uocatur; diuinae uero sophiae speculatores communem uitam appellant. Quae dum sit particeps illius unius uitae, quae per se substantialis est, omnisque uitae fons et creatrix suis diuisionibus uisibilium et inuisibilium uitas iuxta diuinam ordinationem distribuit, quemadmodum sol iste sensibus notus radios suos ubique diffundi. (PP III, 728D–729A, pp. 157–8).

[13] Augustine, *De consensu evangelistarum libri quattuor*. Ed. F. Weihrich, (Wien, 1904), pp. i, 23, 25.

84 CATHERINE KAVANAGH

to bear on the question of God's relation with the world, and adds to Augustine's position.[14] The first of these is the radical negative theology of ps.Dionysius,[15] the second is the concept of theophany and return found in Maximus the Confessor,[16] and they are related.

As far as Eriugena is concerned, the creation, as described in Genesis, is a theophany,[17] in other words, a manifestation of God, and therefore it has something of His nature. The life of the world—that is, the existence of the world—is the divine life communicating itself, right down to the lowest levels of existence. In that sense then, the world is not so radically separated from Him: He is in it, and this presence is what keeps the universe in existence, and this presence at work in the world can quite legitimately be called the Holy Spirit. On the other hand, God, as He is in himself is utterly unknowable; Eriugena's conception of God is very close to Plotinus' conception of the One. (Insofar as he is a Christian theologian, the crucial question is the extent to which the One is actually trinitarian.)[18] Eriugena considers the Greek description of the Trinity—Essence, Power and Operation—to be the most accurate, and this is a triad which can exist on several different levels. Insofar as we can know God, the First Person, and the essence, is the Father, the Second is the *Logos*, the Power of the Essence, and the third is the Operation of God, the Holy Spirit, but the Divine Life in itself is utterly unknowable and at the highest level, ineffable. As we move through the lower levels of creation, however, we can see it more clearly. It is reflected—that is to say, present in particular way—in the

---

[14] See also Sheldon-Williams, I. P., *Periphyseon III*, Scriptores Latini Hiberniae XI, (Dublin, 1981), p. 322, n. 74.

[15] See Roques, R. *L'univers dionysien. Structure hiérarchique du monde selon le Pseudo-Denys.* (Paris, 1954). See also: *Structures théologiques*; also Rorem, P. Rorem, *Ps-Dionysius: a commentary on the texts and an introduction to their influence* (New York, 1993).

[16] See Maximus the Confessor, PG 91:1084C, 1113B, 1385BC; Maximi Confessoris *Ambigua ad Iohannem iuxta Iohannis Scotti Eriugenae latinam interpretationem.* Ed. Jeauneau, É., CCSG 18 (Turnhout, 1988), pp. 31, 48–9, 238.

[17] E.g., PP I 449A–450B; PP II, 633B–634A.

[18] See Beierwaltes, W. *Eriugena. Grundzüge seines Denkens*, (Frankfurt: Klostermann, 1994), Ch VII, in which he discusses the question of Eriugena's trinitarianism, concluding that for Eriugena the Trinity is not purely subjective, that is to say, characteristic of human thinking about God, but actually characterises the divine essence also. In very late Neoplatonism, the question as to whether or not mixture can be found in the One seems also to have become an issue; see the recent work of Sarah Rappe on Damascius' recasting of Proclus' metaphysics, in particular, his criticism of Proclus' doctrine of strongly hierarchical Henads (Rappe, S. Presentation to the Symposium of the International Plato Society, Dublin, July 2007).

THE NATURE OF THE SOUL ACCORDING TO ERIUGENA   85

world in general, created through the power of the Son by the essence of the Father showing, or manifesting, itself through the operation of the Holy Spirit: operation makes things manifest, and it is therefore well applied to that operation which is the life or soul of the world. However, because the Trinity as it is in itself is utterly unknowable, and always remains as such above the world, we avoid the problem of making God subject to limitation, place and time. Eriugena does not specifically identify the World Soul here with the Holy Spirit, but because of his strong emphasis on negative theology, it is possible to say that the World Soul is the Operation of the *Logos* at the level of created reality, or being, and is therefore *in a very particular sense* the Holy Spirit, not as he is in himself, which is ineffable, but as he operates in the created world. This identification is therefore less problematic for him than for Augustine, since it need not necessarily affect the third person of the Trinity in and of itself, as found in the One.

Following the principle of Soul in general comes the first division in the universal soul, which is between rational and irrational soul. The latter refers to the animals, whereas the former

> ... is distributed between angels and men, but whereas in angels it is called intellectual as though for a special meaning, in men it is called rational—although in actual fact, the truth is that in both angels and men it is both intellectual and rational; and therefore intellectual and rational life is predicated of both as a common form.... I[he] can think of no ... reason why the angelic life should not be called rational soul or the rational soul of man intellect, especially as angels possess heavenly bodies of their own.... unless it be merely ... to draw a verbal distinction—for that angels are made in the image of God we do not doubt.... [19]

He goes on to observe that irrational soul is divided into two types: the sensitive in animals, and the auctive in plants, and that all four of these types of soul are found in Man: intellect, as with angels, rational, as with man, sensitive, as with animals, and life (which is the primary

---

[19] .... rationalis quidem vita angelis hominibusque distributa est, sed in angelis ueluti specialis significationis causa intellectualis dicitur, in hominibus uero rationalis. Veruntamen consulta ueritate et in angelis et et in hominibus intellectualis et rationalis est; ideoque de communiter de eis praedicatur uita intellectualis et rationalis. Ad differentiam tamen relinquitur ut ipsa uita intellectus in angelis, in hominibus anima uocitetur. Non enim mihi alia ratio occurrit quae prohibeat angelicam uitam animam uocari rationalem quemadmodum non prohibet humanam rationalem intellectum, praesertim dum angeli caelestia sua corpora ... possident.... nisi sola uocabularum differentia, quomodo et angelos ad imaginem dei factos non dubitamus. PP III, 732C–732D, pp. 162–3.

86 CATHERINE KAVANAGH

characteristic of soul), like the plants, and subsistence in existence, and for this reason, man is called the workshop of all creatures (*creaturarum omnium officina*); angels do not participate in corporeal life, and therefore lack sensitivity. He has some difficulty with this division, since the division between rational/intellectual, which is immortal, on the one hand, and sensitive/auctive, which dies, on the other seems to him an absolute one, and it seems as though two mutually contradictory species (one characterized by possession, the other by privation, of life) are included in one genus of "soul". Given that the bodies of plants and animals "survive," so to speak, as elements after their deaths, given that in every creature, the triad of Essence, Power and Operation is to be found, and given that soul of any kind is higher than bodies made of elements, it seems to him contradictory to say that irrational soul does not in some manner survive, which is what the Fathers, both Eastern and Western, say.[20] Nor does he succeed in resolving this problem, but he suggests that when the individuals perish, the soul is preserved in the genera, and that the Holy Fathers had taught otherwise for the benefit of "men totally given up to the flesh like brutes," to give them a salutary fright, and to raise themselves to the dignity of the rational creature in which they were created!

He then goes on to discuss the characteristics of the human soul in particular. The human soul is always considered as an aspect of human nature as a whole, although the extent to which human nature can be identified with the soul alone is an important one: in fact, it cannot. He writes:

> Now man is body and soul; but if he is always man, then he is always soul and body, and although the parts of man may be separated from one another—for soul abandons the control of the body which it had assumed after its generation, and the body, deserted by it, is dissolved and its parts return each to its proper place among the elements, yet by the reason of their nature [naturali tamen ratione] neither do the parts cease to be always inseparably related to the whole, nor the whole to the parts. For the reason of their relation can never cease to be. Thus, what to the corporeal sense seems to be separated, must on a higher view of things always subsist as it was inseparably. For indeed the human body whether alive or dead, is the body of a man. Similarly the human soul, whether it is controlling its body as gathered together in a unity or ceases

---

[20] See his discussion of this issue in PP III, 736C–739D, where he concludes that the Fathers must have had some deeper meaning for saying something which to all appearances is so contradictory.

THE NATURE OF THE SOUL ACCORDING TO ERIUGENA 87

to control it...yet does not cease to be the soul of a man, and....continues to govern a body distributed among the elements no less than one which is bound together in the structural unity of its members....For if the soul is a spirit, and the elements also into which the body is resolved are closely akin to the spiritual nature, why should it surprise us if the incorporeal soul should control the part of the body preserved in natures akin to itself?[21]

In this passage, we see Eriugena struggling to reconcile the immortal soul with the corruptible body; finally coming to the conclusion the even in dissolution, the body remains somehow attached to the soul. In this, he is inheriting a solution—Maximus'—to a question which had been closely argued in the Byzantine world. From being a dissoluble relation between two loosely conjoined substances, with the soul being seen as the reality and the body being the image, or shadow of it, the relation between body and soul had been made far closer, moving through Leontius of Byzantium's model of two substances in one hypostasis to Maximus' assertion that body and soul were joined indissolubly, even after the death of the former, and that human nature itself was one substance, composed of form (soul) and matter (body); he takes the Aristotelian view that form and matter are intellectually distinguishable but really inseparable in any given reality. Human nature has only one logos in God, not two which are subsequently joined together. This leads Eriugena to consider how the soul animates, or ensouls the body; he rejects the idea of the body as a "container" for the soul, or as some kind of automaton controlled by the soul. Rather, in knowing the world and living in it, soul and body work in harmony. Because it

---

[21] Homo autem corpus et anima est. Si autem semper homo, semper igitur anima et corpus. Et quamuis partes hominis a se inuicem segregentur—anima enim deserit usitatum post generationem sui corporis regimen; qua deserente corpus soluitur, partesque illius propriis elementorum sedibus redduntur—naturali tamen ratione et partes ad totum referri non desinunt semper et inseparabiliter, et totum ad partes. Relationis siquidem ratio nunquam potest perire. Proinde quod corporeo sensui uidetur segregari, altiori rerum speculatione semper simul et inseparabiliter subsistere necesse est. Nam et corpus humanum, siue uiuum, siue mortuum, corpus hominis est. Similiter anima humana, siue corpus suum simul collectum regat, siue in partes dissolutum, ut uidetur sensibus, regere desinat, anima tamen hominis esse non cessat. Ac per hoc datur intelligi altiori rerum intimatione, non minus eam administrare corpus per elementa dispersum, quam una compagine membrorum coniunctum...Si enim anima spiritus est, per se omni corporea crassitudine carens, ipsa quoque elementa in quae corpus soluitur, quantum per se simpliciter subsistunt, spirituali naturae proxima sunt, quid mirum, si incorporea anima partes corporis sui in proximis sibi naturis custoditas rexerit? (PP III, 729C–730A, pp. 158–9).

88 CATHERINE KAVANAGH

is immaterial and immortal, of course, soul must be "located", but it does work in a very real way through the body. The soul uses the body, and its instruments, the senses to form impressions, and by this very activity of synthesis, which in fact gives significance to the experience of the body, the true greatness of soul is revealed: "in a potential sense it is present to receive the phantasies which are everywhere formed in the instruments of its senses; and by this reasoning, we come to know how great is its natural power and placelessness." It receives all the sense impressions simultaneously, and assesses them spiritually "stor[ing] them according to memory...order[ing] them by reason and...evaluat[ing]them by the intellect according to the divine numbers of which she receives knowledge from above"[22] "Contemplating their exemplars it forms judgments both about the numbers which are constituted within itself and about the corporeal and sensible numbers, both of which are outside it." Rational soul continues its activity after death in much the same way as before death since it is never really "contained" by the body at all.

In Book IV, he begins to consider in more depth human nature, as being both body and soul, which is composed of sense, reason, intellect and vital motion, rather than soul as such. However, here again, his interest is primarily in the soul, which is the definitive part of human nature. The human soul is simple; the various elements noted in it are not different parts, but rather different functions.

> For she herself is everywhere in herself whole and individual, but her movements...are designated by different names. For when she is occupied in contemplative activity about her Creator, transcending herself, and transcending the understanding of all creation, she is called intellect or mind or spirit; when by what might be called the secondary activity of her nature, she investigates the causes of nature, she is called reason; when having found them she distinguishes and defines them, she is called interior sense; when she receives through the organs of her bodily senses the phantasies of the sensibles, she is called exterior sense....and yet she is of the most simple....essence...From this we may understand that the whole human soul is made in the image of God, since it is wholly an intellect which intellects, wholly a reason which reasons, wholly a sense in the interior sense and sensing, wholly life and life-giving.[23]

---

[22] See Sheldon-Williams I. P., ed. *Periphyseon* Book III (Dublin, 1981) Introduction, p. 21; following this quotation, he gives a summary of the eight orders of number according to which the sense impressions are structured and made intelligible—in conformity with the intelligible universe.

[23] Ipsa siquidem in seipsa tota ubique est et indiuidua; motus tamen ipsius diuersis

THE NATURE OF THE SOUL ACCORDING TO ERIUGENA   89

Eriugena's anthropology is very strongly spiritualized. Whereas Augustine
had been quite content to read the physical account of creation as being,
on one level, an account of the body, male and female, as we have it
now, Eriugena considered this gross materialism. In fact, Eriugena's
account of the body seems, on one level, really to be an account of
another aspect of the soul. The material body we inhabit now, as far
as he is concerned, is not the body we were intended to have. As man
was originally created, he was neither male nor female, but the perfect
image of God; sexual division came about as a result of the Fall. He tells
us, as above, that God is a Trinity, *ousia, dunamis* and *energeia*, and
this is also the structure of the human soul, which is the true "imago
dei". As God has created the soul in his own image and likeness, so
the soul chooses a body in its own likeness: the body is a likeness of
the likeness of God. He writes:

> ...the whole man is said to consist of mind, the material life principle
> and matter itself. And indeed the mind, in which all the virtue of the soul
> subsists, is made in the image of God, and is the mirror of the Supreme
> Good, since in it the incomprehensible form of Divine essence is present
> in an ineffable and incomprehensible way. But the material life principle,
> whose specific activity centres about matter, and which for that reason
> is called material, seeing that it is involved in the mutable matter of the
> body, is a kind of image of the mind and...a reflection of a reflection:
> so that the mind is a form of the Divine nature, but the vital motion...is
> the form of mind, as it were a second image, through which the mind
> produces even a form of matter. And thus in a way, through the linking
> of human nature, the whole man can suitably be described as fashioned
> after the image of God, though really and primarily it is only in the mind
> that the image can be seen to subsist.[24]

---

appellationibus significantur. Dum enim circa creatorem suum, super seipsam et super
totius creaturae intelligentiam contemplatiuo motu uersatur, intellectus, seu mens seu
animus; dum rationes rerum ueluti secundo motu naturali inuestigat, ratio; dum inuenit
eas et discernit atque definit, sensus interior; dum rerum sensibilium phantasias per
organa corporalium sensuum recipit, sensus exterior....dum sit ipsa [*sc.* corpus]
simplicissimae et indiuiduae et impartibilis essentiae...Hinc datur intelligi totam
animam humanam ad imaginem Dei factam, quia tota intellectus est intelligens, tota
ratio disputans, tota sensus in interiori sensu et sentiens, tota uita et uiuificans. (PP
IV, 787C–788A, pp. 67–8).

[24] ...ita ut totus homo animo et materiali uita et ipsa materia constare intelligatur.
Et animus quidem, in quo tota animae uirtus constat, ad imaginem dei factus, et
summi boni speculum, quoniam in eo diuinae essentiae incomprehensibilis forma
ineffabili et incomprehensibili modo resultat. Materialis autem uita, quae specialiter
circa materiam uersatur, et propterea materialis dicitur, quia mutabilitati materiae (id
est corporis) adhaeret, imago quaedam animi est, et, ut ipse dicit, speculum speculi;
ita ut animus diuinae naturae forma sit, uitalis autem motus....forma sit animi, ac

90 CATHERINE KAVANAGH

In a passage where he uses a lot of mathematical imagery to illustrate the idea that all things are contained in their unified principles, Eriugena observes, that "In the soul, under a unitary mode, are the powers of the whole body which provide for all things separately,"[25] that is to say, that the body depends on the soul for life and existence, and is, so to speak, contained in the soul. Therefore, very often, when Eriugena talks about the body, and above all when he talks about the incorruptible/resurrected body, he is not talking about the flesh and blood which we inhabit now, but the transformed, spiritualized body we were meant to have before the Fall, and which we will eventually have in imitation of Christ. Therefore, the body was not strictly speaking a punishment for the Fall, but it was very strongly modified by the Fall, in particular by being made material, and in the resurrection, it will once again be de-materialized and made spiritual. He says:

> That body which was created at the establishment of man in the beginning I should say was spiritual and immortal, and either like or identical with that which we shall possess after the Resurrection...it is quite apparent to the reason that if the same body which was made at the first creation of man before the Fall is after the Fall itself changed and made corruptible, then that corruptible body would not be a superstructure, but simply the spiritual and incorruptible body transformed into an earthly and corruptible body(800B–C)...the form of the soul is the interior body (803A)[26]

The expansion of God which we see in Creation is only one aspect of His motion, however; the other aspect is the Return, in which all created things will return to Him. Eriugena took most of his ideas on the Return from Maximus, whose ideas are by and large as follows: The point of the cosmic Return is Man himself, since he contains all strands of existence: both a rational soul, which likens him to God, and a material body, which relates him to the world. As a creature, man is both body and soul: he consists of one species, humanity, both soul

---

ueluti secunda imago, per quam animus etiam materiae speciem praestat. Ac per hoc quadam ratione per humanae naturae consequentiam totus homo ad imaginem dei factus non incongrue dicitur, quamuis proprie et principaliter in solo animo imago subsistere intelligatur...(PP. IV 790C–790D).

[25] PP III, 618B.

[26] Illud corpus, quod in constitutione hominis primitus est factum, spirituale et immortale crediderim esse, ac tale aut ipsum, quale post resurrectionem habituri sumus....maxime, cum manifesta ratio perdoceat, si id ipsum corpus, quod in prima conditione hominis factum est, ante delictum mox conuersum est et factum corruptibile post delictum, non erat illud supermachinatum, sed de spirituali et incorruptibili in terrenum et corruptibile transmutatum, (PP IV 800B–C).

THE NATURE OF THE SOUL ACCORDING TO ERIUGENA 91

and body, and not two, the species of soul on the one hand, and the species of body on the other. The *Logos* of man in God is one, body and soul. The Incarnation and Resurrection of Christ are the great pattern of the Return, and as Christ was resurrected in the flesh, so too will all mankind be resurrected. The traditional teaching on the human soul was that it was the form of the body, but Origen maintained that the body was a punishment for the soul for man's sin at the time of the Fall. Maximus certainly preserved the doctrine of personal immortality, but he modifies the doctrine quite substantially. For Maximus, the body is not a punishment, but was always intended by God for man. Man is one nature—a composite nature, to be sure, but human nature cannot be split up into body and soul. The human body and the human soul enjoy a relationship of mutual dependence: the soul relies on the body for its activity in this world, whereas the body relies on the intellect of the soul for guidance as to its proper activity. We can see here the influence of Plato's three-part psychology, sense, emotion and reason. For Maximus, the human being consists of sense, reason, and intellect which informs the reason. The proper end of the human being is the contemplation of the divine, and insofar as the sense is guided by the reason, and the reason is guided by the intellect, then the human creature will turn towards God, and attain its proper end, which is reunification with the Divine. However, insofar as man is distracted by material things, the reason turns away from the intellect, and the intellect loses sight of God, and man descends lower and lower. On the whole, reason and intellect are properties of the soul, whereas sense is identified with the body, but the soul has its own kind of sense also. There is always a question as to whether the soul and the intellect are different, or whether the intellect is the higher part of the soul. In Book IV of the *Periphyseon*, Eriugena will declare that soul and intellect, for all practical purposes, are synonymous.

The process of the Return is essentially a process of contemplation: as intellect or mind contemplates the Divinity, it is drawn closer and closer to it. The resurrected body is likewise involved in this process of contemplation, until eventually it is absorbed into the soul, and the soul into divinity. For Maximus this does not mean a loss of identity: he uses the famous simile of iron in fire to illustrate the process of unification, a simile which is repeated by Eriugena in the first book of the *Periphyseon*.[27]

---

[27] PP I 450B.

92 CATHERINE KAVANAGH

Eriugena takes all of this Maximian doctrine on board. He is particularly interested in the question of the Return, and it is at this point that his differences with the Western tradition emerge most strongly. The Western Fathers generally maintain that in the resurrection and Beatific vision, the material body, although certainly transformed and glorified, would nevertheless remain itself. Eriugena, on the other hand, maintains that the glorification of the body means its absorption into soul, and their absorption into God. It is still the Beatific Vision, since all of this happens by a process of contemplation, but a very dynamic version of it. For Eriugena, as for Maximus, individuality is still preserved; in fact, it has to be, if the transcendence of God is to be preserved.

Conclusion

The term soul or *anima* covers a variety of ideas in the work of Eriugena, all linked by the fundamental concept of "that which gives life, causes autonomous growth and change." Individual soul is an aspect of the universal, or world soul, the dynamic energy which underpins all creation, and is an aspect of the divine *Logos*. The individual soul in turn has several differenct aspects, ranging from the pure intellect found in angels through the sensitivity found in animals to the purely auctive soul found in plants. He draws on a variety of sources both Eastern and Western, but it is the Greek teaching on the subject which eventually dominates his own thought. The aspect which is of most interest to him is that of intellectual, or rational soul, which he sees as coming to contain, or re-assume, all of the other aspects of soul, sensitive and auctive. It is a dynamic reality, and its fundamental goal and purpose is the contemplation of the divine. It is, from the start, an expression of God's nature—the *imago dei* of the Bible, having the power to create itself the body in the same likeness, and its fundamental desire is to draw continually closer to the nature of which it is the image; and in the return, whilst retaining its individuality, it is eventually re-absorbed by the divine nature.

C. ISLAMIC TRADITION

ARISTOTLE'S *CATEGORIES* AND THE SOUL:
AN ANNOTATED TRANSLATION OF AL-KINDĪ'S
THAT THERE ARE SEPARATE SUBSTANCES

Peter Adamson and Peter E. Pormann*

One of the first philosophical works available to authors writing in Arabic was Aristotle's *Categories*. This should come as no surprise. Logic occupied the first place within the Aristotelian curriculum both in the Arabic and the earlier Greek traditions.[1] And the first works within the standard logical textbook, the *organon*, were Porphyry's *Introduction* (*Isagoge*) and Aristotle's *Categories*. In fact, the *Categories* gained considerable importance amongst Christian authors of the Syriac tradition, which bridged the gap between late Greek and early Arabic thought.[2] In a critique of the doctrine of the Trinity, al-Kindī himself implicitly confirms that these basic logical texts enjoyed great popularity among Christians of his own day. He mentions that he has used ideas drawn from the *Isagoge* because it is well-known to his Christian opponents, and more generally because it is a text known even to students.[3] Moreover, the *Categories* also played a role within

---

* Adamson: Kings' College London, Pormann: University of Warwick, Coventry.

[1] That al-Kindī regarded logic as the starting-point of philosophical study is clear from his *On the Quantity of Aristotle's Books*, in M. Abū Rīda (ed.) al-Kindī, *Rasāʾil al-Kindī al-Falsafiyya*, 2 vols (Cairo: 1950/1953), vol. 1, p. 364. Hereafter *Rasāʾil* will refer to volume one of this edition of al-Kindī's works. This work is also edited in M. Guidi and R. Walzer, *Uno Scritto Introduttivo allo Studio di Aristotele* (Rome: 1940).

[2] Authors writing in Syriac produced not only multiple translations of the *Categories* but also numerous commentaries. On this see the studies of S. Brock, for instance "The yriac Commentary Tradition," in C. Burnett (ed.), *Glosses and Commentaries on Aristotelian Logical Texts: the Syriac, Arabic and Medieval Latin Traditions* (London: 1993), pp. 3–18, and H. Hugonnard-Roche, such as his study in the same volume, "Remarques sur la tradition arabe de l'*Organon* d'après le manuscrit Paris, Bibliothèque nationale, ar. 2346," pp. 19–28 and H. Hugonnard-Roche, "Sur les versions syriaques des *Catégories* d'Aristote," *Journal Asiatique* 275 (1987), pp. 205–22. See further R. J. H. Gottheil, "The Syriac Versions of the *Categories* of Aristotle," *Hebraica* 9 (1892–3), pp. 166–215 and K. Georr, *Les Catégories d'Aristote dans leurs versions syro-arabes* (Beirut: 1948).

[3] See A. Périer, "Un traité de Yaḥyā ben ʿAdī. Défense du dogme de la Trinité contre les objections d'al-Kindī," *Revue de l'orient christian* 3rd series, 22 (1920–1), pp. 3–21. Al-Kindī's arguments, without the response of Ibn ʿAdī, are edited and translated in R. Rashed and J. Jolivet, *Oeuvres Philosophiques & Scientifiques d'al-Kindī: Volume 2, Métaphysique et cosmologie* (Leiden: 1998).

96   PETER ADAMSON AND PETER E. PORMANN

the medical teaching of late antique Alexandria.[4] After all, Galen had
insisted that the best physician is also a philosopher, and consequently,
Aristotelian concepts occur in the *Alexandrian Summaries* and other
didactic texts of the period. In Arabic, the *Categories* continued to be
central to the transmission of Greek thought. It was a frequent subject
of commentary and epitome, and al-Kindī himself reportedly wrote an
epitome of the work, as did his student al-Sarakhsī.[5]

Given the prominence of the *Isagoge* and *Categories* it is no wonder
that ideas drawn from these works would have been pressed into service
in areas other than logic. A prominent example would be al-Kindī's use
of the *Isagoge* to discuss divine attributes in his best-known work, *On
First Philosophy*. But it does come as a surprise to see him attempting
to mount an argument for the immateriality of the soul which draws
almost exclusively on the *Categories*. He does so in a short epistolary
treatise preserved in a single manuscript held in Istanbul, which in fact
contains unique copies of many of al-Kindī's philosophical epistles. Its
title is *On [the Fact That] There are Separate Substances*, or more literally *Substances Which Are Not Bodies (Fī annahu jawāhir lā ajsām)*.[6]
The purpose of the present offering is to provide the first translation
of this work,[7] along with explanatory notes.

First, a brief overview of the argument may be helpful. Though the
work sets out to show that there are incorporeal substances, souls
are the central example given of such substances. Al-Kindī says, as
is his wont, that a thorough demonstration is not needed for present
purposes. But he suggests that the proof he will give is supported by
certain "logical principles (*al-awā'il al-manṭiqiyya*)." These may be the
ideas drawn from the *Categories* in what follows. The main such idea
is the distinction between univocal and non-univocal or equivocal

---

[4] See P. E. Pormann, 'The Alexandrian Summary (*Jawāmi'*) of Galen's *On the Sects
for Beginners*: Commentary or Abridgment?', in P. Adamson et al. (eds.), *Philosophy,
Science and Exegesis in Greek, Arabic and Latin Commentaries, Bulletin of the Institute
of Classical Studies*. Supplement 83, 2 vols (London, 2004), vol. 2, 11–33, on p. 17; and
Pormann, 'Medisch Onderwijs in de Late Oudheid: Van Alexandrië naar Montpellier',
Nederlands Tijdschrift voor Geneeskunde [forthcoming].

[5] See F. E. Peters, *Aristoteles Arabus: the Oriental Translations and Commentaries
on the Aristotelian Corpus* (Leiden: 1968), pp. 7–11. In fact Ibn al-Nadīm's *Fihrist*
seems to say that there were two distinct works by al-Kindī based on the *Categories*;
unfortunately no such work is extant.

[6] The work is edited at *Rasā'il* 265–9.

[7] This translation will also appear in P. Adamson and P. E. Pormann, *The Philosophical Works of al-Kindī*, which is forthcoming from Oxford University Press.

ARISTOTLE'S *CATEGORIES* AND THE SOUL 97

predication (*na't mutawāṭa'* and *na't mutashābih*). This distinction from *Categories* ch. 1 is assimilated to the distinction between "said of (*legetai*)" and "present in (*en*)" from *Categories* ch. 2: al-Kindī states that what is said of something else univocally gives that thing its name and definition. (We find the same conflation in al-Kindī's *On the Quantity of Aristotle's Books*; see our note 12 below.) To put this in language not used in the *Categories* itself, al-Kindī is here associating univocal predication with essential predication and non-univocal predication with accidental predication.

Armed with this distinction, al-Kindī continues by arguing that the body must have an extrinsic source of life, because body is not essentially alive. The extrinsic source of life is soul. Now, soul is "said of," and not "present in," the body of the living thing. This might seem surprising, because al-Kindī has just said that bodies are not essentially alive. But he seems to mean that any living thing is *as such* essentially alive: for instance man is essentially alive. So even if soul is only accidentally "in" each body *qua* body, it will be essentially "said of" each living body *qua* living body. Now if this is right, then soul will share a name and definition with the living body. But the living body is a substance; therefore the soul will have the name and definition of substance.

One might object that al-Kindī's argument mistakenly shows that the soul will share the name and definition of body, if it is said essentially of the body. If so, the soul will be a corporeal, not incorporeal, substance. Would it be helpful to repeat the point just made above, namely that soul is not said "univocally" of body as such, but only of living body? We might then say that soul is essentially alive and essentially substance, but not essentially bodily. Unfortunately, this will not work either: the non-living body is just as much substance as the living body. It is not the fact that the living body is *living* that makes it a substance. There thus seems no reason to say that substantiality is transferred to the soul but corporeality is not. Al-Kindī would, one might think, have done better to argue that soul is essentially alive rather than essentially a substance. Had he done so, the argument would be even closer to a text that may be in the background here, namely Plato's *Phaedo* (see our note 16 below).

On the other hand, the thrust of this epistle is not, as in the *Phaedo*, to show that the soul is immortal. It is to show that there are incorporeal substances, where the soul is only one example. As the treatise progresses, the argument becomes more general, and it seems that al-Kindī wants to say that *any* form is a substance. Consider, for instance, the form of a stone. This form will be a substance because it is said of, and thus shares the name and definition of, the substance that is the stone. Again, the difficulty will be that al-Kindī has given us no reason for transferring the predicate "substantiality" to the form, and not other predicates, in particular the predicate "corporeality." So the objection still stands: the argument seems to show that forms said of corporeal substances will themselves be corporeal substances.

However, al-Kindī has a way of arguing that these forms are not in fact corporeal. This argument begins at §7. Again the central example is soul, but the strategy seems applicable to other forms as well. And again, he uses ideas from the *Categories*, recalling that what is "said of" a thing is in the first instance the *species* of that thing. He infers from this that the soul of the living thing is its species, and then launches into a complicated defense of the claim that species are incorporeal. In fact this is the proposition which receives the most detailed discussion in the epistle, even though the incorporeality of species would seem relatively uncontroversial. Much more controversial, and indeed apparently non-sensical, is the idea that my soul is the same as my species. And maddeningly, this idea receives no defense at all. One might, though, make two points in al-Kindī's defense. First, the use of the Greek word *eidos* for both "form" and "species" confuses the issue: soul, as we know from the *De Anima*, is the "form of the body" even though it is not the species of the body. Second, it is of course a matter of intense controversy how Aristotelian forms relate to universals, and whether they should themselves be considered as particular or not. Still, al-Kindī's assimilation of the human soul to a secondary substance from the *Categories* is not likely to strike many readers as plausible.

So it looks as though we can identify several dubious philosophical moves in this epistle. But this does not deprive it of interest. If anything, the flaws in al-Kindī's reasoning show how he is straining to demonstrate a standard Platonic doctrine—the immateriality of soul—using rather impoverished Aristotelian materials. This way of using Aristotle is familiar from the Greek tradition and will be a commonplace of the later Arabic tradition. Consider, for instance, the way that ideas from the *De Anima* are confidently used in both traditions to argue for the immortality and immateriality of soul, a topic only glancingly touched upon by Aristotle himself. In fact it is striking that al-Kindī restricts himself to the *Categories* here, rather than drawing on the *De Anima* (except for the characterization of soul as "form of the body," which

ARISTOTLE'S *CATEGORIES* AND THE SOUL 99

hardly requires having first-hand acquaintance with the *De Anima* itself). Two mutually compatible explanations for this suggest themselves. First, this epistle may have been written before al-Kindī gained access to the *De Anima* in Arabic (see our note 17 below). Second, he may have wanted to use the *Categories* here for the same reason he used the *Isagoge* in arguing against the Trinity: because of its familiarity and importance as a beginning text in the Aristotelian, but also the medical curriculum.[8]

Translation: al-Kindī's That There are Separate Substances

(1) [265] May God help you to achieve truth, and bring you in agreement with its path! I have understood that you asked me to outline my statement that there are incorporeal substances. To do this well presupposes a knowledge of natural things, in order that the logical principles used in [the study of] natural things may be evident to the one making this inquiry.[9] I have outlined for you what I believe to be sufficient (10) for your question. For, it requires a discussion of many propositions which serve as a basis, because of the need for an extensive discussion in order to make the issue clear, and in order to steer you towards enlightenment on the way to the answer to your question. Through God we succeed.

(2) The proof that there are incorporeal substances in the parts of the natural world comes after our first establishing the quiddity of body, namely extension in three dimensions, [266] i.e. length, width and depth; and after our knowing the concomitants of substance that distinguish it from other things: that it subsists in itself (*bi-dhātihi*), has no need for anything else in its stability, is the bearer for the differentia,

---

[8] Our thanks for comments on this material from audiences in Dublin and Cambridge. Peter Adamson would like to thank the Leverhulme Trust, whose funding supported the research into this topic. Peter E. Pormann acknowledges his gratitude to the Warburg Institute for electing him as Frances A. Yates Long-Term Research Fellow, and thus allowing him to pursue this research.

[9] What "logical principles used in [the study of] natural things" are invoked in the subsequent treatise? The only obvious *physical* principle is the first sentence of §2: that the quiddity of body is extension in three dimensions. However Tony Street has suggested to us that we understand the term "logical" to refer to the ideas from Aristotle's *Categories* in what follows.

100   PETER ADAMSON AND PETER E. PORMANN

is identical to itself[10] and unchanging, and is characterized by all the categories.[11] There are, however, [two kinds of characterizations]: univocal characterizations and equivocal characterizations.[12] A univocal characterization (5) is the characterization that gives what is characterized both its name and its definition. The equivocal characterization is

---

[10] *Huwa huwa fī ʿayn.* In what follows the term *ʿayn*, which al-Kindī sometimes uses to mean simply an "individual," seems to mean "essence" and to serve as a synonym for *dhāt*.

[11] Cf. *Categories* 2a34ff: secondary substances and accidents are said of or present in primary substance, but primary substance is not said of or present in anything; the other things exist through it. More puzzling is the claim that substance is "unchanging (*lam yatabaddal*)," already anticipated by the reference to substance's "stability (*thabāt*)." Does Aristotle not say precisely that they are receptive of contraries, at *Categories* 4a10ff? What al-Kindī may mean here is that the substance *persists through change*, the point made most famously at *Physics* I.7. Cf. *On First Philosophy* 27 [Rashed/Jolivet ed.]: "the first bearer of predication, which is being, does not change, because the corruption of something that corrupts has nothing to do with the 'making be' of its being."

[12] Here the three-fold Aristotelian distinction (*Categories*, ch. 1) between synonymy, homonomy, and paronymy has been simplified into a two-fold distinction. (Our thanks to Paul Thom for stressing this point.) For the same ideas see further *On the Quantity of Aristotle's Books*, at *Rasāʾil* 365–6:

> There are eight books on logic. The first is called the *Categories*, and deals with terms, I mean subject and predicate. The subject is what is called "substance," whereas the predicate is what is called an "accident," predicated of the substance, but not giving [the substance] its name or its definition. For "predicate" is said in two ways. In the first, the predicate gives its name and definition to [the subject]. For example "animal (*al-ḥayy*)" is said of man, and man is called animal and defined by the definition of animal (namely "a substance having the capacity for sensation and self-motion"). Likewise, "quality" is said of whiteness, because quality is that which applies to it and is said of it: this whiteness is similar to that whiteness, or this whiteness is not similar to that whiteness; or this shape is similar to that shape, or this shape is not similar to that shape. So "quality," being said of the various kinds of qualities, gives to the kinds of qualities their name and definition. The other way that a predicate is said is when it is said of its subject equivocally, rather than univocally, and does not give it its name or definition. For example, "whiteness (*al-bayāḍ*)" is predicated of the white (*al-abyaḍ*), that is, the white body (*al-jism al-abyaḍ*). "White (*abyaḍ*)," that is, the word "white," is derived from "whiteness (*bayāḍ*)," not from anything else. Whiteness is a color that blocks vision, whereas the white, that is, the white body, is not a color that blocks vision. So whiteness does not give [white] its definition or its name, properly speaking, but rather ["white"] is a derived term, since "white" is derived from "whiteness."

It is not clear whether "equivocal" in these passages is supposed to cover both homonymy and paronymy. Perhaps here in *That There are Separate Substances*, al-Kindī goes on to distinguish them in that in the paronymous case a name is shared (i.e. genuinely, not homonymously) but only "in a derivative fashion." In any case the two-fold distinction will smooth the way for what follows, where al-Kindī conflates this distinction between types of "characterization" with the two-fold distinction between substantial and accidental predication.

ARISTOTLE'S *CATEGORIES* AND THE SOUL 101

one that gives what is characterized neither its name nor its definition. If it does give it [its] name, then it does so only in a derivative fashion, not according to the proper sense of the name, and does not provide any characterization of it. Once this is known it can be established that incorporeal substances do exist.

(3) For, living bodies must have their life in them either essentially (*dhātiyya*), (10) or accidentally and from something else. By what is "essentially in something" I mean what is such that, if it is separated from the thing, the thing is destroyed.[13] Whereas the accidental is what can be separated from that in which it is without the latter being destroyed. If life is in the living thing essentially, then when it is separated from the living thing, the living thing must be destroyed. And indeed we find that when life is separated from living beings then they are destroyed. However the body which we find to be living or non-living is still a body, since, when life is separated from it, its corporeality is not destroyed. (15) Therefore it is clear that life is in body accidentally and from something else.

(4) Now, we call the quiddity of life in the body "soul." So we must now examine whether the soul is a substance or an accident; [267] and if it is a substance, whether it is body, or not body.

(5) We say that things are different either in essence or only in name. Two things the essence of which have the same definition, and which have the same name, differ neither in name nor in essence, since they do not differ in the definition of their essence. The nature of things that do not differ in their essence is the same. (5) So one thing that describes another by giving it its name and its definition is of the nature of what it describes. If what it describes is a substance, then it is substance. But if what it describes is an accident, then it is an accident. On the other hand, that which describes what it describes neither with its own name nor with its own definition does not have the same nature as what it

---

[13] Cf. *On First Philosophy* 43: "By 'the essential' I mean that which makes subsist the essence of the thing: through its existence is the subsistence and stability of the thing's being, and through its absence is the destruction and corruption of the thing. For example life is essential to the living thing. The essential is called 'substantial' because it causes the substance of the thing to subsist."

102   PETER ADAMSON AND PETER E. PORMANN

describes.[14] That whose nature is not the nature of what it describes[15] is extraneous to what it describes. And that which is extraneous to what it describes is what we call an "accident" in what it describes, because it is not of [the described thing's] essence, but is rather an accident in it.[16]

(6) (10) That through which a thing is what it is, is the form of the thing, be it sensible or intellectual.[17] The substance is what it is through itself (*bi-'l-nafs*). The soul (*al-nafs*),[18] then, is the intellectual form of the

---

[14] Cf. *Categories* 1b10–13 (Ackrill trans., modified): "Whenever one thing is said of another as of a subject, all things said of what is predicated will be said of the subject also. For example, man is said of the individual man, and animal of man; so animal will be said of the individual man also." However the notion of "nature (*ṭabīʿa*)" is not found in the *Categories*, and al-Kindī's way of putting the point seems problematic in a way that Aristotle's is not. For al-Kindī seems to be saying that if X is "said of" Y (i.e. if X gives Y its name and definition) then they will share a *nature*, which seems to be a more symmetrical relationship than the one Aristotle has in mind. Animal is said of man, and thus of any given man. But the reverse is not the case: not everything said of man (or a given man) is said of animal. Thus man and animal do not "share a nature," even though animal gives man its name and definition.

[15] Omitting *huwa*.

[16] The whole paragraph is based on *Categories* chs. 2–3. What al-Kindī is doing here is to set up the idea that if soul is "said of" the living body, and if the living body is a substance, then soul too must be a substance. For soul is essential to the living body, so that it will share the living body's nature (i.e. substantiality). This argument is reminiscent of *Phaedo* 105c–e, where Plato has Socrates argue that since soul always brings life to the body, soul itself is essentially alive. It is worth noting that al-Kindī may have known the *Phaedo*, albeit perhaps indirectly. See D. Gutas, "Plato's *Symposion* in the Arabic Tradition," *Oriens* 31 (1988), pp. 36–60, and P. Adamson, *Al-Kindī* (New York: 2007), pp. 131–2.

[17] Of course the idea that the soul is the form of the body is from the *De Anima*, whereas the doctrine of form and matter is notoriously absent from the *Categories*. The hint here that the soul could be the "intellectual (*ʿaqlī*)" form seems to be simply un-Aristotelian. This is an important move on al-Kindī's part, since it sets up the dubious conflation between soul and species. (Note that "intellectual" here does not mean that the soul is or has an intellect, but that it is the sort of form *grasped* by intellects: hence the contrast to "sensible.") The passage raises the question of whether al-Kindī knew the *De Anima* when he wrote the present treatise. It seems likely that he did not, and that the idea of soul as "form of the body" has just filtered through to him as a piece of common knowledge about the Greek tradition. This would explain his assumption in the next sentence that species and form mean the same thing (given only the resources of the *Categories*, what else *could* "form" mean?), and his failure to use any other ideas from the *De Anima* in this treatise. This may mark the treatise as an early work. For elsewhere, al-Kindī does use the *De Anima*, and in fact we have an Arabic version of that work which he seems to have used: the one edited and translated in R. Arnzen, *Aristoteles' De Anima. Eine verlorene spätantike Paraphrase in arabischer und persischer Überlieferung* (Leiden: 1998). For one example of his use of this version, see P. Adamson, "Vision, Light and Color in al-Kindī, Ptolemy and the Ancient Commentators," *Arabic Sciences and Philosophy* 16 (2006), pp. 207–236.

[18] The passage plays on the ambiguity of the word *nafs*. Any substance may be said to exist or be what it is "through itself (*bi-'l-nafs*)." But in the case of a substance

ARISTOTLE'S *CATEGORIES* AND THE SOUL

103

living thing, and is its species.[19] Then, the living thing is a substance, and the species of the substance is a substance. Therefore the soul is a substance, and since it is substance, and is the substance of the species,[20] it is (15) not a body. For the species is not a body,[21] but is that which is common to all its individuals which are bodies, since the individuals that are alive[22] are bodies. Thus it is apparent that the soul is not a body, and is a substance. So it is clear that there are both corporeal and incorporeal substances.[23]

(7) Also, if the species gives its individuals its name and definition, then it is of the nature [268] of its individual. If its individual is a substance, then it too is a substance. But if it [the individual] is an accident, then it [the species] too is an accident. The living, sensible thing is a substance,

---

that is a living being, the "self (*nafs*)" through which the being is what it is, is none other than the soul (*nafs*). How much work does this apparent equivocation do in the argument? Not very much: the foregoing argument based on *Categories* 2–3 would already establish that if soul "describes" the living body then it shares a nature, i.e. substantiality, with the living body.

[19] This move is more problematic: the identification of soul with the *species* of the living body. This seems to be the result of the following line of reasoning. Soul is the body's form; there are only two kinds of forms, sensible and intellectual; and the soul is not the sensible form of the body. It may seem puzzling to identify soul with a species, not least because while Socrates and Plato share the same species, they presumably have distinct souls (see further Adamson, *Al-Kindī*, 109). On the other hand it is tempting, within the Platonizing Aristotelianism familiar from al-Kindī's other works (especially *On the Intellect*), to assimilate species to intellectual forms. So in fact al-Kindī may be depending above all on the apparently innocuous assumption that all forms are either intellectual or sensible.

[20] *Hiya jawhar al-nawʿ*: the genitive in this construct state, the *muḍāf ilayhi*, should perhaps be understood as epexegetical, i.e. "the substance that is species."

[21] This apparently uncontroversial claim will shortly be proven by extensive argument, from §7 onwards.

[22] *Ashkhāṣ al-ḥayy*, literally "the individuals of the living thing." Here al-Kindī means all the individuals that belong to the species "living thing," i.e. all individual living things.

[23] This is, in theory at least, the point under examination in the epistle as a whole: that there are incorporeal, as well as corporeal, substances. The soul is the only example given of a sensible substance. But the argument would presumably be applicable to any intellectual form that "describes" a bodily substance. Such a form would share the nature of substantiality with the bodily substance, and thus itself be a substance. Al-Kindī's argument, rather ironically given its source in the *Categories*, is thus an all-purpose demonstration for something like Platonic Forms. Of course one might say that Aristotle too, in the *Categories* itself, accepts that species and genera are themselves substances. But not only does al-Kindī omit the caveat that they are merely "secondary" substances. He also lets stand the assertion in §2 that any substance will be "subsisting through itself"; if this applies to intellectual forms (i.e. species) as well as bodily substances, we have something much closer to Platonism.

104 PETER ADAMSON AND PETER E. PORMANN

so its species are substances, since the substance gives the substance its name and its definition.[24] The species is either a body or it is not a body. (5) Suppose then that the species is a body, and the individual is also a body. But the species is necessarily one,[25] while the individual is necessarily many.[26] So if the species is one, but common to many, and if it is a body, then it will be in every one of the bodies either as (A) a whole or (B) a part.[27]

(8) [Against (A):] The species is composed of different things, for example "man" is composed of animal, (10) rational, and mortal. Every one of its genera and differentiae are also composed of what defines them, i.e. of that from which its definition is assembled. Therefore, the parts from which it is composed are different from one another. Since the species is not made up of similar parts, if the species is completely present in one of its individual members, then how can it be completely present in another [member of the same species]?[28]

---

[24] Here al-Kindī draws the consequences from the considerations given above in §5. A curious feature of the text is that the argument here in §7 does not follow immediately on from §5, but is instead preceded by the considerations about form in §6.

[25] Omitting *aw kathīr*.

[26] This last assertion would seem to mean that the class of individuals is multiple, i.e. for the single species "man" there are many individual men. This is where al-Kindī might have stopped to consider the problem that individual men have many souls, but as he says here, only one species.

[27] The rest of the epistle consists in a dilemmatic or dichotomous argument by exclusion, a strategy used frequently by al-Kindī; see Adamson, *Al-Kindī*, pp. 37–8 on the structure and limitations of these arguments. The options presented here are reminiscent of Plato, *Parmenides* 131a–b. Arguably, al-Kindī's solution to the question of how a species is completely "in" all its members gets at the truth lurking in Socrates' suggestion that a Form is "in" its participants the way a single day is present in many places. Like the day, a species can be present in many members because it is incorporeal.

[28] The argument of this paragraph seems to presuppose that, had the species been homogeneous (and not "made up of dissimilar parts," i.e. the genus and differentiae), then it *could* be completely present in two members. Here it is important to remember that we are also presupposing (for the purposes of the *reductio*) that the species is a body. And it seems right that a heterogeneous body A cannot be completely present in two distinct bodies B and C: one part of the heterogeneous body would have to be in B, and another in C. But one might doubt whether even a homogeneous body can be completely present in two different objects. Perhaps al-Kindī has in mind a case like water being completely present in two sponges (as suggested in Adamson, *Al-Kindī*, p. 110). But in that case is the water in one sponge not a different body than the water in the other sponge? Al-Kindī might say that if so, the water is not, after all, genuinely homogeneous: the water in one sponge is actually a distinct "part" from the water in the other sponge. But he seems to be thinking that homogeneity means that the parts of a thing are similar, not identical. And this must be right, for otherwise nothing homogeneous could have more than one part.

ARISTOTLE'S *CATEGORIES* AND THE SOUL 105

(9) [Against (B):] (15) But if only a part [of the species] is in each of its individual members, and its individual members are potentially infinite [in number], then its parts will be potentially infinite. Therefore it is composed from what is potentially infinite. But composition cannot have anything potential in it, because it has already come into actuality.[29] Therefore it is impossible that its parts are potentially infinite; yet its parts must be (20) potentially infinite [because, as just stated, there is no limit to the number of possible members of a species]. [269] This is an impossible contradiction. [Suppose then that] each of the individual members [of the species], having in it one part [of the species] that is distinct from any other part, is distinct from all the other individual members by one of the parts of the species. But the individual members are potentially infinite, and we have just said above that it is absurd that something be composed from potentially infinite parts. (5) Therefore in each of the individual members [of the species] there is [supposedly] a part, different from the part in every other [member] of the species; yet it is impossible that there be in each of the individual members one of the parts of the species. So this is possible and impossible, which is a most objectionable contradiction.

(10) Therefore it is impossible that there be in each of the individual members a part of the species, a part distinct from the part in any other [member]. And it is apparent that it is impossible for [the species] to be in each of its individuals as a whole. Since, then, [the species] (10) cannot be in its individual members either as a whole or as a part, if it is a body, the species of the substance is therefore not a body. Yet it is a substance, as we have said. So necessarily there are many incorporeal substances.[30]

---

[29] This argument is rather clever. If we suppose that each member of the species is one of its parts, then the species will never actually exist. For some of its parts—for instance, future members of the species—do not actually exist. Thus the whole does not actually exist. But the species is here identified with the whole of the "parts" which are the species' members. (Problematic here would be a case like the species "sun" which has, and can have, only one member.) For al-Kindī's views on potential infinity, see *On First Philosophy*, 29ff. He discusses wholes and parts at *On First Philosophy*, 45–7, and in *On Definitions*, items 49–52, where the definitions distinguish between wholes made up of similar parts and those made up of dissimilar parts. The first sort of whole is called a *kull* and the second is called a *jamiʿ*.

[30] Here al-Kindī alludes to the overall purpose of the epistle, which is to establish the existence of incorporeal substances generally, as opposed to establishing only the incorporeality of soul. And in fact, the argument of §§8–10 shows that every species is

(11) This is sufficient for what you have asked. May God make you sufficient in all your duties, and safeguard you from all harm and pains! (15) This is the end of the epistle. Praise be to God, ruler of the worlds, and blessings and peace upon both the Prophet Muḥammad and his entire family!

---

incorporeal. This might invite us to reconsider the structure of the epistle as a whole. Though al-Kindī's main goal is apparently to prove the incorporeality of the soul, he could omit the points about soul and retain an argument that there are incorporeal substances, as follows: (a) If X gives Y its name and definition, X shares a nature with Y; (b) species give bodily substances their names and definitions; (c) species therefore share substantiality with bodily substances; (d) species are incorporeal; (e) therefore species are both substances and incorporeal. This is arguably a line of reasoning that Aristotle would accept, since he is happy to call species "substances," albeit in a secondary sense.

PRIVATE CAVES AND PUBLIC ISLANDS:
ISLAM, PLATO AND THE IKHWĀN AL-ṢAFĀ'[1]

Ian Richard Netton*

Medieval Islamic philosophy may usefully be compared with a large cauldron containing a diversity of ingredients. Some blend with others, some retain their own individual identity throughout the cooking process. Let me now interpret my image: the cauldron is the Islamic Middle Ages in the 10th and 11th centuries A.D. The brew which it contains is, in large measure, the Islamic religion of one kind or another. But this Islam shares the pot, happily sometimes, uneasily at others, with a number of other potent ingredients: Neopythagoreanism, Aristotelianism, Neoplatonism, Hermeticism, Mazdaism, astrology, folklore, magic.[2]

The intellectual cosmopolitanism of the age is mirrored in miniature in the cosmopolitanism of the City of Basra in what is now modern Iraq.[3] Basra is famous in the intellectual history of Islam as having been one of the cradles of Arabic philology. But it had other claims to fame as well. It was here that many of the foundations of Arab culture were laid. The City stood at a commercial crossroads; it had come under the influence of civilizations as diverse as those of Persia and India; it was familiar with the peoples of Sind and the Malay peninsula. Its inhabitants included Jews and Christians as well as Muslims and it boasted an expertise in numerous industrial and agricultural crafts. And just as its cosmopolitanism and eclecticism mirror the broader cosmopolitanism and eclecticism of *Dār al-Islām*, culturally, religiously and intellectually, so too we may say that the encyclopaedic *Epistles* (*Rasā'il*)[4] of the Brethren of Purity (Ikhwān al-Ṣafā') neatly mirror the

---

* Exeter University.

[1] This article was originally published in Volume 15 of *Sacred Web: A Journal of Tradition and Modernity*, published in Vancouver, Canada, June 2005: ISSN 1480-6584.

[2] For a general orientation, see inter alia, Majid Fakhry, *A History of Islamic Philosophy* 2nd edn., (London: 1983).

[3] Ch. Pellat & S. H. Longrigg, art. "al Basra", *Encyclopaedia of Islam*, 2nd edn. (EI2), (Leiden, 1960), vol. 1, pp. 1085–1087. See also Ch. Pellat, *Le Milieu Basrien et la formation de Gahiz*, (Paris, 1953).

[4] Ikhwān al-Ṣafā', *Rasā'il Ikhwān al-Ṣafā'*, 4 vols, (Beirut, 1957) [Hereafter referred to as *R.*] For a general orientation and introduction in English, see Ian Richard Netton,

108   IAN RICHARD NETTON

cosmopolitanism and eclecticism of the City of Basra. The majority of scholars today believe that Basra was home to this group of 10th or 11th century A.D. philosophers whom we call the Brethren of Purity.

Their writings, collected in fifty-two *Epistles* (*Rasā'il*), are indeed eclectic, purveying a dual and, at times, incoherent vision of God[5] who is by turns the Creator God of the Holy Qur'an and the Unknowable One of classical Plotinian Neoplatonic thought. The text of the Epistles is saturated not only with the key doctrines, elements and motifs of Islam—most notably derived from the Qur'an—but also with Greek, Judaeo-Christian, Persian, Indian, Buddhist, Zoroastrian and Manichaen references as well. The most casual reading of the text convinces us that the Eastern world (*al-Mashriq*) was as familiar to the Brethren as the Western (*al Maghrib*): indeed, their encyclopedic scope trascended the imperial *ḥudūd* of the Pax Islamica to embrace lands as far afield as China. And as intellectual magpies they thought nothing of deploying elements of Greek and Persian vocabulary as well as anecdotes deriving from classical Indian sources which survey the life of the Buddha.[6]

I do not propose here to enter the perennial debate about the authorship and dating of the *Rasā'il*.[7] Such debates can be sterile. I propose, instead, to concentrate on the textual and the intertextual, taking as a frame the text of the fifty two *Rasā'il* of the Brethren, a group of, probably, Basran encyclopaedist philosophers of the 10th or 11th centuries A.D. who, like Denis Diderot (1713–1784) many centuries later, articulated their manifold interests in encyclopaedic form. Those interests may be collected neatly under the broad headings of mathematica, the natural sciences, the rational sciences and theology. Within those groupings they embrace subjects as diverse, difficult and diffuse as arithmetic, music, logic, mineralogy, botany, embryology, philosophy and magic. The *Epistles* may have been the product, even minutes, of the Brethren's meetings which they held every twelve days; such was

---

Muslim Neoplatonists: An Introduction to the Thought of the Brethren of Purity (Ikhwān al-Ṣafā'), (London, 2002). [Hereafter referred to as Netton, *MNP*]

[5] See Ian Richard Netton, "Foreign Influences and Recurring Ismā'īlī Motifs in *Rasā'il* of the Brethren of Purity" in idem, *Seek Knowledge: Thought and Travel in the House of Islam*, (Richmond, 1996), pp. 27–41.

[6] E.g. see *R.* 1, p. 414, *R.* 2 p. 249. *R.* 4 pp. 162–164.

[7] For a succinct summary of the general state of scholarship in these areas, see Netton, *MNP*, pp. 1–8.

PRIVATE CAVES AND PUBLIC ISLANDS 109

the very plausible theory of A. L. Ṭībawī.[8] Whatever the truth of that however, and whatever else they may be, one cannot avoid characterizing the *Rasā'il* as a species of *adab*. These Epistles belong as much to the genre of *adab* as the writings of the great medieval Arabic *adīb* Abū 'Uthmān 'Amr b. Baḥr al-Jāḥiẓ (c. 776–868/9), though they are, perhaps, shorn of the latter's predilection for the rare (*nawādir*), the exotic ('*ajā'ib*) and the difficult.[9]

Philosophically, the *Rasā'il* of the Ikhwān constitute a marvelous epitome of the mixing of Aristotelianism and Neoplatonism in the cauldron of Islamic intellectual endeavour; to deploy a further metaphor, it is a focal point at which the pendulum of Islamic intellectual development has temporarily stuck, having swung backwards and forwards over several hundred years between the structured lure of Aristotle (cf. al-Kindī who died after A.D. 866)[10] and the emanationist exoticism of Plotinus (cf. al-Fārābī (870–950) and Ibn Sīnā (979–1037)).[11]

The *Rasā'il*, then, are imbued with Greek thought, underpinned both by frequent quotations from the Qur'an[12] and the borrowed moral authority of the prophet Muhammad himself: the Ikhwān note that the Prophet claimed in a tradition that Aristotle would certainly have become a Muslim had he lived in the Age of Muhammad.[13] Thus it is to Aristotle, together with Pythagoras and Plotinus, that we will now briefly turn, before we embark on a more extensive examination of the impact of Plato on the *Rasā'il Ikhwān al-Ṣafā'*. As we do so, we bear in mind the necessary dictum of F. E. Peters that Aristotle and Aristotelianism (especially of the kind encountered in Arabic texts such as the *Rasā'il*), may be two very different things.[14] What may be stressed here is that the Ikhwān use the moral authority of the Greek philosophers too, setting out and elaborating in their text a Greek substratum derived

---

[8] A. L. Ṭībawī, "Ikhwān as-Ṣafā' and their Rasā'il: A Critical Review of a Century and a half of Research", *Islamic Quarterly*, vol. 2:1 (1955), p. 37.

[9] See, for example, al-Jāḥiẓ, *Kitāb al-Tarbī' wa'l-Tadwīr*, ed. Charles Pellai, (Damascus, 1955).

[10] See, for example, al-Kindī, *fi'l-Falsafa al-Ūla* in M. A. H. Abū Rīda, *Rasā'il al-Kindī al-Falsafiyya*, (2 vols., Cairo, 1950–1953), vol. 1.

[11] See, al-Fārābī, *al-Madīna al-Fāḍila* in Richard Walzer, *Al-Fārābī on the Perfect State: Abū Naṣr al-Fārābī's Mabādi' Arā' Ahl al-Madīna al-Fāḍila*, Oxford: Clarendon Press, 1985). See also Ibn Sina, *al-Shifā'* Vol. 2: *al-Ilāhiyyāt*, ed. M. Y. Moussa, S. Dunya & S. Zayed, rev. By I. Madkour, (Cairo, 1960).

[12] See Netton, *MNP*, pp. 78–89.

[13] See *R.* 4 p. 179.

[14] F. E. Peters, *Aristotle and the Arabs*, (New York/London, 1968), p. 3.

110 IAN RICHARD NETTON

from the "private" textual arena of Greek metaphysics, and applied to the domain of public order and soteriology, for the Greeks and their doctrines underpin that Ship of Salvation (*safīnat al-najāt*), beloved by these Ikhwān,[15] whose primary rudder is *ta'āwun*, co-operation.[16] They are ranked among the Blessed elect of the Brethren.[17] As we shall also see shortly, a Greek Platonic paradigm lies behind the building of an *actual* ship of salvation. The key here is the classical Platonic motif of learning as recollection.[18] The great English Romantic poet William Wordsworth (1770–1850) in a much later age, would also deploy that motif to startling effect.[19]

Pythagoras

The sixth century B.C. Pythagoras, and even more his disciples, were, according to Aristotle passionate about numbers. He noted the Pythagorean belief that number was the key to the entire universe.[20] This idea clearly fascinated the Ikhwān. They refer specifically to the Pythagorean belief that "the nature of created things is in accordance with the nature of number" and insist: "This is how we think too."[21] Their own particular passion was for the number four. For example, in a quadrivium duplicated in the European Middle Ages they divided the mathematical sciences into the four parts of Arithmetic, Geometry, Astronomy and Music.[22] And there was much else in their cosmos that was grouped in lists of four. We note, inter alia, the four elements, the four directions and the four humours of medieval medicine (yellow bile, black bile, blood and phlegm).[23] For the Ikhwān this universe of "fours" constituted a marvellous parallel—indeed representation—of the four hypostases at the top of their Neoplatonic hierarchy: The Creator, Intellect, Soul and Matter.[24] What they did manage to avoid was the

---

[15] See *R.* 4 p. 18; see also the concluding chapter of Netton, *MNP*, pp. 105–108.
[16] See, for example, *R.* 4 p. 20.
[17] See *R.* 4 pp. 57–58, 174–175.
[18] See Plato, *Phaedo* 72Eff.; *R.* 3 p. 424.
[19] See the famous poem by William Wordsworth entitled *Ode on the Intimations of Immortality from Early Childhood*.
[20] Aristotle, *Metaphysics* A 985–987.
[21] *R.* 3 p. 200.
[22] *R.* 1 p. 49.
[23] *R.* 1 pp. 116–117.
[24] *R.* 1. pp. 52–53.

PRIVATE CAVES AND PUBLIC ISLANDS 111

grievous error, noted by Aristotle, of the Pythagoreans who confused number and the thing numbered.[25]

However, the Ikhwān did enjoy other elements of the Pythagorean intellectual universe like the idea of a musical firmament: Pythagoras is portrayed listening to the tunes created by the movements of the various stars and other spheres.[26] What they did firmly reject was any idea of *tanāsukh*, transmigration of the soul.[27] Spiritual purification leading to salvation was to be achieved by co-operation (*taʿāwun*) with one's brethren in a single life, rather than as the result of a cycle of transmigrations of the soul in the manner espoused by Hinduism.[28]

Aristotle

Aristotle, who lived from 384–322 B.C., also had a major impact on the thought of the Brethren of Purity, even though it was a "Middle Easternised" Aristotle whom they encountered intellectually. It is clear that they were familiar with many of his logical treatises.[29] How much they really understood is open to debate. Similarly it is difficult to assess the precise quality of the Aristotelian texts in their possession or those extant in Basra. And could they read them in the original Greek or only through the medium of Arabic translation?

Perhaps the greatest Aristotelian influence, albeit often Neoplatonised, lay in the sphere of philosophical terminology: Aristotle's terminology is all-pervasive in the *Rasāʾil* and embraces, inter alia, substance and accidents, matter and form, potentiality and actuality and the four causes.[30]

But the thought of Plotinus, founding father and progenitor of Neoplatonism, is often lurking in the wings. At one point the efficient cause of Aristotle[31]—in Arabic *al-ʿilla al-fāʿiliyya*—is defined by the Ikhwān as "the power of the Universal Spirit".[32] This is sufficient evidence, if evidence were needed, that the thought of the Brethren

---

[25] Aristotle, *Metaphysics* A 987 a.
[26] R. 1 pp. 23, 206–208, 255, R. 3 pp. 94, 125.
[27] R. 3 p. 365.
[28] See Karl Werner, art. "Transmigration" in idem, *A Popular Dictionary of Hinduism*, (Richmond, 1994), pp. 160–161.
[29] See especially *Rasāʾil*, vol. 1 passim.
[30] See my survey in Netton, *MNP*, pp. 19–32.
[31] See Aristotle, *Metaphysics*, bk. 5 1013 a.
[32] R. 2 p. 155.

112   IAN RICHARD NETTON

of Purity is capable of moving a long way from the original texts of
Aristotle, even when they invoke him.

Plotinus (A.D. 204–270)

The *Rasā'il* are soaked in Neoplatonic thought, elements of which are
often in conflict with aspects of their thought articulated elsewhere
in their text. Yet no attempt is made to present a totally harmonious
corpus of doctrines in which all the variegated facets of the Brethren's
intellectual universe cohere.

Three distinctly Neoplatonic elements stand out: their emphasis
on hierarchy, their emphasis on emanation and their Neoplatonic
view of God which remains unreconciled with the Qur'anic view of
God espoused elsewhere in the *Rasā'il*. As with the Syrian Iamblichus
(c. A.D. 250–c. 326),[33] there is a wild multiplication of hypostases over
the original Plotinian three of The One, Universal Intellect and Universal
Soul.[34] Indeed, the Ikhwān posit nine major hypostases of which the
first three correspond to Plotinus' well-known triad.[35] The device or
"motor" which links them all is that of *fayḍ*, emanation.[36] However,
contrary to the Plotinian paradigm,[37] emanation, and the eventual
material universe which results, are not involuntary.[38]

It is, however, in the Ikhwān's portrayal of God in the *Rasā'il* that
much, if not most, of the Neoplatonic interest lies. On the one hand,
the deity of the Ikhwān bestrides "a complex hierarchy of emanation
which goes considerably beyond the simplicity of the Plotinian triad
of One, Intellect and Soul, and comprises nine tiers of being."[39] The
Ikhwān's deity participates in the unknowableness of Plotinus' One in
the *Rasā'il*'s rejection of anthropomorphic terminology.[40] On the other
hand, however, the God of the *Rasā'il* is characterized, traditionally,

---

[33] See Iamblichus, *On the Mysteries*; ed. E. Des Places, *Jamblique. Les Mysteres
d'Egypt*, (Paris, 1989).
[34] See Plotinus, *Enneads*, trans. A. H. Armstrong, Loeb Classical Library, (7 vol.,
Cambridge, Mass, 1966–1988), passim.
[35] *R.* 3 pp. 56, 181–182.
[36] *R.* 3 pp. 196–197.
[37] Plotinus, *Enneads*, 111.2.2.
[38] See *R.* 3 p. 338.
[39] See Netton, "Foreign Influences" in idem, *Seek Knowledge*, p. 35.
[40] E.g. see *R.* 3 p. 403, R. 4 p. 387.

PRIVATE CAVES AND PUBLIC ISLANDS 113

as one who both guides His creation and has mercy upon it.[41] The traditional *basmala* heads nearly every *Epistle*.

There is, then, a Quranic "voice" and a Neoplatonic "voice" in the *Epistles* of the Brethren and nowhere is this seen more clearly than in their theological portrayal of Deity. Logic prevents their ultimate reconciliation and the Brethren attempt no such reconciliation. Whether they are actually espousing, consciously or unconsciously, a "double truth" doctrine akin to what Ibn Rushd (1126–1198) was accused of in medieval Europe is wide open for debate.

Plato (c. B.C. 428–c. 348)

We turn finally, though not of course chronologically, to Plato. For it is his thought, as percolated through, and elaborated by, the *Rasāʾil* of the Brethren of Purity which constitutes the major substratum for our thesis in this essay. Yves Marquet notes the primordial impact of Plato's *Republic* on the Ikhwān's doctrine, while acknowledging that Plato's text was seen by the Brethren through Neoplatonic spectacles.[42] The Ikhwān certainly knew something of *The Republic* as well as the *Phaedo* and *Crito* dialogues.[43] Socrates wins their admiration as a man of stature and wisdom who bravely accepts a death which, as we know from the *Crito*, was not utterly inevitable.[44] The body is characterized, Platonically, in the *Rasāʾil* as a prison for soul.[45] Indeed, the soul is like a man imprisoned in a lavatory, with the faults of the body resembling the filth of that lavatory.[46] Where the Ikhwān do diverge from Plato is their lack of interest in his doctrine of *ideai* and their insistence that knowledge *can* be gained from the world of matter and sensory perception.[47] Finally they claim at one point to reject the Platonic concept of learning as recollection of things which were encountered and known before birth.[48] In what follow we shall re-open and re-examine

---

[41] E.g. see *R.* 4 pp. 62–63, 40, *R.* 3 p. 286.
[42] Yves Marquet, *La Philosophie des Ikhwān al-Ṣafāʾ*, (Algiers, 1975), p. 21.
[43] See *R.* 4 pp. 287–288: compare Plato, *Republic*, 359d–369b; see also *R.* 4 pp. 304, 271, 34–35, 73–74.
[44] See Plato, *Crito*, passim.
[45] *R.* 4 p. 25.
[46] *R.* 3 p. 49.
[47] *R.* 3 p. 424.
[48] *R.* 2 p. 424. See Plato, *Republic*, bk. 7 518b–e; Nicholas P. White, *Companion to Plato's Republic* (Indianapolis/Cambridge, 1979), p. 188.

114 IAN RICHARD NETTON

this statement in the light of other passages and statements of theirs which appear in the *Rasā'il.*

Plato's Simile of the Cave

Of all the passages in Plato's writings, perhaps the Simile of the Cave is one of the most famous.[49] It is designed as a graphic illustration of Plato's doctrine of *ideai* or forms. Philosophy, for Plato, was "construed as intellectual activity concerning the Forms. The simile of the cave has the primary effect of dramatizing this idea by setting forth the relation between the sensible and the intelligible so as to highlight what Plato regards as the far greater attractiveness of the latter."[50]

It has been suggested that "the best way to understand the simile is to replace 'the clumsier apparatus' of the cave by the cinema, though today television is an even better comparison. It is the moral and intellectual condition of the average man from which Plato starts; and though clearly the ordinary man knows the difference between substance and shadow in the physical world, the simile suggests that his moral and intellectual opinions often bear as little relation to the truth as the average film or television program does to real life."[51]

Plato asks us to imagine "an underground chamber like a cave."[52] Prisoners are detained within, pinioned in such a way that they can only look in one direction. There is a fire behind them and a wall in front of them. They perceive their own shadows and the shadows of other objects cast on the wall in front of them by the firelight. For the prisoners in the cave, these shadows are the only reality they know.

It is only when someone is first able to see the fire and then actually able to escape from the cave into the sunlight, that he actually perceives reality and becomes aware of the true nature of those shadows. He may then feel it his duty to liberate his fellow captives but he will encounter difficulties in this: his perception of the shadows will now be less clear than theirs.[53] For Plato, "the realm revealed by sight corresponds to the prison, and the light of the fire in the prison to the power of

---

[49] Plato, *The Republic*, bk 7 514aff.; see Desmond Lee (trans.), *Plato: The Republic*, 2nd rev. edn., (Harmondsworth/London, 1987), pp. 256ff.

[50] White, *Companion*, p. 184.

[51] Lee (trans.), *Republic*, pp. 255–256 citing F. M. Cornford.

[52] Ibid., p. 256; Plato, *The Republic*, bk. 7 514a.

[53] Plato, *The Republic*, bk. 7 514a.

PRIVATE CAVES AND PUBLIC ISLANDS 115

the sun...the final thing to be perceived in the intelligible region, and perceived only with difficulty, is the form of the good [in the world of ideas]."[54] But it is still possible for the philosopher who has returned (i.e. from the world of the *ideai*) to become used to seeing in the dark again and to perceive and distinguish the shadows better than his fellows.[55]

Desmond Lee outlines the following correspondences (the emphases are mine):[56]

"Tied prisoner in the cave	*Illusion*
Freed prisoner in the cave	*Belief*
Looking at shadows and reflections in the world outside the cave and the ascent thereto.	*Reason*
Looking at real things in the world outside the cave	*Intelligence*
Looking at the sun	*Vision of the form of the good.*"[56]

Bertrand Russell notes: "Now the world of ideas is what we see when the object is illumined by the sun, while the world of passing things is a confused twilight world. The eye is compared to the soul, and the sun, as the source of light, to truth or goodness."[57] In sum, the ordinary person can only apprehend appearances; the philosopher can apprehend reality and "the Forms are apprehended only by those philosophers who are fully accustomed to activity of the intellect outside the cave."[58]

Plato notes, significantly for our study of the passage which follows, in reference to the "escaped prisoner" who has sought the "world of the *ideai*":

> And when he thought of his first home and
> what passed for wisdom there, and of his
> fellow prisoners, don't you think he
> would congratulate himself on his good
> fortune and be sorry for them?[59]

---

[54] Lee (trans.), *Republic*, pp. 259–260; Plato, *The Republic*, bk. 7 517.
[55] See Plato, *The Republic*, bk. 7 520c.
[56] Lee (trans.), *Republic*, p. 259 n. 2.
[57] Bertrand Russell, *History of Western Philosophy*, 2nd edn., (London, 1971), p. 140.
[58] White, *Companion*, p. 186.
[59] Lee (trans.), *Republic*, p. 258; Plato, *The Republic*, bk. 7 516.

116   IAN RICHARD NETTON

The Two Islands Simile of the Ikhwān al-Ṣafāʾ

In one of the most extended illustrations of their perennial themes, most notably that of *taʿāwun*, co-operation,[60] the Brethren present us with a striking simile of two islands.[61]

Dominated by a city on top of a mountain, one has a delightful climate and abundant flora and fauna. Its inhabitants descend from a common ancestor and live in mutual love and harmony. The Ikhwān characterize the city of these people as *Al-Madīna Al-Fāḍila*, 'The Virtuous City', a name which cannot fail to resonate with any reader of al-Fārābī's seminal text.[62]

A group of those people then set sail and are shipwrecked on another island whose character is the exact opposite of the one they have left. Worst of all, its native inhabitants are monkeys (*qirada*).[63] Every so often they are attacked by a huge bird of prey which seizes a number of those monkeys. The survivors of the shipwreck scatter over the island, seeking sustenance and shelter. They interbreed with the monkeys and produce many offspring. Ultimately they become used to their condition and forget their real homeland (*nasū baladahum*).[64] Greed, competition, envy and war become commonplace.

However, one of those who were shipwrecked and settled on the new island returns *in a dream* to his native land. He is made extremely welcome by the inhabitants of that City which he had left so many years before. At the city gate they cleanse him of the impurities of his journey in a spring, dress him in new clothes and carry him in state into the City, where he narrates his story. Then he awakes from the dream and is overwhelmed with sadness.[65]

He tells his dream to a compatriot and they ask: "How can one return and be saved from this place?" (*Kayfa al-sabīl ilā al-rujūʿ wa kayfa al-najāt min hunā?*). They decide to co-operate (*yataʿāwanān*)[66] and build a boat in which to return to their former homeland. Others

---

[60] See n. 16 above.

[61] See *R.* 4 pp. 37–40.

[62] See n. 11. See also Ian Richard Netton, *Al-Fārābī and His School*, (Richmond, repr. 1999), pp. 4–7, 53, 90, 102 n. 119.

[63] *R.* 4 p. 38.

[64] Ibid.

[65] *R.* 4 p. 39.

[66] Ibid.

PRIVATE CAVES AND PUBLIC ISLANDS 117

are recruited to help with the boat building by being reminded of the City they have left behind.

However, in the midst of their frenzied shipbuilding activities, the great bird swoops again and seizes one of the men, rather than its usual diet of monkey. The bird eventually drops the man on a roof of a house in the native City whence he has come. The delighted man begins to wish that all his exiled compatriots will meet a similar fate.

It is a different story on the island of the monkeys. His compatriots, ignorant of his true fate, begin to weep for him. The Ikhwān comment that, had they known what the bird had really done with their friend, they would have desired the same fate.[67]

The Brethren then proceed, in their typically didactic style, to provide the following *tafsīr*:

- Our terrestrial world (*al-dunyā*) resembles the island of the shipwreck.
- Human beings resemble those monkeys.
- Death is like that Great Bird.
- The "Friends of God" (*Awliyā' Allah*) are like the people who were shipwrecked.
- Paradise (*Dār al-Ākhira*) is like the great mountain City whence those shipwrecked people originally came.[68]

Here knowledge of reality is indeed recollection. The "dreamer" among the shipwrecked men gains real knowledge by the device of the dream. At the end of this *Risāla* (no. 44 in their corpus of 52) the Ikhwān counsel their Brethren to wake "from the sleep of negligence and the slumber of ignorance" (*min nawm al-ghafla wa raqda al-jahāla*),[69] a common motif: the world is full of deception and trials and the intelligent man should not seek immortality (*al-khulūd*) therein.[70]

Behind all this lies the common Platonic theme of the soul having had a previous existence to which it eventually returns. But other themes jostle for our attention as well: the idea of life as a voyage, going back, perhaps to that supreme archetype, Homer's *Odyssey* itself; the idea of life as a quest neatly illustrated by Jason and the Argonauts and the

---

[67] R. 4 p. 40.
[68] R. 4 p. 40.
[69] Ibid.
[70] Ibid.

118 IAN RICHARD NETTON

search for the golden fleece;[71] the theme of salvation being associated with a boat: here the ark (*fulk*) of Noah (Nūḥ) in both *Genesis* and the Qur'an[72] immediately springs to mind as well as the ancient Egyptian myth of the barque of the God, *Amen Ra*.[73] Salvation from shipwreck and an ensuing ultimate conversion evokes the shipwreck of Paul on Malta described so vividly in the *Acts of the Apostles*.[74] The intertext is massive.

Yet there is another major theme to be extrapolated from the narrative of the Ikhwān as well: as we have already noted, Plato, in Book 7 of *The Republic*, gives us his famous Simile of the Cave in which he illustrates the difference between shadow and reality, between the hidden, "private", individual vision of confused sensory perception and the open "public", vision of an enlightened intellect, mediated via *da'wa*. The "privacy" of Plato's cave embraces a privation of both perception and intellect; the open "public" arena outside the cave represents illumination of both.

The Island of the Monkeys is a dark, private, wild, harsh and hidden world, hidden, that is, from the majority of mankind and illuminated intellection. The monkeys by their very nature are pale imitations of humanity. They are cut off, private on their remote island, from real human beings with whom they have no contact until the arrival of the shipwrecked men from the Virtuous City.

The latter are quick to discover the privacy and privations of their new island: the "cave" motif, which we discovered firstly in Plato's text is resumed in the Ikhwān's text: the survivors of the wreck seek refuge by night in "the caves" (*al-maghārāt*)[75] of their new island from the heat and the cold (*min al-ḥarr wa'l-bard*).[76] These caves are specifically and pointedly characterized as "dark caves" (*maghārāt muẓlima*).[77] Their private trauma ("private" because it is unknown to their former compatriots) embraces a multitude of privations. And the monkeys also

---

[71] See Tim Severin, *The Jason Voyage: The Quest for the Golden Fleece*, (London, 1985), *passim*.

[72] See *Genesis* 6–8; Qur'an 7:59–64.

[73] Or Amon-Re. See Erik Hornung, *Conceptions of God in Ancient Egypt: The One and the Many*, (London, 1983), esp. p. 281 *sv* 'Re'; see also George Hart, *A Dictionary of Egyptian Gods and Goddesses*, (London & New York, 1988), pp. 179–182 *sv* 'Re'.

[74] See *Acts of the Apostles*, 27–28.

[75] *R.* 4 p. 38.

[76] Ibid.

[77] Ibid.

PRIVATE CAVES AND PUBLIC ISLANDS 119

represent both temptation and sin. The "public" reality of the Virtuous City may only be revisited at first in the world of dreams which also stresses the need for public cleansing, after which "illumination" follows. When the true reality emerges, or rather is encountered again, unfettered by a dream world, with the Great Bird as catalyst, the man who has been returned to his former state recognizes his former country, home, people and relatives.[78] Now he is in the public domain of an eternal, intellectual illumination. And he has had some prior knowledge of this. The 'learning' of a present state equates to a 'recollection' of that same state at a previous time. Learning is indeed recollection.

Sāmī S. Ḥawī has noted a "distinct and significant resemblance between Plato's Allegory of the Cave" and the *Ḥayy b. Yaqzān* of Ibn Ṭufayl (died A.D. 1185/6)[79] though "we cannot establish for certain that Ibn Ṭufayl had read Plato."[80] Ḥayy becomes "a self-taught plilosopher."[81] In the *Rasāʾil* of the Ikhwān al-Ṣafāʾ the shipwrecked men are identified as *awliyāʾ Allah* but they could just as easily be characterized as *falāsifa* since they have a prior knowledge or *ḥikma* concerning a better state. They could also be said to bear the charism of prophethood since their mission is to avoid temptation, identify salvation and lead others to it by identifying the true reality: what Plato might characterize as the Form of the Good. Alienation from that Reality or Good has no role in the great scheme of things, either for Plato or the Ikhwān al-Ṣafāʾ.[82]

Did the Ikhwān read either the whole, or parts of, Plato's *Republic* in the Greek original or in Arabic translation? At the very least we have clear evidence in their own text that they knew of this Platonic work;[83] at first or second hand, they absorbed in their *Rasāʾil* a number of Platonic themes and motifs.[84] A survey of the Platonic impulses adumbrated so clearly in their Simile of the Two Islands, yields the following fundamental paradigm: real authority and illumination, which work for the public good (*pro bono populorum, maṣlaḥa*) and produce

---

[78] *R.* 4 p. 39.
[79] See Ibn Ṭufayl, *Ḥayy B. Yaqzān* in Ahmad Amīn (ed.), *Ḥayy B. Yaqzān li Ibn Sīnā wa Ibn Ṭufayl waʾl-Suhrawardī, Dhakhaʾir al-Arab*, no. 8, (Cairo, 1952).
[80] Sāmī S. Ḥawī, *Islamic Naturalism and Mysticism: A Philosophic Study of Ibn Ṭufayl's Ḥayy Bin Yaqzān*, (Leiden, 1974) p. 18 n. 7.
[81] Ḥawī, *Islamic Naturalism*, p. 23.
[82] For a philosophical study of alienation, see Nathan Rotenstreich, *Alienation: The Concept and its Reception, Philosophy of History and Culture*, vol. 3, (Leiden and New York, 1989).
[83] *R.* 4 pp. 287–288.
[84] See Netton, *MNP*, pp. 16–19.

120   IAN RICHARD NETTON

structures of order, dwell within the Virtuous City. Its heralds are the *awliyā' Allah*. The alienation, privacy and privations of the desolate island, the Island of the Monkeys, bespeak a world where law and order has broken down. Enmity, hatred and the fires of war—absent from the original island of bliss and tranquility[85]—are the fruit of a literally God-forsaken island whose intellectual illumination and conversion is devoutly to be wished.[86]

There is a final paradigm: the Ikhwān, through the use of *ta'āwun*, co-operation, within the *umma*, build and climb aboard their own Noah's Ark, their *Ship of Salvation* which is the Brotherhood, and sail in it from the privacy and privation of a world of sin towards the universal, immortal, "public" arena, offered to all in the revelation of the Qur'an, the Paradise Garden of the illuminated intellect and enlightened Spirit.

---

[85] See *R.* 4 pp. 37–38.
[86] See *R.* 4 p. 38.

TRADITION AND INNOVATION IN THE PSYCHOLOGY OF FAKHR AL-DĪN AL-RĀZĪ

Maha Elkaisy-Friemuth[*]

Fakhr al-Dīn al-Rāzī is one of the last encyclopaedic writers of Islamic philosophy in its relation to theology who followed in the footsteps of Abū Ḥāmid al-Ghazālī. He was born in Rayy in 1149 A.D. and, like the scholars of the medieval period, he travelled extensively to different towns in Persia. Finally he settled in Herat (Persia) where he enjoyed the favour and admiration of 'Alā' al-Dīn Khawārīzm and worked in his court. It seems that al-Rāzī was unfortunate in being surrounded by several enemies, one of whom was his own brother, which made him ask his students to hide the place of his tomb before he died in Herat in 1207 A.D.[1]

Al-Rāzī left a very rich corpus of philosophical and theological works. In general he was most influenced by Ibn Sīnā (d. A.D. 1037), Abū al-Barakāt al-Baghdādī (d. A.D. 1168) and Abū Ḥāmid al-Ghazālī (d. A.D. 1111). Although he wrote extensively on philosophical as well as theological subjects, his style of writing is usually difficult to identify as either theological or philosophical. He uses philosophical terminology widely also in his theological writings. *Al-Mabāḥith al-Mashriqiyya* and his last work *al-Maṭālib al-'Āliyya* are usually regarded as his most important philosophical works. He also wrote commentaries on three works of Ibn Sīnā: *al-Ishārāt, 'Uyūn al-Ḥikma* and *al-Mabāḥith*. In the latter work he, following al-Ghazālī, criticises Ibn Sīnā's concept of emanation.[2] He found no logical ground for the concept that the One can produce only one entity, which is considered one of the basics of the Neoplatonic concept of emanation, as we will learn below.[3] He also criticises Ibn Sīnā's view that God cannot know particulars. He sees no ground for considering that the act of knowing should be unified with the knowable, which would entail multiplicity in the divine knowledge

---

[*] Katholieke Universiteit Leuven.
[1] M. Ṣāliḥ al-Zurkān, *Fakhr al-Dīn al-Rāzī*, (Cairo, 1963), pp. 15–25.
[2] Ibid., pp. 17–19.
[3] Ibid., p. 343.

122 MAHA ELKAISY-FRIEMUTH

and therefore threaten God's unity. Knowledge, for al-Rāzī, is an especial relationship to the object known: to know a subject means that you build a relationship with it through understanding, analysing or evaluating. Yet to do so means that you attempt to know something new about the object, which Ibn Sīnā and other philosophers regard as not appropriate for God. Although his argument is plausible, al-Ghazālī, before al-Rāzī, presented a more convincing argument in which he explained that God knows the material world through his eternal knowledge of it.[4] However, while al-Rāzī's refutation of Ibn Sīnā is considered more thorough and less aggressive than that of al-Ghazālī, it actually does not surpass it.

Al-Rāzī's originality, however, may be found in many of his theological and philosophical arguments; his study of the human soul is to be considered, in my opinion, as his best contribution in this field. The details of his concept of the soul are found mainly in three different philosophical works: *al-Mabāḥith al-Mashriqiyya*, *Kitāb al-Rūḥ wa al-Nafs* and in his last encyclopaedic work, *al-Maṭālib al-ʿĀliyya*. *Al-Mabāḥith* is considered his earliest work on philosophy, which he wrote at an early stage of his life, and *Kitāb al-Rūḥ wa al-Nafs* concentrates mainly on ethical subjects, so I will concentrate here particularly on *al-Maṭālib al-ʿĀliyya*, for it is his latest philosophical work and expresses his final opinion on this subject. In this article I will start by examining the nature of the human soul, and then I will move to look at his concept of *al-Rūḥ* as a mediator between *al-Nafs* and the bodily organs. I will also devote considerable attention to his discussion of the perception of the rational soul and its ability to perceive particular and universal knowledge. This latter discussion demonstrates the source of al-Rāzī's originality and his particular contribution to the study of the human soul. Finally, I will examine his argument as to whether the soul is created or eternal and whether it survives the death of its body and what future it will enjoy.

The Nature of the Human Soul

Al-Rāzī presents this subject in a certain systematic arrangement. He starts his discussion by arguing that the majority of thinkers agree that

---

[4] Ibid., pp. 300–10.

TRADITION AND INNOVATION IN THE PSYCHOLOGY OF AL-RĀZĪ   123

there are two kinds of beings: necessary (*wājib*) and contingent (*mumkin*) beings. The former designation is applicable only to God, while all other beings in the world are characterised as contingent (*mumkin*) existents. However, here, he argues, like all Muslim philosophers, that some contingent (*mumkin*) beings can have material bodies while others can exist in an immaterial form, either in connection with a body or as pure intellect. He starts his discussion of the human soul by, first, proving the existence of immaterial contingent beings, answering those Muslim theologians (*mutakalimūn*) who claim that all possible beings must either be limited in space or attributes, which they call accidents and which inhere in material beings. In short, the theologians argue that all contingent (*mumkin*) beings or substances must have material existence.[5]

In contrast, al-Rāzī, while he seems to adopt the atomist theory, believes that human and animal bodies function through the inherence of a soul which he regards as an independent substance. He considers that the theologians are mistaken to think that whatever exists in an immaterial form would be equivalent to God, and therefore deem it to be in association with God. Al-Rāzī argues here that having an immaterial nature does not automatically correspond to being equivalent to God, because sharing a negative attribute with God (such as having no material body) does not mean sharing all His other positive attributes, such as omnipotence or omniscience. Moreover, every two species under one genus share many attributes, but nevertheless they are not totally identical. Since this is evidently true, then there is no obvious reason why it is not possible to share immateriality with God without sharing His divinity?[6]

After providing the proofs for the existence of immaterial contingent (*mumkin*) beings—or mainly showing that there is no logical ground for rejecting the philosophical possibility of the existence of immaterial beings—he proposes that the human soul belongs to this class of beings. His proofs of the immateriality of the soul are given at length in *Maṭālib* and other works, but nevertheless they do not go beyond those of Ibn Sīnā or other philosophers before him. His two main strong proofs are Avicennian: first, we notice that the body gets older and weaker, while the soul remains the same or even gets wiser; the

---

[5] Fakhr al-Dīn Al-Rāzī, *al-Maṭālib al-ʿĀliyya* (Beirut 1999), vol. 7, pp. 15–16.
[6] Ibid., pp. 17–19.

124 MAHA ELKAISY-FRIEMUTH

second argument is that the consciousness of oneself does not cease in the person when some or all of his limbs are cut off, which proves that the soul is consciously independent of its body.[7] However, in his famous commentary on the Qur'an, *Mafātīḥ al-Ghayb*, al-Rāzī combines this latter argument with more elaboration and proofs of his own, but in this case speaking as a theologian who considers that the soul consists of a very fine airy matter:

> Say: 'The Spirit is of the bidding of my Lord'". Intuition alone tells us that the spirit is what man means when he says "I". But can this "I" be the organic body when it is well-known that its parts are always changing and being replaced? If man is not this body, is he a body in which the earthly element predominates, since this would be made of bone, flesh, fat and sinews, and nobody identifies man with these "thick, heavy and dark" tissues. It cannot be a body in which the aqueous element predominates, since this would be one of the four humours, and none of these is man, except that some consider that an exception should be made for the blood, since the loss of it brings death. Bodies in which there predominate the elements of air and fire are the spirits, bodies composed of air mingled with natural heat (*al-ḥarāra al-gharīziyya*) and engendered in the heart and in the brain. Spirits cannot dissolve or decline. They are noble, celestial and divine bodies, which penetrate into the organism as soon as it is formed and completely prepared to receive them. They remain there so long as the body is in good health, but when there arise thick humours which prevent their circulation (*sarayān*), they leave it, and this is death.[8]

Al-Rāzī, then, turns to examine whether all souls are united in definition and reality. First, following his style in *Maṭālib*, he sets out the opinions of the philosophers before him. I will give here a short example: some philosophers consider that the souls of humans and animals are similar in definition and reality, but they differ when they are connected to their bodies, using different bodily organs, and therefore they differ only in their function but not in their reality.[9] In contrast, Ibn Sīnā considers, as al-Rāzī claims, that the souls of animals are of different kind to those of humans. Human rational souls are immaterial and have the ability to perceive the divine world while the animal souls are of material substance and have the ability to perceive only the mate-

---

[7] Ibid., pp. 35–41.
[8] Commentary on Sura XVII, 85; Arnaldez, R. "Insān." *Encyclopaedia of Islam 2*, Brill online, 2008.
[9] Al-Rāzī, *Maṭālib*, pp. 85–89.

TRADITION AND INNOVATION IN THE PSYCHOLOGY OF AL-RĀZĪ   125

rial world.[10] Another group of physicians claim that each human soul is different in its reality; and others, whom al-Rāzī does not identify, consider that the human souls are divided into different species, each of which have certain qualities which are influenced by one of the souls of the planets.[11] It seems here, however, that al-Rāzī prefers this latter opinion, which was also the opinion of the philosopher Abū al-Barakāt al-Baghdādī in his famous book *al-Mu'tabir fī al-Ḥikma*. According to Ṣāliḥ al-Zurkān, al-Rāzī was greatly influenced by Abū al-Barakāt and made good use of his book *al-Mu'tabir* in different studies.[12]

Thus al-Rāzī regards the human soul as an immaterial substance taking full control over the body and directing its journey towards knowledge. The human souls, according to al-Rāzī, seem to belong to different species of souls which, though similar in their reality and definition, are influenced by the souls of the different planets. In a long separate section on the souls of the planets in *Maṭālib*, al-Rāzī studies these souls and shows their influences on earthly life and events. This section, and similar studies in other works of his, were the occasion for accusing him of heterodoxy, as Ibn Taymiyya declared him to be a heretical theologian. However, besides his study on the soul (*al-nafs*) he also drew attention to the role of another entity similar to the soul, known in Islam as *al-rūḥ*. What follows explains his understanding of it and its relationship to the human soul.

Al-Rūḥ *wa* al-Nafs

It seems that most Muslim theologians used the term *rūḥ* as synonymous to the term *nafs* (soul). Before presenting al-Rāzī's opinion on this issue we need here to explain these concepts among theologians and philosophers of his time. Since early theologians adopted the atomist theory in explaining the nature of the world, they considered that the soul can fall either under the heading of material substance (which they call *jawhar*), or under that of immaterial attributes which they called accident (in Arabic *'araḍ*). But they considered the body as a substance (*jawhar*); thus the soul which inheres in the body must, for them, be an accident, since, for them, all possible beings are either

---

[10]   Ibid., p. 85 & p. 179.
[11]   Ibid., pp. 85–95.
[12]   Al-Zurkān, *al-Rāzī*, pp. 484–86.

126   MAHA ELKAISY-FRIEMUTH

substances or accidents. Strict atomist theologians, such as many of the Basrian Mu'tazilites, consider that humans are composite beings who are observed as functioning units. They are living through the accident of life, which is classed as an accident inherent in the whole body, and similar to it is ability and knowledge. Life entails the accident of perception and identifies living beings as those who can perceive warmth, coldness and pain. Sight, taste and hearing are accidents which inhere only in certain parts of the body, and a defect in an organ can occur without stopping the accident of living.[13]

A group of theologians, however, called the Baghdādī Mu'tazilites, seems to be very much influenced by the Platonic concept of the soul. However, at this early stage it is not clear whether they read Platonic sources or were influenced by the Christian discussion of the subject. Al-Naẓẓām, an early theologian from the Baghdādī Mu'tazilites, regards the human soul as light which is spread throughout the body and causes all its activities. The soul has ability, will, life, and knowledge on its own merits. This means that the human soul for him does not depend on knowledge or ability from outside but, similar to Plato's concept of the soul, it has knowledge, ability, and the other qualities within itself. This argument, however, did not convince other Muslim theologians who did not see a logical ground for this claim.[14] For them the body has a great importance, for it will have eternal life in Paradise, as the Qur'an declares. Later Muslim theologians talked about the human being in terms of matter and form or soul and body. Al-Rāzī informs us here that several later Ash'arites argue that the soul consists of a very thin material (like the Aristotelian *aithêr*) which inheres in all organs of the body.[15] They all however, made no distinction between the term *nafs* and the term *rūḥ*, although both terms are mentioned in the Qur'an. The Qur'an mentions three levels of *nafs: al-'ammāra bi l-sū'*, commanding to evil (Q. 13:53), *al-lawwāma*, self-reproaching which recognises evil and asks for God's guidance, (Q 75:2), and *al- muṭma'inna*, the tranquil soul which has achieved peace with God (Q. 82:27).[16]

The term *rūḥ*, however, has more esoteric features. The Qur'an speaks of *rūḥ* in connection with the creation of Adam as a breath from

---

[13] M. Elkaisy-Friemuth, *God and Humans in Islamic Thought* (London, 2006), p. 52.
[14] Ibid., p. 53.
[15] Al-Rāzī, *Maṭālib*, p. 22.
[16] Elkaisy-Friemuth, 'al-Rūh wa al-Nafs', in *Encyclopaedia of Islamic Religion and Culture* (London, 2007).

TRADITION AND INNOVATION IN THE PSYCHOLOGY OF AL-RĀZĪ   127

God's spirit, *rūḥ minhu* (15:29), and as the spirit which is breathed into the womb of Mary (21:19). It is also referred to as a divine secret "say (that) the spirit (cometh) by the command of my Lord (*qul al-rūḥ min amri rabbī*)" (17:85). It also refers to certain angels as *al-rūḥ al amīn*, the faithful spirits who came to Muhammad (26:193), or *rūḥ al-qudus*, who is mainly known as the spirit which sends down revelation (16:102). Sufis such as Junayd and al-Ghazālī, in his late work *Kimiyā' al-Saʿāda*, identified the human soul mainly with the Qur'anic esoteric *rūḥ* and believed that the human spirit is a divine secret within the human body so that it may acknowledge its divine origin through its earthly experience.[17]

Al-Rāzī, in contrast, speaks of *al-rūḥ* in terms of the Aristotelian *pneuma*, and he admits that his concept of *al-rūḥ* comes from Ibn Sīnā's book *al-Qanūn* in medicine. However, he probably also had read the translation of Aristotle's *De Anima*, or Ibn Sānā's commentary on it. *Al-rūḥ* is a tenuous fine matter which has its source around the heart. However al-Rāzī believes that this *rūḥ* emerges from the hot airy element in the sperm, since he believes that the sperm contains the four elements: heat, coldness, liquid and earthly matter. When the human is formed in the mother's womb the airy and hot element of the sperm separates itself from the heavy thick elements and become an independent spirit, *al-rūḥ*. The heart, as he argues, is the first organ to be formed in the body and the *rūḥ*, which is the hot tenuous element, is collected around the heart and moves from there up to the brain and down to the liver and all organs of the body.[18] This theory that *al-rūḥ* emerges from the hot air in the sperm reminds us of the Ikhwān al-Ṣafā's theory of how the human is formed in accordance with the Qur'anic development in which the human starts as *nuṭfa*, then *ʿalaqa*, then *muḍgha*:

> The development of the human embryo according to the months and the astral influences. In the first month, under the action of Saturn, whose property is to cause form to take shape in matter, the *nuṭfa* is placed in the matrix. In the second month, under the dominant influence of the spiritual forces of Jupiter, heat is engendered in the *ʿalaqa* and produces in it the balance of the humours. In the third month, under the influence of Mars, the *ʿalaqa*, moved more vigorously, receives an excess of heat which transforms it into *muḍgha*. In the fourth month, it is the sun which

---

[17] Ibid.
[18] Ibid., pp. 111–13.

128 MAHA ELKAISY-FRIEMUTH

guides the development: its spiritual forces exert a major influence on the *muḍgha*; the vital powers breathe on it and it receives the animal soul.[19]

Al-rūḥ, since it consists of this fine tenuous matter, has the ability to mediate between the immaterial *nafs* and the material bodily organs. However, its main role here seems to be conveying the orders of the immaterial soul to the bodily organs. We will see below that al-Rāzī, in contrast to the Aristotelian tradition, does not consider that *al-rūḥ* plays any role in the process of knowledge, since he regards the imaginative and the conceptual processes as being taken over directly by *al-nafs* in a pure immaterial mode.[20] Al-Rāzī argues here, on the one hand, that the human soul, *al-nafs*, with its three faculties, the rational, the animal and vegetative, is an immaterial substance inherent in the body.[21] On the other hand, he presents *al-rūḥ* as another independent entity, which has a material form, in order to explain the relationship between the immaterial *nafs* and the material body. However the relationship between the immaterial *nafs* and the material world is not established through the *rūḥ* but rather through the nature of the material images and their conversion to immaterial substances as soon as they enter the body, as will be explained in the section to follow.[22] In doing so, he accepts both the philosophical immaterial *nafs* and the theological material soul.

As we noticed above, none of the Muslim thinkers treated *al-rūḥ* in the way al-Rāzī did. They usually confused it with *al-nafs*, some considering it a substance, but others deeming it one of the different attributes or powers of the body. Al-Rāzī, however, here introduces his theory about the nature of *al-rūḥ* in connection to Ibn Sīnā's two books, *al-Shifā'* and the *Medicine of the Heart*. Here we understand that Ibn Sīnā connects *al-rūḥ* to the vegetative and animal soul and considers that it carries their functions, as al-Rāzī informs us in *Maṭālib*.[23]

At any rate, al-Rāzī also presents here a long discussion as to whether *al-rūḥ* is connected to the heart, from where it spreads throughout the body, or is mainly connected to the brain. In this discussion, he is influenced by the Aristotelian tradition which prefers to connect the *pneuma*, which could be identified with al-Rāzī's *rūḥ*, to the heart.

---

[19] Arnaldez, R. "Insān." *Encyclopaedia of Islam 2*, Brill online, 2008.
[20] Al-Rāzī, *Maṭālib*, pp. 152–54.
[21] Al-Zurkān, *al-Rāzī*, pp. 482–83.
[22] Al-Rāzī, *Maṭālib*, pp. 153–54.
[23] Ibid., p. 111.

TRADITION AND INNOVATION IN THE PSYCHOLOGY OF AL-RĀZĪ   129

However, he seems here to have read primarily an Arabic translation of this conflict between the followers of Galen and the followers of Aristotle, because he gives all the details of this conflict and the arguments of both parties without referring to either Ibn Sīnā or to any of the Arab philosophers.[24]

In any case, al-Rāzī here makes a clear distinction between *al-rūḥ* and *al-nafs* with its tripartite divisions. He gives *al-rūḥ* the minor role of carrying orders from *al-nafs* to the different parts of the body. The three faculties of *al-nafs* he considers as powers which influence the system of the body and the process of knowledge without being in direct connection with the body. Thus al-Rāzī's purpose in giving importance to the role of *al-rūḥ* here lies in attempting to consider *al-nafs* with all its three faculties functioning as an absolute immaterial power in the body, as will be demonstrated in the following section.

The Functions of al-Nafs

Al-Rāzī, like all other Muslim and Arab philosophers, accepted the tripartite division of the soul, though with some important modifications. He was certainly influenced by al-Fārābī and Ibn Sīnā's studies concerning the different faculties of the soul and its role in perceiving knowledge.[25] Al-Fārābī (d. 950 A.D.) was the earliest to introduce a systematic study on the soul and its faculties. He considered, following Aristotle, that the activities of all living beings are related to the powers of the soul, *al-nafs*. There are three kinds of souls in the psychology of al-Fārābī: the eternal soul of God, which has no beginning and no relation to matter; the eternal souls of the angels, which have a beginning but exist without any connection to matter (*'aql mufāriq*); and finally the earthly soul, which exists in matter and can only be eternal through possession of knowledge. The earthly souls are also of three kinds: the vegetative soul which explains the nourishing of the thing and its growth, the animal soul which is responsible for all emotions and desires, and finally the rational soul which has the capacity to attain knowledge of the immaterial world and is only attributed to humans. The function of the human soul, however, includes the activities of both the vegetative and the animal soul, but it presents the possibility

---

[24] Ibid., pp. 98–111.
[25] Al-Zurkān, *al-Rāzī*, pp. 484–85.

130 MAHA ELKAISY-FRIEMUTH

for humans to reach the level of the angelic souls. The human soul controls all the functions of the body and uses it as its own instrument, which relates the soul to the other beings in the earthly world. The soul for al-Fārābī has only one hope, and that is to control the desires of the body and to lead the rational part of the soul to contemplate the divine world.[26]

Ibn Sīnā, for his part, considers that the rational soul is the only soul which has the ability to reach the angelic level, while the animal and the vegetative souls remain tied to the material world and face its fate. He hints in some of his writings, as al-Rāzī reports, that both souls are not purely immaterial, since they are able to carry information concerning the material world and transform it into immaterial images. Surely, they must be of a very fine tenuous material nature.[27]

Al-Rāzī in his study of the soul did not follow blindly al-Fārābī and Ibn Sīnā but criticised them and their Greek teachers, Aristotle and Plato, first, for their unwillingness to attribute to animals rational souls. In a long section in *Maṭālib* he argues that animals have rational abilities which sometimes exceed the human rational soul in some fields of knowledge. But he admits that if rationality for Arab philosophers means rational thinking in all fields of knowledge then obviously animals are not rational beings. However, we must also admit that humans also fail to perceive all kinds of knowledge.[28]

This argument, though, is mainly directed against the concept that animal souls are of material substance with no hope of an eternal future, here al-Rāzī is attempting to show the weakness in the philosophers' epistemology, which is dependent on the idea that the animal material soul is the mediator between the rational soul and the bodily sense-faculties. Al-Rāzī here asks: is the human soul one simple entity in reality or does the human have three souls, each of which is responsible for a certain function and has a different nature? Although al-Rāzī acknowledges that the Aristotelian tripartite division describes the different functions of the one soul, he argues that the nature of the three souls must be equally also identical.

Al-Rāzī here discovered a clear confusion in the Aristotelian tripartition; while the Arab philosophers acknowledge the soul as one

---

[26] Al-Fārābī, *Risāla fī al-ʿaql*, ed. M. Bouyges, (Beirut, 1938), pp. 5–40.
[27] Al-Rāzī, *Maṭālib*, p. 147.
[28] Ibid., pp. 179–84.

TRADITION AND INNOVATION IN THE PSYCHOLOGY OF AL-RĀZĪ 131

unity with different functions, they admit that only the rational soul is of pure immaterial immortal nature. He raises here an interesting question: how could it be that the soul is one, but a part of it has a material nature and the other part is pure intellect?[29] Although the Aristotelian concept clearly is attempting, by means of the tripartite model, to explain the relationship between the immaterial soul and the material information which it receives from the senses, as well as directing all bodily organs, this theory, in al-Rāzī's opinion, is not without contradictions. Principally, he argues that *al-nafs* is able to perceive particular as well as universal knowledge by demonstrating that the images of the material world become immaterial as soon as they enter the body through the senses; for example, seeing does not mean that the thing itself enters into the eye, but only an immaterial image of it. The soul for him is able to perceive the material information directly without any assistance from a material mediator because these items of information are transformed into immaterial images as soon as they make contact with the human or animal's organs.[30]

Yet the relationship between the *nafs* and the inner bodily organs and the inner senses seems to be conducted through the powers of *al-rūḥ*. *Al-rūḥ* has the ability, as we showed above, to convey orders from the brain to all parts of the body and to transfer information of all bodily experiences back to the brain. *Al-rūḥ* in this case is considered as a material substance running though all parts of the body, similar to the way in which Muslim theologians believe that the soul runs through the body, as oil in olives. In the process of knowledge, however, al-Rāzī argues that *al-nafs* is able to conduct all kinds of knowledge without assistance from any material mediator.[31]

This claim that *al-nafs* is able to perceive the material world without an intermediate material substance is indeed al-Rāzī's contribution and the source of his originality in this study. His proofs that *al-nafs* is able to perceive the material image and to judge over it and organise it in a certain hierarchy are, in fact, quite simple. He first presents the principle that a judgement on two things means in the first place possessing the knowledge of these two things, in order to be able to make such a decision. This is evidently true: simply, when we see a person

---

[29] Ibid., pp. 147–51.
[30] Al-Rāzī, *Maṭālib*, pp. 149–51.
[31] Ibid., pp. 111–13; see also al-Zurkān, *al-Rāzī*, pp. 480–82.

132   MAHA ELKAISY-FRIEMUTH

we are immediately able to judge that it is a human. The rational ability here must possess the knowledge of the particular person and the knowledge of the quality of the human and therefore in one process it recognises both kinds of knowledge.[32]

In addition, since we consider that the soul is an immaterial substance which controls and runs all the activities of the body, it is clear that it acknowledges in all these activities the particular as well as the universal; otherwise how could it make a decision about those activities? This proof, as al-Zurkān explains in his book on al-Rāzī, is also mentioned by Abū al-Barakāt al-Baghdādī who influenced al-Rāzī greatly in his concept of the human soul. However, Abū al-Barakāt considers that *al-nafs* is even aware of the process of digestion and all inner activities of the body, but it does not remember this, because these activities happen at a very high speed, which is nearly impossible to remember or to be actively recognised.[33]

Moreover, al-Rāzī explains that reaching universal concepts comes usually through necessary and particular premises which make the connection between particular objects to a certain universal concept like the relationship between 'Alī and the human; only because we know 'Alī and other particular persons we conclude that they all belong to the class 'human'. Thus the universal concepts are indeed derived from the particulars which means the genus is, in fact, dependent on the species members of it; without those particular members the genus would not have any reality. For example, the concept 'justice' depends fully on knowing the particular good and the particular evil and only through this particular knowledge can our concept of 'justice' have sense. Here al-Rāzī insists that understanding the universal depends on understanding the particular and therefore they belong to the same perception process: the one who perceives the universal must in the same time have the ability to perceive the particular members of the universal.[34]

In his explanation of the process of perception, al-Rāzī also criticises the notion of the pure mental image which is purified by the faculty of imagination. He believes that each mental image is in the first place

---

[32] Al-Rāzī, *Maṭālib*, pp. 152–3.
[33] Al-Zurkān, *al-Rāzī*, p. 485.
[34] See Al-Rāzī, *Maṭālib*, p. 182; in this sense al-Rāzī argues in many of his works that God must have the ability to perceive the particular as well as the universal for these two processes are inseparable.

a personal image, for each one of us perceives things in accordance with his/her own perception and mood and compares it to his/her own knowledge. Thus how could we consider any mental image as a pure universal image when it must be connected to the one who perceives it?[35]

Indeed the discussion above put the emphasis on the reality of *al-nafs* in its perception of the world and its awareness of this perception. Al-Rāzī here is attempting to show that the claim that the rational soul which is mainly interested in judgements and universal impersonal knowledge cannot, in fact, stand alone and obviously cannot represent the whole person, since it omits all his/her personal and real experience. He believes that since the rational soul perceives itself as a particular soul belonging to a certain person, then in fact it has the ability to perceive itself as a particular and as a part of the universal rational soul.

Undoubtedly, al-Rāzī here is attempting to explain what will be the nature of the human soul after the death of the body. In a short section in *Maṭālib* he explains that *al-nafs*, after its departure from the body, remains acquainted with worldly events, since it has the ability to perceive the particular as well as the universal.[36] Through this theory, al-Rāzī is attempting to argue for the assurance that the human soul will be able in eternity to know itself and recognise others, since we can infer that in *Maṭālib* he hints at the possibility that the afterlife is purely spiritual. This possibility can be argued for, since he devotes a fairly long section to maintaining that spiritual pleasure is much higher and more fitting to the nature of the human than material pleasure. Here he implies that the divine promise must be spiritual pleasure. In what follows we will examine closely his concept of the fate of the human soul in the afterlife.

The Origin and Future of the Human Soul

The origin of the human soul is an important element in the discussion of its essence and its relationship to other immaterial beings. Al-Rāzī clearly rejects the possibility that the human soul has a necessary existence in itself because for him the only necessary existent is God. He, then, discusses the other two possibilities: whether it is created in

---

[35] Al-Rāzī, *Maṭālib*, pp. 182–3.
[36] Ibid., p. 155.

134 MAHA ELKAISY-FRIEMUTH

time or created eternally.[37] Here however the important question is whether al-Rāzī connects the human soul to an eternal universal soul or considers it created by the creator directly. Before setting out his argument in this connection we need first to give a brief summary of his cosmology.

Although al-Rāzī does not reject the theory of emanation, he argues against the theory that "the One can only produce one". He sees no logical reason for the philosophers' assumption that God cannot emanate multiplicity, while the intellects can. He also argues that if the first intellect comes under the class of 'contingent (*mumkin*) beings', as Ibn Sīnā and most Arab philosophers argue, which includes possessing two natures of existence and essence. This must conclude that the first intellect includes multiplicity within itself, which all philosophers would agree about, however this must also conclude that the One did produce multiplicity, in which case we cannot consider that the One (God) emanates a single entity.[38] This, indeed, proves that the One can only produce multiplicity, since the only pure One is God. However, he continues to refute their defence that God can be the cause of only one part of the two parts of the first intellect, which is its necessity of existence; but al-Rāzī answers that if this can be done to the first intellect, why should not God be the cause of the necessary part of each being, meaning that God can emanate existence to all possible being?[39]

Although al-Rāzī rejects the theory of emanation as expounded by other Muslim philosophers, he argues that existence can only be given by God. However, he believes that some beings come directly from God, and these are the intellects and the souls of the different planets, while others need a preparatory stage in order to be able to receive their existence from God. The souls of humans and animals, therefore, are related in his opinion to the latter kinds of beings. They need a preparatory stage, which comes about by certain movements of the stars and planets, but the actual existence of these souls will finally be provided by God Himself.[40] In this case we can consider that al-Rāzī advocates the theory of primary and secondary causes—though, as an Ash'arite, he believes that the only creator and provider of existence is God. This reminds us, however, that on Ibn Sīnā's theory each being receives

[37] Al-Rāzī, *Maṭālib*, pp. 8–9.
[38] Al-Zurkān, *al-Rāzī*, p. 344.
[39] Ibid., pp. 344–45.
[40] Ibid., p. 483.

TRADITION AND INNOVATION IN THE PSYCHOLOGY OF AL-RĀZĪ   135

its existence from God, while its essence comes from the relationship between matter and form.[41]

From the discussion above we see clearly that there is no room in al-Rāzī's theory of creation for a universal soul which produces all souls, although in some writings he identifies the universal soul with the Qur'anic divine throne.[42] The existence of the human soul is here related to different causes, some of which are the souls of the planets, but when all the conditions for the existence of a certain species of soul emerge, they then will receive their existence from God. Thus, although God is the giver of existence, their direct cause is the different souls of the planets and their particular movements.[43] In this sense al-Rāzī believes, like Ibn Sīnā and Aristotle, that each soul is connected to one specific body and its existence is tied to the existence of its body. However, he goes on further to say that the existence of each body is also made to suit one specific soul, although in a long section in *Maṭālib* he argues that we cannot prove that the soul is tied only to one body, since the soul uses the body for its own benefit, and the possibility that it uses more than one body to reach its goal can not be dismissed. Nevertheless, at the end of the discussion he declares that he, at least, believes that the soul is created for a specific body.[44] Moreover, in other writings he attacks the theory of reincarnation for the main reason that it supposes the eternal existence of the human soul.

Concerning the immortality of the human soul, al-Rāzī shows clearly that the soul is a substance independent of the body and does not perish by its death. His argument for the immortality of the soul is divided into three levels: first, his argument that the soul does not come under the class of beings which decay; second, his argument that the last day is possible; and third, his discussion of the resurrection of the body and its connection to the soul.[45] I will give details of all three arguments.

That the soul does not come under the class of things subject to decay is a fundamental argument in al-Rāzī's concept of the immortality of the soul. The human soul, like all the celestial souls and the universal soul, is immaterial and a simple unity. This means that it does not consist of parts and therefore is indivisibly one. Decay, in contrast, is

---

[41] Elkaisy-Friemuth, *God and Humans*, pp. 88–89.
[42] Al-Zurkān, *al-Rāzī*, pp. 355–56.
[43] Ibid., p. 483.
[44] Al-Rāzī, *Maṭālib*, pp. 145–47.
[45] Ibid., p. 141.

136 MAHA ELKAISY-FRIEMUTH

applicable only to beings which consist of atoms or of matter and form. For decay comes to separate atoms or to destroy the unity of matter and form, and thus immaterial simple entities do not fall under the possibility of decay and cannot be destroyed. Al-Rāzī mentions here also the different opponents of this theory and his refutation of them.[46] The strongest argument against this theory is: if the human soul is created and specified to one body, then it is a contingent (*mumkin*) being in itself and its contingency means that it could exist or remain non-existent; and its existence can only mean its contingency, which must mean that its matter accepted the form of the soul and therefore it could exist. Thus since, in their opinion, it consists of matter and form, it is indeed subject to destruction. This argument is reminiscent of the perishability axiom which faced medieval Christian theologians: all that exists in time must perish in time.[47] Al-Rāzī here, however, considers that the contingent existence of the soul does mean that it has a potential matter but that it received its existence only through the power of the divine creation. In addition, he considers that substances which are contingent (*mumkin*) but do not exist in a material form are nevertheless not subject to decay because decay threatens only entities which actually exist in space and in a place (*maḥal*). Therefore when we say that the soul is created, its possibility of existence does not fall under the category of beings which can be destroyed.[48]

Whether the world will be at some time destroyed and then reconstructed is a theory which is directly connected to the concept of the last day (*al-Maʿād*). In his study of this subject, al-Rāzī informs us that Muslim philosophers in general do not support the concept of the last day for two reasons: first, because they believe that, since God is eternal and everlasting, his main activity, which is emanation, is also eternal and everlasting; secondly, the philosophers also consider that what is perished cannot be reconstructed in its original form.[49] Al-Rāzī discusses the issue of *al-Maʿād* in his book *al-Arbaʿīn fī Uṣūl al-Dīn*, and concludes, in the first place, that emanation, though it could reflect God's activity, in reality is not an act of compulsion but an act of volition, and therefore God is not obliged to keep emanation everlasting. Therefore, this issue, he confirms, cannot be solved by rational proofs,

---

[46] Al-Rāzī, *Maṭālib*, pp. 141–44.
[47] Ibid.
[48] Al-Zurkān, *al-Rāzī*, pp. 407–14.
[49] Ibid., pp. 487–89.

TRADITION AND INNOVATION IN THE PSYCHOLOGY OF AL-RĀZĪ 137

since no one can prove what God wills, but rather by revealed text. As a result, *al-Ma'ād* is a possible future of the world, and if it happens then resurrection is also possible.[50]

In dealing with the question of resurrection we reach the third point in his discussion of the immortality of the soul. Before presenting this discussion it is appropriate here to give a short illustration of al-Rāzī's concept of bodies (*al-ajssām*). It seems from *Maṭālib* and *Kitāb al-Arba'īn* that al-Rāzī, though in his early writings rejecting atomism, in his later writings followed the Muslim theologians in their belief in the indivisible part (*al-jawhar al-fard*).[51] Most Muslim theologians have adopted the theory that all bodies consist of several parts, the smallest of which they called atoms or *jawāhir*. Badawī considers the Mu'tazilite Abū al-Hudhayl to be the earliest to adopt the theory of atoms and accidents. He was probably influenced by the ancient Greek atomists who, however, considered that the smallest part of the body, the atom, existed eternally. Yet the Greeks seem to believe that atoms function through their own qualities, while Muslim theologians consider that movements, convergence, warmth, coldness, and all other attributes do not belong to the atoms but come to inhere in them. Muslim theologians, in addition, considered that atoms are created and destroyed by God. All activities of the atoms are produced by the inherence of what they call accidents, *a'rāḍ*. They used this word in order to explain the nature of change in everything. It is possible to compare accidents with the Aristotelian concept of form which actualizes matter; however, the Arabic concept *a'rāḍ* is more complex because the activity of each moment is explained and interpreted as an inherent quality of a certain accident at a certain moment. *A'rāḍ* are also distinguished from the Aristotelian forms by being created by God at the time when they inhere in the atom, and only God can make them disappear.[52] Al-Rāzī defended this theory in his later writings and considered it to be more plausible than the theory of matter and form because matter, *hule*, can exist only potentially, not actually, and form, Rāzī continues, also is not an independent entity and does not have independent existence. Thus, al-Rāzī argues, how can it be that two substances which do not exist in reality can bring other things into existence?[53]

---

[50] Fakhr al-Dīn al-Rāzī, *al-Arba'īn fī Uṣūl al-Dīn*, (Beirut, 2004), pp. 271–77.
[51] Ibid., pp. 247–57.
[52] Elkaisy-Friemuth, *God and Humans*, pp. 52–55.
[53] Al-Zurkān, *al-Rāzī*, p. 425.

138   MAHA ELKAISY-FRIEMUTH

At any rate, on the question of resurrection, al-Rāzī considers that, for all things that consist of parts, their possibility of existence and non-existence is equal; their existence is based on the fact that their parts came together, and their non-existence means that either their parts perished or separated from each other. In either case, the possibility of reconstructing perished or separated parts exists equally, since all existent things have the possibility of their existence as an essential characteristic of them.[54] Thus this possibility of existence does not cause things to cease when they die, but rather only their actual existence ceases, and therefore the possibility that they can be reconstructed is rationally approved. Muslim theologians, however, differ in their concept of how the atom perish. Some consider that atoms cannot be destroyed, but rather separate from their unity when death destroys the body. This group, al-Rāzī declares, do not believe that perished things can be recreated and therefore they consider that God separates the atoms and brings them together again on the day of resurrection. However al-Rāzī asks here how it is possible that the thing itself comes into existence again, since the person is not only the combination of atoms but what is unique in each person, his/her own characteristic, which is present in the actual person who died. Thus he finds in this theory no guarantee of actual resurrection.[55]

Al-Rāzī, on the other hand, believes that in death humans, animals and plants perish totally and nothing remains from their atoms. Resurrection of humans is rationally possible, but cannot be proved except by referring to revealed texts. However, it is dependent upon two main premises: first, that God has the ability to actualise all possible things; and second, that God knows the particular as well as the universal. Since al-Rāzī believes, as we mentioned previously, that God is the only giver of existence, then all possible beings can only exist if God provides their existence. This means that God is able to turn all possibilities into actuality; this includes the possible existence of perished things which still hold their possibilities in themselves to be resurrected. God also has the ability to bring perished things and beings back to their exact actual characteristics, because He, in al-Rāzī's opinion, knows exactly each particular.[56] Al-Rāzī argues that since God is endowed with

---

[54] Al-Rāzī, al-Arbaʿīn, pp. 274–75.
[55] Ibid., p. 280.
[56] Ibid., p. 282.

TRADITION AND INNOVATION IN THE PSYCHOLOGY OF AL-RĀZĪ 139

omniscience, and this includes knowledge of all particulars, denying to Him this kind of knowledge, he believes, would attribute to Him ignorance of His own creatures, which is impossible and absurd.

Although al-Rāzī in *Kitāb al-Arbaʿān* argues for the possibility of bodily resurrection, it is not necessary that he believes in its actual occurrence. He actually in *Maṭālib*, his last book, does not deal with the issue of *al-Maʿād* in a separate section, but rather dedicates a long section to proving that material pleasure is not appropriate to human nobility. Spiritual happiness is, in fact, what should be the ultimate hope of each human and the goal of their lives.[57]

Nevertheless al-Rāzī, in each of the sections mentioned in this article, admits that there are no guarantees and absolute proofs on the subject of the human soul, and it will for ever remain in the field of possibility, since only God knows with certainty the truth (*al-yaqīn*) about the soul, in respect of its reality, function and future.

---

[57] Ibid.

D. JUDAIC TRADITION

THE SOUL IN JEWISH NEOPLATONISM:
A CASE STUDY OF ABRAHAM IBN EZRA AND
JUDAH HALEVI

Aaron W. Hughes*

The Greek philosophical tradition, as we know, made a large impact on rationalist Arabo-Islamic thinking, especially in the domain of philosophy that we now typically refer to as epistemology. It was speculation about the soul, for example, that provided the impetus for Arabic philosophers to re-define traditional theological monotheistic concepts such as revelation using natural theories of human cognition inherited from the Greeks. This speculative framework made its way into the Jewish philosophical tradition in the eleventh century, and its introduction therein represents the translation of Greco-Arabic terms into the Hebraic vocabularies and categories associated with the Bible.

In order to examine both the dynamics and tensions associated with this translation activity, what follows analyzes the theory of the soul developed by Abraham ibn Ezra (1092–1167), generally considered to be one of the foremost representatives of the medieval Jewish Neoplatonic tradition. Ibn Ezra, a polymath who wrote treatises on many topics, is perhaps most famous for his biblical commentaries, wherein he reads the Bible in light of contemporaneous philosophical and scientific theories. As such, these commentaries provide tremendous insights into the ways that Jewish thinkers overcame the strangeness of philosophical ideas by grounding them within autochthonous categories, thereby naturalizing the philosophical tradition within Judaism.

Although successful on some levels since his commentaries came to be included within the *miqraot gedalot*, or the rabbinic Bible, his synthesis did not go unchallenged. One of the foremost representatives of the critique mounted against philosophy is ibn Ezra's older contemporary and friend, Judah Halevi (1075–1141). Halevi was generally critical of philosophy because he felt that Jewish categories (e.g., prophecy) were *sui generis* and, when framed using non-Jewish vocabularies and understandings, were both unhelpful and ultimately pernicious to

---

* SUNY, Buffalo.

144 AARON W. HUGHES

true belief. To counter the philosophical reading of Judaism provided by the likes of ibn Ezra, Halevi penned one of the greatest paeans to Jewish particularism, the *Kuzari*, which provides an informed (anti-) philosophical critique of philosophy.

In order to show just what is at stake in this debate, I have chosen to focus not simply on ibn Ezra's conjunction of Greco-Arabic philosophy and Judaism, but also on Halevi's critique of this conjunction. By putting the work of these two thinkers in counterpoint, I hope to show something of the struggle over philosophical ideas in general and those over the soul in particular that occurred within medieval Judaism. The debate between these two, for lack of a better term, "worldviews" was not simply an academic one. For how one understood the soul ultimately determined how one conceived of a host of related issues, such as creation, revelation, and redemption. At stake was how to understand Jewish culture: What books should be read? What sources should be deemed authoritative? And, ultimately, what should Judaism's relationship be to other cultures? The universalism of ibn Ezra and the particularism of Halevi, thus, represent two strands of Jewish existence that continue into the present.

To explore these issues in detail, what follows consists of several inter-related parts. After giving brief biographical sketches of both ibn Ezra and Halevi, I move into a descriptive analysis of how each of these thinkers conceptualized the human soul, especially its relationship to the divine world. This, in turn, will enable me to discuss several inter-related topics such as how each articulated theories concerning the origin of the human soul, its cognitive subdivisions, and how the proper care of the soul contributed to the *summum bonum* of human existence. Following this, I shall examine how both ibn Ezra and Halevi conceived of one particular part of the soul, the imagination, showing how this played an important role in their respective notions of prophecy.

Abraham ibn Ezra and Judah Halevi:
Jewish Universalism versus Particularism

In ibn Ezra we witness both the glories and the tensions inherent to the life and times of Andalusi Jewish courtier culture. Drawn to the universal themes of the Arabo-Islamic culture, he was also acutely aware of the particularities of the Jewish people. He was born in 1089 in the town of Tudela (then in al-Andalus) in the northeastern region

THE SOUL IN JEWISH NEOPLATONISM 145

of Castille, most likely the same place as his older contemporary Judah Halevi (see below). The son of a wealthy family, ibn Ezra (and Halevi) would undoubtedly have received a rich education in both Jewish topics (e.g., Bible, Talmud) and non-Jewish ones (e.g., Arabic literature, science, philosophy).[1]

With the fall of Tudela in 1115, ibn Ezra left the city of his birth and began what would amount to a lifetime of peregrinations. He traveled throughout Spain (both Muslim and Christian) and North Africa. And in 1140, the same year that Halevi set sail for the land of Israel, ibn Ezra also left al-Andalus for good. Brought on by the fanaticism of the Muslim Almoravid conquests, he went to France, Italy, and subsequently England. These travels played a major role in the introduction and dissemination of Andalusi philosophical and scientific advancements to Jewish cultures outside of the Iberian Peninsula.

Ibn Ezra not only translated Arabic mathematical and astronomical treatises into Hebrew, thereby developing a technical Hebrew vocabulary for such sciences, he also wrote many synthetic scientific, grammatical, and philosophical treatises. Moreover, he framed many of his philosophical ideas using the genre of the biblical commentary; indeed he often wrote at least two commentaries to each biblical book. Despite his prolific output, there is a paradox in that, to use the words of Tzvi Langermann, "Ibn Ezra contributed virtually nothing to any of the branches of philosophy; he authored little in the way of strictly philosophical tracts and, indeed, there is no reason for us to suppose that he enjoyed any rigorous training in philosophy."[2] Regardless, ibn Ezra's eclecticism and prolific career established him as one of the major thinkers of pre-Maimonidean Jewish philosophy.

Halevi was born in either Toledo or Tudela,[3] in the year 1075. Regardless of his birthplace, he soon made his way to the Castilian court in search of fame and fortune among its Jewish literary circles. Impressed with the poetic gifts and promise of this aspiring young poet, Moshe ibn Ezra (ca. 1055–1138; and no immediate relationship to Abraham

---

[1] Requisite biographies include Hermann Greive, *Studies zum jüdischen Neoplatonismus: Die Religionsphilosophie des Abraham ibn Ezra* (Berlin, 1973); Israel Levin, *Abraham ibn Ezra: His Life and Poetry* [Hebrew] (Tel Aviv, 1969).

[2] Y. Tzvi Langermann, "Ibn Ezra, Abraham," *Stanford Encyclopedia of Philosophy*.

[3] This ambiguity revolves around the manuscript tradition. See the comments in Schirmann, "Where was Judah Halevi Born?" in his *Studies in the History of Hebrew Poetry and Drama*, vol. 1, pp. 247–249.

146 AARON W. HUGHES

ibn Ezra) invited him to Granada.[4] There, Halevi became the darling of the Jewish literati: his poetic brilliance, facility with prosody, and ability to manipulate language quickly ensured for him a prominent place within the pantheon of distinguished Andalusi Jewish poets. He also became an important court physician and respected leader of the Jewish community.[5] Halevi spent much of his youth and middle age mesmerized by the universal poetic and intellectual currents associated with Arabo-Islamic Neoplatonism, creatively framing Judaism in the light of its categories.

By the age of fifty, however, Halevi began to turn his back on the ideals and practices that defined the elite culture in which he was so intimately involved.[6] His disillusionment with its poetic manners and forms,[7] its intellectualist mooring of Judaism, led him to renounce an entire way of life. On one level, then, Halevi was a product of the rich Judeo-Arabic culture,[8] yet on another level his life reveals the ambiguity of this symbiosis at the points at which it was increasingly fragile and most vulnerable:

> They congratulate him for being in the service of kings
> Which to him is like the worship of idols.
> Is it right for a worthy and pious man
> To be glad that he is caught, like a bird by a child,
> In the service of Philistines, Hittites, and descendants of Hagar
> His heart is seduced by alien deities
> To do their will, and forsake the will of God,
> To deceive the Creator and serve His creatures.[9]

---

[4] See, for example, "A Letter of Rabbi Judah Halevi to Rabbi Moses ibn Ezra," 404–407. A poetic version of ibn Ezra's invitation may be found in "*Yaldei yamim*" in *Secular Poems*, vol. 1, pp. 22–23.

[5] S. D. Goitein, *A Mediterranean Society* (Berkeley, 1988), vol. 5, p. 448; Ross Brann, *The Compunctious Poet: Cultural Ambiguity and Hebrew Poetry in Muslim Spain* (Baltimore, 1991), pp. 84–85.

[6] On the literary trope of turning one's back on the folly of youth, see the introduction to Brann, *The Compunctious Poet*.

[7] Brann, *The Compunctious Poet*, pp. 94–106.

[8] Long regarded in secondary scholarship as the "Golden Age," this has in recent years come under increasing interrogation. See, for example, Mark R. Cohen, *Under Crescent and Cross: The Jews in the Middle Ages* (Princeton, 1994), pp. 3–14; Ross Brann, *Power in the Portrayal: Representations of Jews and Muslims in Eleventh- and Twelfth-Century Spain* (Princeton, 2002), pp. 1–21; Aaron W. Hughes, "The 'Golden Age' of Muslim Spain: Religious Identity and the Invention of a Tradition in Modern Jewish Studies," in *Historicizing "Tradition" in the Study of Religion*, edited by Steven Engler and Greg Greive (Berlin, 2005), pp. 51–74.

[9] "*Hayukhlu pegarim*," trans. Goldstein, *The Jewish Poets of Spain*, pp. 37–138.

THE SOUL IN JEWISH NEOPLATONISM   147

As this poem makes explicit, Halevi refuses to connect authentic Jewish existence to the slavish imitation of Arab and Islamicate values. True piety could no longer be defined, as it was for so many of Halevi's Jewish contemporaries, as a set of universal, ahistorical ideals provided by a generic and spiritualized Neoplatonism. In its place, Halevi crafts his *magnum opus*, the *Kuzari*, as a celebration of Jewish particularism, an indictment against attempts to read Judaism in the light of such universal categories. Ironically, however, Halevi composes his defense of Jewish particularism in the Arabic language, using the Arabo-Islamic categories of his day.

Halevi wrote the *Kuzari* over a period of at least twenty years. Not surprisingly, we witness in it the changing attitudes of an individual to the dominant paradigms of Andalusi Jewish culture.[10] Although he began the work while still living in al-Andalus, he completed the work in Egypt in 1040, just before he made his way to the land of Israel.[11] This rather lengthy period of composition has led some to conclude that the final version of the *Kuzari* was hastily put together in an "uncrafted and disconnected manner."[12] Yet the very fact that the *Kuzari* is the product of one of the most creative and distinguished of the medieval Jewish poets should militate against such a reading.

---

[10] Pines argues, for example, that book five of the *Kuzari*, generally regarded as a later addition to the work, was written at a time when Halevi began to know and look favorably upon the work of Avicenna, and that he subsequently reworked a number of his earlier ideas in the light of Avicennian categories. See Pines, "Shi'ite Terms and Conceptions in Judah Halevi's *Kuzari*," *Jerusalem Studies in Arabic and Islam* 2 (1980), pp. 215–217. Also on the subject of the *Kuzari*'s "stratigraphy," Yohanan Silman argues that there exist two distinct layers in the *Kuzari*, an "early" one that is influenced by philosophy, and a "later" one that rejects philosophy in favor of experience and history. See his *Philosopher and Prophet: Judah Halevi, the Kuzari, and the Evolution of His Thought*, translated by Lenn J. Schramm (Albany, 1995), pp. 159–165; 289–307.

[11] Goitein, "The Biography of Rabbi Judah ha-Levi in Light of the Cairo Genizah Documents," *Proceedings of the American Academy of Jewish Research* 28 (1959), pp. 55–56; Touati, introduction to *Le Kuzari: Apologie de la religion méprisée* (Paris, 1994), p. viii.

[12] This is the opinion of Julius Guttmann, "The Relationship Between Religion and Philosophy According to Judah Halevi" (Hebrew) in his *Religion and Knowledge: Essays and Lectures*, edited by S. H. Bergman and N. Rotenstreich (Jerusalem: Magnes Press, 1955), 66. See the comments in Michael S. Berger, "Towards a New Understanding of Judah Halevi's *Kuzari*" *Religion* 72.2 (1992), pp. 210–228. On Halevi's travels from al-Andalus to the land of Israel, see Raymond P. Scheindlin, *Song of the Distant Dove: Judah Halevi's Pilgrimage* (New York, 2008).

148   AARON W. HUGHES

Ibn Ezra's Tripartite Division of the Soul

It is notoriously difficult to lift a monolithic philosophical system from the vast and wide-ranging corpus of Abraham ibn Ezra, let alone a general theory of the soul. Although there exist many suggestive and original philosophical fragments scattered throughout his biblical commentaries and other scientific works, many of these fragments are obscure and their interpretation made difficult owing to the cautious language that he employs, his imprecision in using terms, or his more general unwillingness to provide details. For instance, he is often fond of alluding to weighty matters and subsequently employing the term *ha-maskil yavin* ("the wise person will understand") without ever explaining what exactly it is that he means.

Ibn Ezra's theory of the soul is, for the most part, Neoplatonic in both is structure and its assumptions.[13] He claims that the individual is composed of a body and three souls: the vegetative (*ha-nefesh*), the animal (*ha-ruah*), and the human (*ha-neshamah*).[14] The *nefesh*, which ibn Ezra locates in the liver, is the lowest of the three souls; it is found in plants, animals, and humans, and it is associated with the basic nutritive and reproductive desires. The *ruah*, which he locates in the heart, is the intermediary soul; it is found only in animals and humans, and is associated with the corporeal desires. Both the *nefesh* and the

---

[13] Immediately, however, we are presented with a problem: None of the thinkers of late antiquity or the medieval period would have considered themselves to be "Neoplatonists" or to have belonged to a distinct school referred to by the name "Neoplatonism." Chronologically, it becomes impossible to speak of a, much less *the*, Neoplatonic anything (e.g., cosmology, metaphysics). All those we now refer to as Neoplatonists would undoubtedly have been uncomfortable with the label "neo" owing to the fact that they considered themselves simply to be Platonists. Moreover they were, and this is something that often strikes the modern reader as odd, Platonists who were quite content to read and use Aristotle. As Lloyd Gerson argues in his intriguingly titled *Aristotle and Other Platonists*, from roughly the time of the earliest Platonists in the fourth century B.C.E. to the beginning of the Islamic period, there was a tendency to read Plato and Aristotle harmoniously based on a division of labor: Plato was regarded as authoritative for the supra-lunar world, whereas Aristotle was regarded as authoritative for the sensible one. As a result, there exists a tremendously complex labyrinth of connections between Platonism and Aristotelianism, connections that we often blur by employing the vague and misleading term "Neoplatonism." In this regard, see Lloyd P. Gerson, *Aristotle and Other Platonists* (Ithaca, 2005), pp. 1–12; also see the comments in Maria Luisa Gatti, "Plotinus: The Platonic Tradition and the Foundation of Neoplatonism," in *The Cambridge Companion to Plotinus*, edited by Lloyd P. Gerson (Cambridge, 1996), pp. 22–29.

[14] E.g., *Sefer Yesod Mora ve sod ha-torah*, in *The Ibn Erza Reader*, edited by Israel Levin (Tel Aviv, 1985), p. 330.

THE SOUL IN JEWISH NEOPLATONISM   149

ruah are corporeal and perish with the death of the individual. Above
these two souls is the *neshamah*, found in the brain, which is unique
to humans. This is the rational soul of the philosophers and, according
to ibn Ezra, it is eternal.[15]

This becomes clearer in his commentary to Deuteronomy 6:5 ("You
will love the Lord your God with all your heart [*lev*], with all your soul
[*nefesh*], and with all your might [*me'od*]"). Ibn Ezra argues that the
heart is the part of the body associated with understanding and thus
scripture means by it the intellect.[16] The heart, then, is a metaphor for
the *neshamah* because the heart receives strength from it more than
from any other part of the body. By contrast, he locates the various
sensual desires of the body in the lower soul, *i.e.*, the *nefesh*. The term
"might" refers to all of the power or ability that the individual possesses.
Implicit in his comments is that the love for God must be a complete
love that involves the entire being of the individual with the heart as
the epicenter. In his philosophical epitome, *Yesod Mora* ("Foundation
of Piety") X.2, he argues that this love of God is the foundation of all
wisdom.[17]

In typical Neoplatonic fashion, ibn Ezra describes the *neshamah* as
"likened to God in its essence."[18] In other words, it is indestructible,
eternal, and resides, prior to its association with a human body, in the
universal soul (*nishmat ha-kol*). This universal soul, according to his
comments on *Genesis* 1:26, is part of the third and highest level of the
world, the so-called *olam elyon*. In his long *Commentary to Exodus*
3:15, ibn Ezra clarifies:

> The upper world is the world of the holy angels. They are neither bodies
> nor are they in bodies like the soul [*neshamah*] of man. Their level is
> beyond human understanding. In this world is the Glory [*kavod*] and
> all of it is eternal. It neither moves nor changes its value; its rank does
> not come from itself, but from the glorious Name [*ha-shem ha-nikbad*].
> The soul [*neshamah*] of man is from this upper world and it receives its
> strength from this world.[19]

---

[15] *Commentary to Genesis*, p. 18. I have used the text found in *Commentary to the
Torah*, edited by Asher Weiser (Jerusalem, 1977), p. 18.

[16] Although note the inconsistency with the previous paragraph where ibn Ezra
equates the heart with the animal soul or *nefesh*.

[17] *Sefer Yesod Mora*, p. 337.

[18] *Commentary to Genesis*, p. 19.

[19] This description differs considerable from his commentary to *Daniel* 10:21, where
he claims that the angels occupy a position in the intermediate world. Greive argues

150   AARON W. HUGHES

The *neshamah*, then, is the essence of the individual. It is juxtaposed against to the body, in which it ephemerally finds itself. Moreover, in claiming that the *neshamah* is from the upper world, ibn Ezra seems to argue that because the human soul originally dwells in the realm of the angels, it necessarily preexists the body. In this he differs from Avicenna, one of his main Muslim sources.[20]

When the *neshamah* enters the human body it does so as a tabula rasa (*luah halaq*) and, as a result must become individualized.[21] It consequently rests upon each individual to make the most of his *neshamah*, to develop and sustain it according to its lofty origin. This primarily involves studying and understanding the various scientific disciplines. In the introduction to his commentary on *Qoheleth*, he writes:

> Just as the passerby, who has been taken prisoner, longs to return to his homeland and to be with his family, so does the intellecting spirit yearn to grab hold of the higher rungs, until she ascends to the formations of the living God, which do not dwell in material houses... This will transpire if the spirit whitens, sanctifying herself above the impurities of disgusting bodily lusts which sully what is holy... then what is distant will be like what is near, and night like day; then she will be configured to know the real truth, which will be inscribed upon her in such a way so as not be erased when she departs the body, for the script is the writing of God. She was brought here in order to be shown, and for that reason she was imprisoned until the end of her term.[22]

In this highly literary passage, ibn Ezra argues that the *neshamah* is essentially trapped within the body and at the mercy of sensual and corporeal desires. Since the senses can only perceive accidents, ibn Ezra argues that it is impossible to know God directly.[23] Like many of the medieval Jewish philosophers who will follow him, ibn Ezra informs the reader that God's essence is beyond human comprehension; all that humans can do is approach God through the observation of His traces

---

that angels there, i.e., in the intermediate world, refer to the celestial spheres. See his *Studies zum jüdischen Neuplatonismus*, 90. Elliot R. Wolfson argues that this may come from the thought of Avicenna. See his "God, the Demiurge, and the Active Intellect: On the Usage of the Word *kol* in Abraham Ibn Ezra," *Revue des Études Juives* 149 (1990), p. 86, n. 37.

[20] E.g., Avicenna, *Kitāb ahwāl al-nafs*, edited by Ahmad Fū'ād al-Ahwānī (Cairo, 1952), pp. 99–105; idem, *Al-Shifā': Al-Tabā'iyyat*, vol. 6: *Al-Nafs*, edited by G. C. Anawati and S. Zayed; rev. Ibrahim Madkour (Cairo, 1975), pp. 204–206.

[21] See his comments in *Sefer Yesod Mora*, p. 337.

[22] Levin, *The Ibn Ezra Reader*, p. 288.

[23] *Commentary to Exodus*, p. 214.

THE SOUL IN JEWISH NEOPLATONISM

in the world of nature. As a result, one can only know God by means of the various scientific disciplines, whose subject matter is, for the most part, the world that the senses perceive. By studying and mastering the physical and metaphysical sciences, ibn Ezra argues, one metaphorically fills one's tablet (*luah*) with God's writing.[24]

Ibn Ezra defines the love of God in rationalist terms. He conceives of it as a hierarchical process, in which each science represents a rung in a ladder. One begins with the study of logic, which he calls "the scale employed by every other science."[25] In *Yesod Mora* I.1, he argues that logic is what enables the true believer to abstract universal principles from the 613 commandments. After one has mastered logic, one must observe, understand, and attempt to master the various natural sciences. These sciences enable one to understand the lower world (*ha-olam ha-shafal*), permitting an entry point to the structure and beauty that exists beyond observable sense phenomena.

Once one understands the structure of the lower world it is imperative to investigate the intermediate world (*ha-olam ha-emtsa'i*). This is the world of the stars, planets, and spheres; and the requisite sciences to understand this world includes mathematics, geometry, and astronomy. Mastery of these sciences permits one access to the upper worlds (*ha-olam ha-elyon*). Ibn Ezra says very little about this world except that it involves knowledge of God's throne and the account of the chariot (*ma'aseh merkabah*), i.e., metaphysics.

Like all Neoplatonists, ibn Ezra stresses the importance of self-knowledge. He defines the individual as a microcosm (*olam qatan*). In his commentary to *Exodus* 31:18, for example, he argues that "one cannot know God unless he first knows his own *nefesh, neshamah*, and body; what good is wisdom to him who does not know the essence of his own *nefesh*." In a different passage, ibn Ezra equates this wisdom with the form of the soul.[26] Through self-knowledge and a proper understanding of the sciences, one begins to grasp God's presence behind everything. Constant observation and contemplation of the natural world both produces and sustains in the individual a love for God.[27] This, in turn, leads to the goal of human existence: cleaving (*devequt*) to God. This

---

[24] *Sefer Yesod Mora*, p. 337.
[25] *Sefer Yesod Mora*, p. 318.
[26] *Commentary to Exodus*, pp. 176–177.
[27] *Sefer Yesod Mora*, pp. 322, 342.

152   AARON W. HUGHES

insures the return of one's immortal soul to the upper world.[28] In his comments to *Psalm* 1:6, ibn Ezra argues that the souls of the wicked will perish with the body's corruption.

For ibn Ezra, then, the *summum bonum* of human life is the re-absorption of the rational part of the human soul into the divine soul. This is something that can only be done when the individual has perfected his rational soul through the study of philosophy and science. Here we see the tension inherent to the philosophical reading of Judaism: Are only those who have perfected the various sciences capable of attaining this re-absorption? If so, what is the fate of all those Jewish souls that have not mastered these sciences, but who lead good lives according to the performance of the divine commandments? Moreover, what happens to non-Jewish philosophers? Are they assured of a place in the afterlife over non-philosophical Jews? This brings into stark relief the ambiguities inherent to the philosophical understanding of traditional Jewish concepts.

Halevi takes a different view of both the nature of the human soul and the utility of the sciences in one's intellectual development. This, of course, is not to say that he is unaware of the basic Neoplatonic or Avicennian division of the soul. In book five of the *Kuzari*,[29] for instance, Halevi summarizes the philosophical conception and subdivision of the soul. He writes that

> the existence of the soul [*al-nafs*] is shown in living beings by motion and perception, which is unlike the movement of the elements. The cause of the former is called soul, and is divided into three parts. The first division is common to animals and plants and is called the vegetative power [*al-quwwa al-nabātiyya*]; the second which is common to humans and other living beings is called the vital power [*al-quwwa al-hayawāniyya*]; and the third which is specific to man is called the rational power [*al-quwwa al-natiqiyya*].[30]

---

[28] See the comments in Georges Vajda, *L'amour de Dieu dans la théologie juive du Moyen Age* (Paris, 1957), p. 111.

[29] Here it is worth pointing out Shlomo Pines' argument that book five of the *Kuzari*, generally regarded as a later addition to the work, was written at a time when Halevi began to know and look favorably upon the work of Avicenna, and that he subsequently reworked a number of his earlier ideas in the light of Avicennian categories. See Pines, "Shi'ite Terms and Conceptions in Judah Halevi's *Kuzari*," pp. 215–217.

[30] Halevi, *Kitāb al-radd wa al-dalīl fī al-dīn al-dhalīl*, edited by David H. Baneth and Haggai Ben-Shammai (Jerusalem, 1977), V. 12.

THE SOUL IN JEWISH NEOPLATONISM   153

Much like ibn Ezra, Halevi contends that the soul is the entelechy [*kamāl*] of that in which it exists. Each one of these souls is endowed with a number of faculties, such as nutrition, motion, or intellection. The soul, according to Halevi, is distinct from the body and does not need it because

> the physical powers are weakened by strong influences. For instance, the organ of the eye is damaged by the sun, and the ear by too strong a sound. The rational soul, however, retains whatever stronger knowledge it has obtained. Moreover, old age attacks the body, but not the soul, for the latter is stronger after the fiftieth year while the body begins to decline, the activity of the body is limited but the soul has access to unlimited numbers of geometrical, arithmetical, and logical forms.[31]

Halevi also argues that any union between the human soul and the divine soul is impossible so long as the former resides within a body:

> A complete connection is impossible unless all physical powers are subdued, and it is the body that prevents this connection. Once the soul has separated from the body, it becomes perfected, joins with that which renders it immune to injury, and unites with the noble substance in which all higher knowledge takes place.[32]

Once Halevi provides this very long and detailed Avicennian discourse on the nature, function, and division of the soul, however, he begins immediately to subvert it. In the section immediately following the above, he writes:

> Why should we need such embellishments [*al-tahīl*] in order to prove the life of the soul after the dissolution of the body, considering that we have reliable information regarding the return of the soul, be it spiritual or corporeal. If you spend your time confirming or refuting these views, you will spend your life in vain.[33]

What Halevi means by the phrases "reliable information" refers not to scientific theory, but to the traditions handed down in the Torah. Halevi continues by arguing that the philosophers proffer no proof whatsoever for their theories regarding the soul, but rely on, at best, speculative opinion. Because the philosophers are unable to reach consensus on any number of weighty issues, Halevi argues that it is much better to

---

[31] Halevi, *Kuzari*, V. 12.
[32] Halevi, *Kuzari*, V. 12.
[33] Halevi, *Kuzari*, V. 14.

154   AARON W. HUGHES

rely on the certain knowledge handed down in the pages of the Torah. Such knowledge, according to him, is granted only to the select few:

> These are the souls [al-nufūs] that comprehend the whole universe, know their Lord and His angels, who see one another, and who know each other's secrets...We others however do not know how and by what means this came to pass, except by prophecy [al-nubūwa].[34]

Prophecy, not Greco-Arabic science, is what enables the Jewish people to have access to the secrets of the universe including the true nature of the human soul. These secrets come not from theories of the soul or theories of cognition, but from the true knowledge contained within Torah and authentic Jewish traditions, which Halevi calls a "kind of vision" [kal-mushāhada].[35] Philosophers, on the contrary, are unable to possess such certain knowledge precisely because they lack such access to God-revealed scripture and authentic tradition. Speculation on the soul, and he frames this in direct opposition to ibn Ezra's claim, is not beneficial to religious development because it actually gets in the way of proper understanding. To make his point even stronger, Halevi asks rhetorically: If the substance of all soul is the same, "why did not Aristotle's soul become united to Plato's?"[36]

Imagination and Prophecy

Of central importance for ibn Ezra is the nature of the relationship between the human soul and the divine world and, more precisely, the mechanics behind the human soul's apprehension of that world. In order to examine in closer detail ibn Ezra's use of the imagination and his conceptualization of prophecy, I shall focus on his allegorical *Hay ben Meqitz*.[37] This is a text that works on multiple levels. On one level it is a pastiche of biblical phrases that enabled twelfth century Jews to embrace and legitimate the intellectual and aesthetic ideals of Neoplatonism, in much the same manner that Avicenna did with his

---

[34] Halevi, *Kuzari*, V. 14.
[35] Halevi, *Kuzari*, V. 14.
[36] Halevi, *Kuzari*, V. 14.
[37] For an in-depth examination of this text, and its relationship to Avicenna's and Ibn Tufayl's *Ḥayy ibn Yaqẓān*, see my *Texture of the Divine: Imagination in Medieval Islamic and Jewish Thought* (Bloomington, 2004). All translations of *Hay ben Meqitz* that follow come from my critical English translation found in the appendix to this work.

THE SOUL IN JEWISH NEOPLATONISM

Ḥayy ibn Yaqẓān before him.[38] On another level *Hay ben Meqitz* is a rich philosophical-mystical narrative that culminates in the protagonist's ascent to and ultimate vision of the divine presence.

In the cosmological system we encounter in *Hay ben Meqitz*, ibn Ezra recounts ten spheres in ascending order: the Moon, Mercury, Venus, the Sun, Mars, Jupiter, Saturn, the sphere of the fixed stars, the all-encompassing diurnal sphere which contains no stars, and the sphere of the unembodied angels.[39] This last sphere, which he sometimes calls glory (*kavod*), is of crucial importance for understanding ibn Ezra's discussion of the imagination.

Before examining his conception of the imagination, however, it is worth mentioning that ibn Ezra conceives of a large ontological chasm separating the world of generation and corruption from the one that exists beyond the sphere of the moon (i.e., the superlunar world). Following Avicenna, he argues that God has no knowledge of particulars, except in a universal way.[40] Because of this ontological chasm, ibn Ezra is ambiguous about how embodied individuals can have access to the world that exists above this one. In some of his comments to biblical verses he argues that we can only have knowledge of the divine by means of the created order (i.e., through the divine attributes of action).[41] Yet, in other places he claims that one can receive a direct, quasi-inspirational, form of knowledge if one's soul separates from the body and cleaves to the upper world.[42]

Recalling ibn Ezra's tripartite division of the soul, he regards it as the function of the animal soul (*nefesh*) to function as the intermediary between the higher and lower souls, and to interact with the sensual world through the five senses and process the data associated with these senses. The animal soul is crucial, then, since it can either fall prey to the passions associated with the body or it can be used in the service of the intellect. Ibn Ezra subsequently argues that it is through a combination of theoretical and practical wisdom that the individual

---

[38] On the nature of the relationship between Avicenna's and ibn Ezra's treatises, see my "A Case of Twelfth-Century Plagiarism?: Abraham ibn Ezra's *Ḥay ben Meqitz* and Avicenna's *Ḥayy ibn Yaqẓān*, *Journal of Jewish Studies* 55.2 (2004): pp. 306–331.

[39] *Hay ben Meqitz*, lines 425–663. On the differing, and sometimes contradictory, cosmological accounts in the vast oeuvre of ibn Ezra, see Howard Kreisel, "On the Term *kol* in Abraham Ibn Ezra: A Reappraisal," *Revue des Études Juives* 152 (1994), pp. 61–66.

[40] E.g., *Commentary to Genesis* 18:21; *Short Commentary to Exodus* 33:12.

[41] E.g., *Long Commentary to Exodus* 20:1.

[42] E.g., *Short Commentary to Exodus* 23:20.

156   AARON W. HUGHES

is able to perfect himself, thereby attaining a union (*devequt*) with the Active Intellect:

> Wisdom [*'asa*] and ethics [*musar*] lead an individual to put God before him both day and night and thus his *neshamah* cleaves to the Creator before separating from the body [i.e., at death].[43]

In other passages, ibn Ezra claims that it is the heart (*lev*) that cleaves to the upper world.[44] For it is the heart, as the essence (*iqqar*) of the individual,[45] that functions as the locus whereby one loves God and experiences His presence. However, since the heart (or soul) exists within a corporeal body, it is unable to apprehend the upper world without recourse to vision. It is at this juncture that the imagination, the "eye of the heart" (*'ein ha-lev*) becomes important. For it is this "eye" that enables one to see visions of the upper world. It is the faculty, in other words, that is responsible for giving corporeal forms to incorporeal phenomena.

The upper world of the unembodied angels cannot be apprehended without the aid of a faculty responsible for translation. Since corporeality hinders our ability to grasp the structure of disembodied reality, images become necessary to our understanding. Ibn Ezra puts it this way: "When the soul is directed toward the glory [*kavod*], then it receives new images, forms and visions by the word of God."[46]

Ibn Ezra implies with these comments that when the soul of the righteous cleaves to the upper world, it encounters that world in an unmediated way. The disclosure of this upper world, however, can occur only by the mediation of the imagination: the images that it produces become the symbols by which superlunar reality reveals itself. As a result, an intelligible portrait of the celestial realm can only occur through the familiar images of the world that is lived and experienced. The human soul is able to perceive the celestial world because it is ultimately composed of the same essence as the disembodied angels. It cannot do this, however, without the images provided by the corporeal world; for these images represent the sum and substance of our experience with and in the world.

---

[43] *Commentary to Psalm* 16:8.

[44] E.g., *Commentary to Deuteronomy* 10:20, 11:22. Again, though, it seems that he uses *lev* as a metaphor for the *neshamah* and not for the *nefesh*.

[45] E.g., *Commentary to Deuteronomy* 20:17.

[46] *Short Commentary to Exodus*, 23:20; cf., *Commentary to Psalm* 139:18.

THE SOUL IN JEWISH NEOPLATONISM   157

According to his commentary to *Psalm* 139:18, two paths are open to the individual that grant access to the divine world. One occurs through the various channels associated with ratiocination that we engage in while awake; and the other occurs during dreams:

> [This] is like the appearance of God when the body sleeps and when man's *neshamah* cleaves to the upper *neshamah* so that it sees beautiful images [*temunot nifla'ot*]...yet this is not the path of all dreams.

These special dreams are those in which the soul of the wise man cleaves to the beings associated with the upper world (*ha-elyonim*) that exist without bodies. In *Hay ben Meqitz* ibn Ezra makes this explicit when he claims that one can only experience this world internally, through the "eye of the heart":

> It happened that when we came to its border
>   We approached to cross it.
> I saw wonderful forms [*surot mufla'ot*]
>   And awesome visions [*mar'ot nora'ot*].
> Angels stood guard
>   They were mighty ones.
> Cherubim
>   Enormous and many.
> Seraphim standing
>   Praising and announcing His unity.
> Angels and *ofanim*
>   Lauding and singing.
> Souls [*nefashot*] consecrating
>   Spirits [*ruhot*] glorifying.
> I was afraid and said
>   "How awesome is this place that I see."
> He replied: "From your feet
>   Remove your sandals
> From the matter of your corpse
>   Lift your soul
> Forsake your thoughts
>   Relax your eyelids!
> See by the eyes of your interior
>   The pupils of your heart [*be-ishonei levavakha*]."[47]

It is up to the imagination to give these incorporeal entities an appropriate form. This is something that the intellect cannot do since its epistemological currency is that which exists without image.

---

[47] *Hay ben Meqitz*, lines 648–673.

158   AARON W. HUGHES

What ibn Ezra intimates is that the intellect needs the imagination because it is the faculty responsible for supplying images necessary for thought. These images, to quote his comments to *Psalm* 17:15, do not occur through a "vision of the eye" (*mar'eh ha-'ein*), but through a "vision of wisdom" (*mar'eh shiqqul ha-dat*). This latter vision is the one that occurs when the imagination, in close association with the intellect, encounters the Active Intellect and subsequently transfers the perceived images to the intellect. In typical fashion, ibn Ezra only alludes to his sources: "These are truly visions of God [*mar'ot elohim*] and these are matters that are not appropriate to reveal except to one who has studied the science of the soul [i.e. psychology]."[48]

Halevi's prophetology is, not surprisingly, generally quite critical of that presented by philosophers such as ibn Ezra. For one thing, Halevi denied the self-serving claims put forth by many philosophers that the philosophic act was akin to prophecy, with the only difference between them being the strength of the imaginative faculty that allowed prophets to coin parables for the non-philosophic masses. Halevi, in contrast, underscores the super-rational and super-natural aspects of prophecy. For him prophecy is of a radically different genus from philosophy because it is not based on deduction but direct experience and tasting (*dhawq*). He differentiates between philosophers and prophets by distinguishing different features of God: *Elohim* is the philosophical conception of God, whereas he reserves the Tetragrammaton for the religious conception of God.[49]

On one level, then, Halevi implies that both the philosopher and the prophet experience a union with something that is external to the individual. However, there is a crucial distinction between the *devequt* (Ar. *ittiṣāl*) of the philosopher and that of the prophet. The relationship that develops between the rational part of the philosopher's soul and the Active Intellect is a "slow, gradual, syllogistic process."[50] The relationship between the prophet and God, however, is an immediate one, in which the individual becomes a passive recipient of the divine influx (Ar. *al-'amr al-ilāhī*).[51] So, whereas the most the philosopher

---

[48] *Commentary to Psalm* 17:15.

[49] See the comments in Harry Austryn Wolfson, "Maimonides and Halevi: A Study in Typical Jewish Attitudes toward Greek Philosophy in the Middle Ages," *Jewish Quarterly Review* 2 (1911), pp. 318–322.

[50] Halevi, *Kuzari*, I.1.

[51] There is a huge debate surrounding the meaning of this term in Halevi. I here follow Diana Lobel, who argues that Halevi "detaches the term from its elaborate

THE SOUL IN JEWISH NEOPLATONISM 159

can hope for is a union with the Active Intellect, the prophet cleaves to that which is above this Intellect, to God himself:

> The prophet's eye ['ayn al-nābi] is more penetrating than speculation. His sight reaches up to the heavenly host directly, so that he sees the dwellers in heaven, and the spiritual beings that are near God, and others in human form...These are things that cannot be approached by means of speculation, and that the Greek philosophers have rejected because speculation negates everything that it cannot see.[52]

A good example of the relationship between the prophet and God may be found in Abraham. Abraham's relationship with God resided in his union with the 'amr ilāhī as opposed to rational speculation.[53] Rather than spend his time trying to perfect his rational soul, Abraham trusted his powers of imagination and intuition, and, thus, experienced an unmediated relationship with the divine. Accordingly, the only true relationship that an individual can have with God, referred to now by the Tetragrammaton, is one based on emotion and experience as opposed to the intellect.[54] Halevi subsequently attaches great importance to the commandments, i.e., proper action, and makes this superior to belief or ratiocination. One draws close to God, then, not through reason, but through action.

The relationship between the prophet, or a true believer, is not dependent upon syllogisms or logical arguments, but upon the unswerving and often unquestioned performance of the divine commandments. These commandments in turn have come down to the community through the true tradition (ha-qabbalah ha-amitit) established by the prophets.[55] Like ibn Ezra, Halevi stresses the importance of the commandments; unlike him, however, he does not try to divide them rationally since they all exist within a synecdochical relationship.

Neo-Platonic framework, and uses it as a fluid way to point to the divine." See her *Between Mysticism and Philosophy: Sufi Language of Religious Experience in Judah Ha-Levi's* Kuzari (Albany, 2000), 29–30; on the etymology of the term and interesting implications, see Shlomo Pines, "Shi'ite Terms and Conceptions in Judah Halevi's *Kuzari," Jerusalem Studies in Arabic and Islam* 2 (1980), pp. 172–178.

[52] Halevi, *Kuzari*, IV.3.
[53] Halevi, *Kuzari*, IV.17.
[54] The Arabic term that Halevi employs here is *dhawq* (literally, "taste") and is one that he picked up from the Sufis. See Lobel, *Between Mysticism and Philosophy*, pp. 91–93.
[55] *Kuzari* III.53.

160 AARON W. HUGHES

Unlike ibn Ezra and other philosophers, Halevi argues that cleaving to God by means of the *amr ilāhī* is impossible through syllogistic reasoning or scientific speculation. For Halevi, then, the rational faculty is not an end in and of itself; the goal of life is not to perfect the soul by attaining scientific knowledge so as to bring one's rational soul from a state of passivity to one of activity. On the contrary, true knowledge involves the intuition of phenomena without access to their causes which are often unknown to the human intellect. In the following passage, Halevi brings this distinction into further relief:

> At the same hour when the doubts are removed from the heart of a man that he had before this concerning God, and he mocks all of the logical proofs with whose help he used to try to arrive at an understanding of God, His sovereignty and His unity. Once he arrives at this level of the worship of God through love, he is prepared to surrender his soul from this love, in cleaving to God he finds an incredible pleasure; whereas he who keeps away from God sees the source of all damage and sorrow. This is the opposite of the philosophers, for they see in the worship of God nothing but pleasant politeness.[56]

Conclusions

Philosophical notions of the soul, as the above comments by both ibn Ezra and Halevi clearly show, are intimately connected to larger religious issues such as creation, prophecy, and the afterlife. It is for precisely this reason that the stakes in presenting a coherent theory of the soul were so high. A rationalist interpretation offered by ibn Ezra was intimately connected to his intellectualist program for what he thought Judaism should look like, what its relationship to non-Jewish sources and cultures should be. Judah Halevi, on the other hand, was highly critical of ibn Ezra's universalism and his framing of the soul using Greco-Arabic categories. As a result, he preferred to develop a theory of the soul that he regarded as distinctly Jewish and that was predicated on what he considered to be the uniqueness of the Jewish religious imagination and the ontology of Jewish difference.

Jewish universalism and particularism, then, represent two responses to contact with non-Jewish ideas. Whereas the former seeks to show the compatibility between Jewish and non-Jewish cultures, the latter

---

[56] Halevi, *Kuzari*, IV.5.

THE SOUL IN JEWISH NEOPLATONISM

endeavors to show their incompatibility. So even though both ibn Ezra and Halevi had radically different conceptions of the soul, its function, and its telos their theories ultimately present two contrasting responses to the struggle over philosophy amongst Jews in the medieval period. Speculation on the soul, in other words, provided a catalyst whereby Jewish intellectuals could ruminate on the nature of the relationship between foreign concepts and biblical categories. Whether this relationship was deemed positive, as in the case of ibn Ezra, or negative, as in the case of Halevi, this was not a simple case of acceptance or rejection. For, as ibn Ezra's theory of the soul demonstrates, even an acceptance of Greco-Arabic concepts still had to be translated into autochthonous Hebrew categories. And even Halevi, in his rejections of the case concepts, still had to struggle with them.

MAIMONIDES, THE SOUL AND THE CLASSICAL TRADITION

Oliver Leaman*

Philosophy represents itself as a timeless search for truth, but in fact during different historical periods particular issues and debates became very popular at the expense of other issues and debates. Philosophy is just as much a matter of fashion as other cultural artefacts, and during medieval Jewish philosophy one of the prime areas of debate was over the nature of the soul. This debate was actually very much taken over from Islamic philosophy that formed the warp and woof of its Jewish equivalent. and the major figure here is undoubtedly Moses Maimonides. He was particularly close to one of his Islamic predecessors, al-Fārābī, and especially so on this topic, and the development of the discussion is both interesting and at the same time raises important issues that it fails to resolve.

The role of the soul in Islamic philosophy is itself highly controversial. The Qur'an has a robust notion of both the soul and the afterlife, unlike the Jewish bible, yet most philosophers sought to restrict the role of the soul in a variety of ways, stemming from their application of philosophical techniques to the notion. Aristotle had quite radically described the soul as the form of the body, and the implication of that is that when the body is no more in existence, the soul has nothing to inform, and so evaporates. Plato of course has a more robust notion of the soul as an independent being, operating apart from the body with no problem, indeed, with fewer problems than when embodied. Aristotle's more restricted view of the soul was constructed no doubt to respond to the sorts of arguments that Plato had produced. Aristotle's rather gnomic remarks on the mind at *De anima* III, 5 (430a 10–23) in turn stimulated huge debates in subsequent philosophy, and were the source of a considerable architectonic within Neoplatonic thought. A particularly heated debate arose around the notion of the active intellect, and this has much to do with the issue of whether our

---

* Kentucky University.

164   OLIVER LEAMAN

ability to think abstractly is part of us, or something separate from us that can affect us, and that we can approach. Our material intellect is certainly part of us, but in so far as we can think abstractly, in terms of generalizations and universals. that sort of thought looks like it is independent of us, since although we may be having it, it has a structure and content that is independent of us. If I put two apples in my bag and later on add a third, and then at the end of the day count the apples, what makes them add up to three is not a reflection on my experience, but on something formal about numbers and what they mean, an abstract reasoning process that works independently of my experience of apples in bags. If I discover only two apples at the end of the day I shall suspect that one has dropped out, not that my grasp of the laws of mathematics are at issue. If I think that the apples issue is only a matter of experience then I have seriously misunderstood the situation, like someone staring at a number and trying to make it something else. It is because of this that many philosophers argued that whatever was behind our ability to think abstractly had to be something independent of us, albeit something with which we could get in touch. In Neoplatonic thought a whole range of spheres and planets were identified with different levels of thought and were linked with us by having an effect on us, albeit certainly not in a straitforwardly causal manner. Although the cosmology seems to us today to be fanciful, it does represent nicely that way in which our faculty for thought both seems to be part of us physically, since we are the thinkers, yet also separate from us, since the issues of what thought is and whether it is valid or not are independent of us.

A number of interesting technical issues arose with respect to the soul, and one was how advanced our thinking can actually get. What are the bounds of thought? A limitation on our thinking that the mystics in both Islam and Judaism fought against was the idea that our thought could only get as high as the active intellect, the realm of abstract thought, sometimes identified with the moon. This would obviously seriously interfere with our contemplation of God, for instance, and we would be restricted to thinking in the way that God thinks, to a certain degree. It also then looks like the only valuable form of thought is abstract thought, the sort of thought valued by philosophers and scientists, and this seems to cut out a lot of people who might be leading good and honourable lives, yet whose thought is limited to a rather mundane level of social and religious performance. This seems problematic from a religious perspective, and not only from such a perspective. It seems

MAIMONIDES, THE SOUL AND THE CLASSICAL TRADITION   165

to treat just one sort of knowledge as important, and fails to value the lives of those, surely the majority, for whom intellectual thought is not a major part of their experience of existence.

This is part of a much wider issue, and we are unlikely to resolve it here, since the emphasis is on the soul. But the soul is clearly linked closely to this debate, since the soul on the traditional religious view is something very much like how we are while we are alive, and that is why we care about its fate. The afterlife is only attractive for many people, after all, if something like me survives my death, and for the soul to be like me it has to adopt or include many of my most significant features. This is nicely resolved by bodies being resurrected, of course, since with the body comes a lot of what makes human life both valuable and also individually attractive. Maimonides does talk of the significance of a physical resurrection of the body, it is one of the principles of Judaism which he played a part in defending and certainly the basis of the literal interpretation of the messianic promise, as normally interpreted. It is worth pointing out, though, that Judaism, unlike the two religions that came out of it, has in the Torah a very limited account of the afterlife. The Bible is often sceptical of the possibility of an afterlife and the references to it in a positive light are few and cautious. But what is important here is not the Bible but the commentaries, the Oral Law, and this and especially the Talmud, is full of references to the soul, the next world, our rewards and punishments, and so on, and that is what Maimonides was working with. He was a staunch defender of the oral law, coming at a time not so distant from the period that the Karaites had threatened its pre-eminence, and he certainly appreciated that just as in Islam and Christianity, Judaism had come to adopt a robust notion of the soul and what lay before it in the world that follows this one. It was this notion that lay in the forefront of Maimonides' mind as he defended what he took to be the principles of Jewish belief on the soul, and it is this notion that he sought to reinterpret theologically so that it was both intellectually respectable and also workable from a religious point of view.

In his *Commentary on the Mishnah* Maimonides produced thirteen articles of faith. One of his passions was summarizing and these are supposed to summarize the 613 commandments found in the Torah. In Tractate Sanhedrin, chapter 10, of his commentary he describes these thirteen principles as the fundamental truths of our religion and its very foundations. The thirteenth principle is the belief in the resurrection of the dead. In his *Mishneh Torah* he denounces anyone who does

166 OLIVER LEAMAN

not accept this principle as forfeiting his share of the world to come (*Hilkhot Teshuvah* 3.6), although presumably this is not much of a threat to someone who does not believe in resurrection. He actually returned to this topic a long time later in a specific treatise on resurrection, Here he refers to Daniel (12.2–13), but interestingly much more to the stories, prayers, wishes and so on of the prophets and sages from the Talmud and the Midrash. And although we might be surprised at the paucity of comment on this in the Bible, the commentaries and prayer book are indeed replete with such references, and as Maimonides says, the doctrine of resurrection had, at least in his time, become very much one of the principles of the religion. One might reflect that the later works found themselves in an environment where competing religions such as Christianity, and later on still Islam, had attractive views on a very lively afterlife and Judaism felt the need to compete on a equal level.

There can be no serious doubt that Maimonides takes on board the whole of the philosophical account then current on the mind. When philosophy produces conclusions with which he disagrees, such as on prophecy and the origin of the world, he quite bluntly points this out, and refers to problems he perceives in the philosophical account. In the *Guide* he never questions the theory of the mind, in particular its origins in a particular interpretation of Aristotle at the hands of al-Farabi. Here the active intellect is compared to the sun, whose light changes the sense of sight from a state of potentiality to one of actuality, and does the same with the category of visible objects. The soul becomes, or can become, closer to the active intellect by thinking about purer and purer topics, until finally it can transcend matter altogether and achieve ultimate happiness and the afterlife. This is very different from the normal account of the afterlife, of course, and it is worth pointing out also that no divine influence is required for this passage to perfection. Al-Fārābī sometimes describes this spiritual ascent as revelation, but it is not at all clear what role this religious language is expected to play, since what is supposed to take place is that something outside of us, the active intellect, can affect us and take us in a certain direction. This is not a process that it decides to undertake, since the active intellect is constantly, as its name suggests, in action and it is only limited in its effectiveness by the matter that it confronts, or by something impeding it. If the matter is in the right state to receive it, then nothing can prevent it from informing it, and so the contemplative ascent is then automatic.

MAIMONIDES, THE SOUL AND THE CLASSICAL TRADITION 167

Yet on this account of the human mind it is difficult to understand how a person could be resurrected from the dead. Our minds are irretrievably connected to our bodies, or so it would seem, and are only independent of them in so far as we can think abstractly, since abstractions operate independently of the physical. Normally we use our imagination to make sense of abstractions, since we can then apply them to our everyday world and understand how to use them better in a practical sense. But this is not the sort of thinking that could survive death, since imagination is irretrievably physical and makes uses of our senses and what we can derive from our senses. Without senses the imagination would have no role, and this is a good thing, according to Maimonides, since without imagination we can confront sheer abstraction and come much closer to the way things really are. One might add, we can become much closer to the ways in which God himself thinks. When God does mathematics he does not, unlike us, need to think in terms of natural objects, but can operate entirely formally. Perhaps this sort of thinking is available to even us after death, it might be more available to us then since we are no longer distracted by our bodies, but we should point out again that this sort of resurrection seems to be very different from how it is described by the commentators and the rabbis in the Talmud and the Midrash. For one thing, how are we to be rewarded or punished if we do not have bodies? I suppose our attempts to do mathematics might be constantly frustrated as a form of punishment, or helped as reward, but this seems small beer when brought up against a life of vice or virtue and what the authorities suggest ought to be its appropriate recompense.

A major obstacle to a notion of physical resurrection for Maimonides is his rather contemptuous attitude to the physical. The body gets in the way, since "matter is a strong veil preventing the apprehension of that which is separate from matter as it truly is" (*GP* III, 9; 436). This suggests that we should look forward to decrepitude since when "the strength of the body fails...the mind will be free to comprehend what it will then encompass" (*Mishneh Torah*, Foundations of the Torah 7:2). In the *Guide* we are told that "in the measure according to which the faculties of the body are weakened...the intellect is strengthened, its lights achieve a wider extension, its apprehension is purified, and it rejoices in what it apprehends" (*GP* III, 51; 627—further references to the Guide are given in terms of volume, chapter and page in the Pines translation). The body links us very closely to the rest of the animal world, with its narrow interests and sensation-directed mentality. Yet

168   OLIVER LEAMAN

our form is of course "the image and likeness of God" (*GP* III, 8; 431). By contrast, in the Introduction to the *Guide* the parable of the married harlot is interpreted as a critique of the senses, which she symbolizes, and which lie at the heart of all sin and human imperfection. By contrast, "all... virtues are consequent upon his form" (*GP* III, 8; 431). One might think that Maimonides would counsel the subjugation of the body by the mind, but he does not, since this would be to interfere with the principle of moderation and balance that he takes so seriously. Although we are in bodies, and they can be a problem, they also provide us with an opportunity to use them to transcend them, or so Maimonides argues. That is the point of social and religious life, and represents a way that God enables us gradually to perfect ourselves. He could miraculously transform us immediately into better people, but that would remove from us the opportunity to trying to do it ourselves, and so our bodies represent for us both an obstacle and also an opportunity.

So the principle that form is good and matter is bad should not be taken too literally. We are material creatures and without matter our chances of finding anything out are very limited. There is no reason either why a virtuous person should not lead a physically satisfying life, based as it would be for Maimonides on moderation and self-control. He uses the faculties which God has given him to improve himself, to become more like God, and this will involve intellectual and moral development, but it might well be matched by an increase in his wealth and physical well being. It is when matter becomes the end, in the sense of the sole end, that it becomes problematic, and gets in the way of our spiritual progress. I think Maimonides would approve of those TV commercials so prevalent in the US which show people changing their lives by first changing their bodies. Of course, physical change would not for him be the end, but then it is is not on those commercials either, it is generally represented as part of a strategy of self-improvement. Matter can assist in such progress, provided that we understand its appropriate role and do not overdo the attention we pay to it. Adam is a good example of how to get things wrong. He became dominated by his imagination to concentrate on the physical pleasures (*GP* I, 2; 25) which meant giving them a status they did not really deserve. This lead him to an overwhelming desire to eat that which he had been forbidden (*GP* I, 2; 26), and this symbolizes going too far in the pursuit of sensual pleasures. This is worth emphasizing since without making this sort of point we seem to form a picture of Maimonides as someone entirely in favour of asceticism and self-denial, Yet for him there is nothing

MAIMONIDES, THE SOUL AND THE CLASSICAL TRADITION   169

wrong with the body provided it is kept in its place. We are physical creatures, as was Adam, so denying the body is to deny what we are, but to concentrate too much on the body is also to deny what we are, beings that are created in the image of God. By this Maimonides thinks is indicated not a physical resemblance, but a potential resemblance in thinking. We can to a degree think like God, if we perfect ourselves intellectually, and this involves as a necessary condition putting the body in its place, but certainly not abandoning it.

On this issue Maimonides represents something of the consensus position in Islamic and Jewish philosophy of this period. Philosophers generally argued for the superiority of the solitary life, the life of the mind, the concentration on the rational intellect, and yet there are many things that we enjoy doing, and feel we need to do, that are not intellectual. In a few minutes time after doing a bit more typing, for example, I shall get up and make myself a cup of tea and eat a chocolate digestive biscuit. That is acceptable, Maimonides would say, provided that it represents a short break to enable me to return to my task of working on philosophy with renewed vigour. We are material beings and so the body has to be satisfied if we are to do anything at all, and satisfying the body does not mean pandering to it. The soul and the body have to work in tandem, but we go awry, Maimonides and the whole tradition that he represents argue, if we do not realize that the soul is far superior and more permanent than the body.

Looking after the body is a matter of joining a society, since the manufacture of the tea and biscuits, together with the house, street and companionship which makes my work possible are all features of people cooperating socially and economically. Although society is important, it is important not in itself, but for what it makes possible, and that is the perfection of the human soul.

In a very important passage Maimonides says that our:

> ultimate perfection is to become rational in actu, I mean to have an intellect in actu; this would consist in his knowing everything concerning all the beings that it is within the capacity of man to know in accordance with his ultimate perfection (*GP* III, 27; 511).

This perfection "is the only cause of permanent preservation" (*GP* III, 27; 511), and he repeats this point later at *GP* III, 54; 635 where he refers to this perfection as what makes us truly what we are. It is not our possessions, what we look like, or even our moral qualities, but solely our intellectual ability that sums up who we really are.

170   OLIVER LEAMAN

A good example here is Moses whose "intellect attained such strength that all the gross faculties in the body ceased to function" (*GP* III, 51; 620). Moses' prophecy was so strong that he did not need to use his imagination, but could relate to God "face to face" and receive prophecy during the day, in the full light of everyday events. But Moses was not entirely unique since Maimonides tells us that he, together with Miriam and Aaron, and even lesser prophets and thinkers, all experienced "death as by a kiss" (*GP* III, 51; 628), the idea that the passage from life to death was so easy that it was barely noticed.

Maimonides is often called an elitist, and his account of human perfection certainly puts the emphasis on our intellectual abilities, abilities that are restricted among humanity. On the other hand, what other alternatives are there? Gazing at myself admiringly in the mirror does not seem plausible as an account of ultimate perfection, nor does eating cucumber sandwiches. Even moral perfection is limited in scope, since our motivation for ethical behaviour can be so varied. Maimonides is very aware of this, in his account of charity he differentiates between a whole range of ways of being charitable (Leaman, 2006, 12–14), and even the highest level of moral action could be something we bring about without thinking much about what we are doing, like praying regularly without really understanding what we are doing or saying. For Maimonides such moral and religious behaviour is worthwhile since it helps us get on the road to perfecting ourselves, but this is very much intellectual perfection, since even moral improvement is essentially limited by our physical faculties. When it comes to charity, for example, we are naturally drawn to those we know, to those more like us, and to those from whom we may expect some response. We can do better than that, and we should, but our behaviour will inevitably be affected by our imagination (which Maimonides often identifies with the evil inclination) since it involves interactions with other people, and that is fraught with personal problems and conflicts.

What this treatment of the soul has so far ignored is the whole Neoplatonic structure of intellects, emanation and the hierarchy of different levels of being, and for historical reasons these details are indeed worth discussing. But only for historical reasons, and there is no reason to discuss them here. This entire architectonic is merely a way of expressing, in the idiom of the time, what we can express much more succinctly and plausibly using modern philosophical vocabulary. This has the result that what we are describing looks far less mysterious than when presented in its Neoplatonic garb, but this is all to the good, since

MAIMONIDES, THE SOUL AND THE CLASSICAL TRADITION   171

what Maimonides and his contemporaries were doing was seeking to understand some fairly common features of thought, which they then went on to describe using the philosophical machinery of the time. We respect them and their work more if we eschew the antiquated language they actually used and reformulated their ideas in more modern ways, since then we can see that they are part of a continuing debate that has taken place in philosophy over the nature of the soul and what it is for human beings to think.

Yet one aspect of the discussion that seems to be quite distinctive is Maimonides' apparently presenting at least two distinct accounts of the soul, one rather Aristotelian and the other more fitted to religious orthodoxy. On the former view the soul is irretrievably attached to the body, except in very special circumstances that are difficult to follow. On the latter the soul and the body in some way come back together after death and continue to live in some sort of partnership into the future, indeed, the eternal future. Although it is certainly true that the Jewish bible does not contain much of the traditional religious view on the soul, it does appear occasionally, and much more importantly it is replete in the later commentary literature, which is so significant for Maimonides, How do we reconcile these two interpretations of the soul and what lies in wait for it after death?

The first thing to be said, and it has been said already, is that this is hardly an issue just for the soul, but occurs right across Maimonides' works. It is settled in a number of different ways. Some think that his philosophical views are his real views, while his religious views are those he produces for the naive public, hinting to the wise that this could not be his real views. Others suggest that he was not interested in reconciling the two views and just thought that different forms of expression were appropriate for different sorts of language and action. This is not the place to resolve this issue, important though it is, but let us see if we can find within the teaching on the soul some scope to understand how the two views can coexist.

In the part of the United States in which I live it is commonplace to greet someone by saying "How are you?". This is not a request for information, nor is it an expression of concern for the addressee. It is the equivalent of saying "Hello", which in itself is a rather strange way, if one thinks about it, of greeting someone, since it is so empty of content except as a greeting. If one responds to the question "How are you?" with a long list of ailments, real and imagined, the response has not hit the mark, unless one is in hospital or there is some other

172   OLIVER LEAMAN

context to make you think that health is really what the addressor is interested in. Does that mean that the person who asks "How are you?" is insincere in what he says? He is not really interested in the health of the addressee, he is just using a convenient form of words. I remember recently listening to a recent immigrant to the US saying one of the things he liked about the country was that everyone was so concerned about her health that they kept on asking her about it! She had entirely misunderstood what was going on, as one often does when living in a culture in which one is not a native.

So what we say is often not to be taken as literally in accordance with what we say. But this does not seem to work for the soul, since what we have here is a matter of fact, the actual nature of our thinking part, and so a description of it is either true or false. It is not like finding an acceptable way of greeting someone, which really does not convey much in the way of information. The soul is either separate, or separable, from our bodies, or it is not, and so the statement that it is cannot really be a *façon de parler* that it is not.

However, we need to look at Maimonides' theory of language before we reject the idea that both sorts of statements about the soul are capable of co-existence. Our language has a point. It embodies our ideas about reality and gives us the opportunity to refine those ideas. This is important, since for Maimonides the Bible is replete with language that appeals to us as physical creatures, and yet indicates the necessity to go beyond that level of thought. That is why there is so much anthropomorphic language in the Bible about God, together with the firm indication that God is to be taken as being entirely incorporeal and unlike us (according to Maimonides). God is using our existing ideas, and those of earlier generations, and is working with them, talking to us as we are now but providing a route to a higher level of thought. That is the entire point of a religion based on legislation, since the rules and network of customs are designed to elevate us out of the realm of the ways in which we used to live and think to a superior alternative, albeit not one that we can hope to acquire immediately. We are in training, as it were, and cannot expect to become skilled right at once, but if we follow the principles, the eventual end will be realized, and we shall achieve our goals. We shall have changed ourselves, in effect.

The idea that the soul is a ghost in the machine is a very attractive idea, one we form quite naturally and there is no harm in it provided that we do not let it get out of hand. The idea that the soul may survive the body is also acceptable in the sense that it is worth emphasizing

MAIMONIDES, THE SOUL AND THE CLASSICAL TRADITION 173

the distinction between our thoughts and what they are about in the material world, since the thoughts themselves rest on principles of validity that have nothing to do with the material nature of what has them. If we think of the individual surviving into another world after death this is also useful, since it helps us understand that our lives and works have a wider context than just our actual life span. It also allows us to think about the difference between thinking about things that constantly change and are insubstantial and the permanent and pure subject matter of science and philosophy, for instance.

But if we think that after death something much like me now is going to be around, aren't we just being misled? Not necessarily. According to Maimonides, since we are material creatures our imagination makes use of material ideas to persuade us to act in certain ways. Those ideas will certainly be inaccurate, since they are material, but they may point to the truth.

This might seem like a terrible example of evasiveness. If Maimonides thinks that there is really no individual afterlife why does he not just say so? He could explain and defend the theory on which such an afterlife has to be ruled out, and then argue for a reinterpretation of religion accordingly. He is not slow to use allegory, after all, when it comes to matters of the philosophy of mind. For example, he says that whenever the Bible talks about angels it means something that was imagined, although in other places he interprets angels in other ways also. He goes on to argue that the different categories of thinker at the foot of Mount Sinai heard different things when God revealed the law to Moses. He is not exactly reticent in providing a challenging reinterpretation of traditional beliefs. He was a controversial thinker during his own time, and he remains controversial today precisely because of the radical issues and arguments he defends.

The answer is surely that we should take seriously the theory of language that he used throughout his work, and adopted very much from al-Fārābī, albeit with many variations. According to this our language rests on a basic logic that can only be revealed using philosophy, or in other words rational techniques. Grammar, theology, law and so on can help us understand the language, but only logic can pierce through to the reality beneath, and assist us in really grasping the issue. Different kinds of language exist and are linked to the same basic logical distinction, and these differences exist because we are all different, with different interests, backgrounds, histories and so on. A superficial understanding makes it look as though the formulations

174 OLIVER LEAMAN

of language stand in contradiction to each other, but in fact this is not the case. They are merely different ways of saying the same thing, or so Maimonides would have us believe.

In a recent book on the soul the authors say "We do not need to understand ourselves theoretically to get on in the world" (Martin, R. and Barresi, J. p. 303 (2006). They make this point to contrast the ordinary everyday understanding of the self and soul with what they take to be more complex philosophical and scientific accounts, and this does seem a reasonable approach. We cannot expect everyone to appreciate the theoretical controversies that surround the notion of us as thinking beings, as the sorts of selves that we are. Maimonides could not disagree more with this point. Of course, he would agree that different people have different degrees of understanding of the mind, and many people know very little about it. But everyone has through religion a route to come to understand the mind in the way that is suitable for that individual, and that route is one which is capable of bearing theoretical fruit, if it is tended in the right way. Even our prayers and stories that portray the soul as very much like us as embodied creatures is capable of raising issues, stimulating questions, suggesting developments that lead the practitioner of the religion, slowly or quickly, to engage with more involved theoretical issues. If this view appears to be disingenuous then perhaps it is because we have a rather crude view of how to apply theory to practice. In the amusing story "Portuguese irregular verbs" Alexander McCall Smith describes a group of holidaying German philologists confronted for the first time with a tennis court, and asking for the rule book to work out how to play. Since they have no practical experience of the game they have no skill at it, and no idea how to apply the rules to produce a pleasurable, and finite resolution of the competition (the rule book comes before the device of the tie breaker). The other hotel guests are amused at their behaviour, and look forward to their next enterprise, which is to tackle swimming, where again all they have to help them are the official rules, the theory, and no practical background at all. Why this makes them, and us, laugh is because we know that theory and practice have to be blended together in activities like sport, and sport is merely a form of human behaviour like religion, or knowing who we are. The point of religion for Maimonides is not just to get us to behave in appropriate ways but to understand why, and so theory is very much what religion is pushing us, albeit gradually, towards.

MAIMONIDES, THE SOUL AND THE CLASSICAL TRADITION

A contrast is often made between his *Guide of the Perplexed*, his main philosophical text, and the *Mishneh Torah*, his commentary on the Mishnah, his main legal or halakhic work. It is not a matter of irrelevance that the first book of the latter is what he calls the "Book of Knowledge" and this lays out the theoretical underpinning of the whole work, an underpinning that of course is in line with his general philosophical views. And in the *Guide* he says explicitly that he has not written a philosophical book, since "the books composed concerning these matters are adequate" (*GP* II, 2: 253). This tidy dichotomy between philosophy and theology, like that between theory and practice, does not really work when looking at many of the chief works of Maimonides, nor does it shed much light on his views on the soul.

E. LATER MEDIEVAL PERIOD

ST. THOMAS AQUINAS'S CONCEPT OF THE HUMAN SOUL AND THE INFLUENCE OF PLATONISM

Patrick Quinn[*]

Aquinas's Use of Platonism

What has often gone unnoticed or at least is not commented on is the way in which St. Thomas Aquinas used Platonic insights in order to explain what the soul is and how it functions in extraordinary situations before and after death. Such Platonism typically occurs when Aquinas sets out to explain why and how it is that the human soul needs to function independently of the senses. The reason for such independence is that the mind can see God unhindered by any sensory input when God is seen face to face. How it occurs is explained by Aquinas in terms of an intense intellectual attentiveness to God which occurs with the necessary aid of a supernatural disposition which allows God to be seen in the divine essence itself. This encounter is described as *visio Dei*, the face to face vision of God. In order for the mind to operate in this way, sensory activity must, according to Aquinas's account, cease since, according to Thomas, if the senses continued to operate in their natural way of providing potentially intelligible data for mental abstraction, this would prevent the possibility of such an encounter occurring:

> ...for the understanding to be raised to the vision of the
> divine essence, one's whole attention must be concentrated
> on this vision, since this (the vision of God) is the most
> Intensely intelligible object, and the understanding can
> reach it only by striving for it with total effort. Therefore
> it is necessary to have complete abstraction from the bodily
> senses when the mind is raised to the vision of God.
>
> (*De Veritate, 13.3*)

Indeed, Aquinas implies that were the senses to be somehow involved, this would result in a form of sensory pollution that would taint the purity of the mental act of seeing God's essence:

---

[*] All Hallows College, Dublin.

180   PATRICK QUINN

> Nevertheless, in so far as the purity of intellectual
> knowledge is not wholly obscured in human understanding, as
> happens in the senses whose knowledge cannot go
> beyond material things, it has the power to consider things
> which are purely immaterial by the very fact that it retains
> some purity. Therefore, if (the mind) is ever raised beyond
> its ordinary level of immaterial things, namely, the divine
> essence, it must be wholly cut off from the sight of
> material things during that act. Hence, since the sensory
> powers can only deal with material things, one cannot be
> raised to the vision of God unless he/she is wholly deprived
> of the use of the bodily senses. (*De Ver.13.3*)

While this may seem a plausible possibility after death when the soul is separated from the body and bodily existence altogether, it does present a problem for Aquinas's Aristotelian interpretation of how knowledge is acquired in life before death. Yet, St. Thomas insists that the mind acts in this purely mental way, without any sensory input whatsoever, during the experience of rapture (*raptus*) or religious ecstasy when God is seen in what might be described as a temporary beatific vision. While this is an exceptional experience granted only to a privileged few, Aquinas does believe that such a vision is really possible in life before death and he selects as an example of this extraordinary experience, the description that is given by St. Paul in his second letter to the people of Corinth, 2 Cor. 12.1–7.[1] This temporary vision of God described by St. Paul could only have occurred, according to Thomas's explanation, because the activities of the sensory powers were completely suspended so that the mind could approach God's essence wholly non-impeded, all of this in the context of Paul's biological life still continuing. This conclusion allows St. Thomas to retain his conviction that the soul-body unity which enables Paul as a human being to function in a psycho-physical way, is intrinsic to his constitution as a composite entity, essentially defined as such.

By contrast with rapture, the final beatific vision after death is the destiny of all humankind and is open to everyone who conscientiously seeks God. This ultimate experience, which also occurs by supernatural dispensation, enables one to see God after death and in the ultimate state of bodily resurrection. What is significant here too is that such knowledge does not occur in the mode of cognising reality, which, for

---

[1] See *De Veritate Q.13* and *Summa Theologica II–II.Q.175*.

ST. THOMAS AQUINAS'S CONCEPT OF THE HUMAN SOUL   181

human beings, means using the senses to produce potentially intelligible images (*phantasmata*) which are then rendered actually intelligible by the power of the mind. Instead, as in rapture, the intellect acts quite independently of the senses, which, Aquinas insists, is not natural to it, although not unnatural either.[2] The latter fine distinction may or may not be plausible but even if granted, it still remains true, at least for St. Thomas, that our natural way of acquiring knowledge is based on our sensory and bodily powers. This is why Aquinas regards Aristotle's account of cognition as being so acceptable in the natural human circumstances of life compared with the account that Plato gives. However, it is also why Thomas admits, in *Summa Theologica.I.89.1*, for example, that an Aristotelian explanation will not serve to explain how we can understand anything after death in the absence of bodily life with the dissolution of our sensory organs.

Committed as he is to the metaphysical nature of the mind and, more importantly to his Christian belief that our destiny is to share God's life fully in a wholly spiritual way after death, it is clear why Aquinas looks to Platonism to account for how it might be possible to continue to function intelligently in some way after we die. For Plato, this does not seem to present any problem as his dialogue, *Phaedo*, indicates, where there is a clear message that not only do we continue our noetic activity after death but indeed function at a much more enhanced intelligent level in the state of blessedness.[3] This is made possible because when our intelligent psyche is liberated from its bodily life, it resumes its natural psychic state where it can once more function independently of the body which in life before death has impeded our search for knowledge by imprisoning our souls in material being. The psyche's destiny for Plato clearly lies in a form of disembodied psychic existence where reality can then be seen at its most sublime. This because, for Plato, it is our *psyche* that essentially constitutes our true existence and ultimate destiny and way of existing and so death can then be philosophically welcomed as the liberator of our psychic being from its material and physical constraints.

---

[2] See *Summa Theologica I.89.1*.
[3] *Phaedo 66b–67b*.

182 PATRICK QUINN

Aquinas's Point of View

This, however, is not a point of view to which St. Thomas subscribes. He insists in a number of places that the human being "is made up of body and soul as two things that constitute a third thing which is neither one of them, for (the human being) is neither soul nor body."[4] This is the Aristotelian viewpoint, although Thomas's description of soul and body as "things" should be noted. Aristotle regards *psyche* as the first principle of life and as the substantial form of a living being and while Aquinas accepts this, he does go on to argue for the substantial independence of the soul. Thus the Thomistic soul (*anima*) is described as an intelligent substance, a claim which he makes very clear in *On Being and Essence* when he comes to analyse the nature of simple substances. In fact, as an early text, this investigation of how the essence of a thing is related to what a thing is, makes the complexity of the status of the human soul quite explicit. The soul on the one hand, he says, is part of the human being as its substantial form which makes each of us to be the kind of composite beings we are. Yet *anima* is also a simple intelligent substance which, though naturally related to its human body and indeed constituting the latter *as* a human body, is nonetheless essentially independent of it because of the soul's intelligent nature. The human body is thus naturally intelligent because it is so ensouled, runs the argument, but the soul as the form and essence of such an intelligent being by virtue of that fact transcends bodily existence, which is also the source and meaning of all our intelligent behaviour, especially at the highest level, where the divine essence is seen for what it is, if not understood.

This complexity is formulated by Aquinas in terms of regarding the human being and the human soul itself as having an intermediate state of existence between the physical bodily and temporal world of sensory experience, on the one hand, and the immaterial, eternal and intelligible realm of divine spiritual existence, on the other.

---

[4] See the section in Aquinas's early metaphysical text, *De Ente et Essentia* (*On Being and Essence*) where he discusses how essence is found in composite substances.

ST. THOMAS AQUINAS'S CONCEPT OF THE HUMAN SOUL   183

Being on the Boundary

This notion emerges in some of Aquinas's earliest writings, including in his commentary on the Sentences of St. Peter Lombard.[5] Here it comes up in connection with St. Thomas's claim that to be human is to be *minor mundus*, a micro-universe personifying existence, life and thought. This theme is developed at considerable length in other texts, notably in Aquinas's *Summa Contra Gentiles* and also in his *Summa Theologica* and *De Anima*. In *Contra Gentiles 2.68*, he discusses it in the context of examining how an intelligent substance (the soul) can also be the form of the body. He accounts for this in the context of the interconnectedness of things in the hierarchy of being where the human body as an intelligent body is supreme in the category of bodies whereas the intelligent soul is the lowest of all the intelligent substances precisely because of its natural dependence for knowledge on the bodily senses. These factors constitute the human soul "on the *horizon* and confines (*quasi quidem horizon et confinium*) of bodily and non-bodily things inasmuch as it is an intelligent substance, and yet the form of a body." The status of the human being for Aquinas thus becomes one in which its intelligent part, the soul, is an intelligent substance which functions at the lowest level of such intelligences because it naturally operates through the body whereas its bodily part constitutes the human being as supreme in the category of bodily substances. A somewhat similar account is given by Aquinas in *De Anima Q.1* where St. Thomas concludes that the soul's cognitive nature marks it as being transcendent over matter and subsistent in being. In *Contra Gentiles 2.81*, in the context of discussing whether the soul perishes when death occurs, he states that the human soul when separated from the body in death can subsequently understand reality in a different and much better way, similar to the kind of cognition that occurs in separate or angelic substances. By withdrawing from the world of the senses, the soul's capacity for knowledge increases, according to Thomas (a claim which is strongly reminiscent of Plato's *Phaedo*):

> ...since the human soul...is on the boundary line of bodily and non-bodily substances *as though it were*

---

[5] See *Comm.II.Scriptum Super Sententiis, d.1.q.2.a.3.*

184   PATRICK QUINN

on the horizon of eternity and time, by withdrawing
from the lower world it approaches the higher. (*SCG.2.81*)

He expands on this claim in *SCG.3.61* by concluding that it is because
the intelligent soul is created by God "*on the borderline between eternity
and time* as stated in *De Causis*" that the beatified can come to see the
vision of God. The reference to *De Causis* is significant from the point
of view of Platonism in that Aquinas had issued his own commentary
on this text where he explicitly states that he knows *De Causis* to be a
summary of Proclus' *Elements of Theology*. In doing so, Aquinas also
makes clear that he distilled from this commentary his own thoughts
on the boundary soul. Finally in Book 4 of *Summa Contra Gentiles*,
he employs his "boundary" formula, this time in order to justify the
Christian belief in why God became human. It is precisely, he says,
because human existence as lived out in the course of our changing
lives allows us the prospect of forgiveness that the salvific act of God
in the humanity of Jesus Christ can address this essential feature of our
lives in a redemptive manner.

Aquinas's Preference for Human Existence as a Boundary Form of Living

It seems clear then that St. Thomas had a significant preference for
describing our human way of being as being on the boundary of this
physical world of time and of the non-physical eternal world to come.
The variety of powers in the soul, he states in *Summa Theologica I.72.2*,
precisely constitutes us as beings that can function in a physically
intelligent way because the human soul "is on the confines of spiritual
and bodily creatures, and therefore the powers of both meet together
in the soul". This preference goes all the way back to his metaphysical
treatise, *On Being and Essence*, where, perhaps most clearly, as was
mentioned, Aquinas maps out the simplicity yet complex duality of our
nature and existence. This is portrayed as a unified complexity of our
constitution as being human in body and soul while yet being formally
substantial as intelligent substances. As a consequence, in the beatified
state of bodily resurrection, the vision of God will be fully experienced
not just by us as intelligent souls (which occurs after death when the
soul is separated from the body) but ultimately in our bodily being too
which itself becomes enhanced to the point where each person's human

ST. THOMAS AQUINAS'S CONCEPT OF THE HUMAN SOUL   185

body will be transformed into a *corpus spirituale*, a spiritualised body, brilliant and glorious in the sight of God, and totally in tune with our souls. In that state, our boundary existence becomes a wholly unified blissful one which is no longer fragmented as can be experienced in life before death, or more tragically and permanently definitive of the state of damnation where perpetual turmoil and ongoing distress reigns in the awful awareness of the eternal loss of God for all eternity.[6] The nature of the human soul is central to all of this in providing us with the means of coming to know God by defining our physical life as an enquiring and intelligent one aimed towards that which can only truly and sufficiently satisfy us in all our personal and interpersonal intelligent needs.

---

[6] See *Summa Contra Gentiles* Book 4 and *Aquinas, Platonism and the Knowledge of God* (1996), Patrick Quinn, Guildford: Avebury, Ashgate, pp. 81–90.

INTELLECT AS INTRINSIC FORMAL CAUSE IN THE SOUL ACCORDING TO AQUINAS AND AVERROES

Richard C. Taylor*

The study of Averroes and his influence is changing. In recent years some scholars working in the thought of Thomas Aquinas have moved away from the very common focus on the conflict of Aquinas with Averroes and Averroists on the nature of the soul as found in the *De unitate intellectus*[1] and other works.[2] Many now see the positive value of the philosophical thought of Averroes to the development of the thought of Aquinas and thinkers of the Thirteenth century generally. They have come to appreciate the positive contributions of the philosophical psychology of Averroes to the development of the accounts of Aquinas concerning epistemological issues such as the grounding of the content of knowledge in the apprehension of the natures of things of the world rather than in illumination from God (according to Augustine and the tradition he gave rise to) or from a transcendent Agent Intellect (according to Avicenna in some fashion).[3] Deborah

---

* Marquette University.

[1] Representative among recent contributions containing positive assessments of the success of the critique of Averroes by Aquinas are Alain de Libera, *L'Unité de l intellect de Thomas d Aquin* (Paris, 2004) and the interpretive essays of Ralph McInerny in his *Aquinas Against the Averroists: On There Being Only One Intellect* (West Lafayette, Indiana, 1993). Particular attention should be given to Deborah Black's critical review of McInerny's account in *Review of Metaphysics* 49 (1995), pp. 147–148.

[2] Edward P. Mahoney provides a list of the most important encounters of Aquinas with Averroes on the issue of the intellect in "Aquinas's Critique of Averroes' Doctrine of the Unity of the Intellect," in *Thomas Aquinas and His Legacy*, David M. Gallagher, ed. (Washington, D.C., 1994), pp. 83–106. Those encounters are identified as (1) *In 2 Sent.* d. 17, q. 2, a. 1; (2) *Summa Contra Gentiles* 2, cc. 59–73; (3) *Summa Theologiae*, prima pars, q. 76; (4) *Quaestiones disputatae de spiritualibus creaturis*, articles 2 and 9; (5) *Sententia libri de anima*, book 3, c. 1 (see the discussion below for the precise citation); (6) *Compendia theologiae*, c. 85; and (7) *De unitate intellectus contra Averroistas*, pages. Also see the remarks of R. A. Gauthier in his introduction to the critical edition of Aquinas's *Commentary on the De Anima* in Ch. 4, "Les sources du commentaire, II. Le commentaire d'Averroès, section 2. Le Grand commentaire sur le Livre de l'Âme dans l'oeuvre de Saint Thomas," in *Thomas Aquinas, Sentencia libri de anima* (*Opera omnia*, XLV, 1) *220a–*225a. (Rome: Commissio Leonina; Paris, 1984.)

[3] For many years B. Carlos Bazán has shared his valuable insights in a number of important articles. See Bernardo C. Bazán, "La Noetica de Averroes (1126–1198),"

188   RICHARD C. TAYLOR

Black has done much to promote the sound and critical understanding
of Averroes and the real value, or rather lack thereof, of attacks on him
by Aquinas, with scholarly precision in a number of recent articles.[4]
Some other contributions have aimed at showing that Averroes' famous
doctrine of the two transcendent intellects, the Agent Intellect and
the Material Intellect, in some fashion shared by all human knowers,
provides an impressively coherent Aristotelian account for the series
of characteristics which Aristotle attributes to the intellectual soul.[5]

Philosophia 38 (1972), pp. 19–49; "*Intellectum Speculativum*: Averroes, Thomas Aquinas,
and Siger of Brabant on the Intelligible Object," *Journal of the History of Philosophy* 19
(1981), pp. 425–446; "The Human Soul: Form and Substance? Thomas Aquinas' Critique
of Eclectic Aristotelianism," *Archives d'histoire doctrinale et litteraire du moyen âge* 64
(1997), pp. 95–126; "Conceptions of the Agent Intellect and the Limits of Metaphysics,"
in *Nach der Verurteilung von 1277: Philosophie und Theologie an der Universität von
Paris im letzten Viertel des 13. Jahrhunderts: Studien und Texte. After the condemnation of 1277: philosophy and theology at the University of Paris in the last quarter of the
thirteenth century: studies and texts*, Jan A. Aertsen, Kent Emery, Jr., and Andreas Speer
(eds.). (*Miscellanea Mediaevalia* 28), pp. 178–210. Berlin and New York: W. de Gruyter,
2001; "13th Century Commentaries on *De Anima*: From Peter of Spain to Thomas
Aquinas," in *In Commento Filosofico nell'Occidente Latino (secoli XIII–XV)*, Gianfranco
Fioravanti, Claudio Leonardi and Stephano Perfetti (eds.), pp. 119–184. (Turnhout, 2002).
In his articles in 1997 and later Bazán has been more appreciative of the insights of
Averroes and their value to Aquinas as well as of the challenge they represented to
Aquinas. Regarding Avicenna the standard view is recounted in Herbert Davidson's
Alfarabi, Avicenna, and Averroes, on Intellect (Oxford: Oxford University Press, 1992).
However, this has been recently criticised. See Dimitri Gutas, "Intuition and Thinking:
The Evolving Structure of Avicenna's Epistemology," in Robert Wisnovsky (ed.), *Aspects
of Avicenna*. (Princeton, 2001) (reprinted from *Princeton Papers: Interdisciplinary Journal
of Middle Eastern Studies*, Vol. IX), pp. 1–38; and by Dag Nikolaus Hasse, "Avicenna
on Abstraction," ibid., pp. 39–72. A critical attempt at conciliation has been set forth
by Jon McGinnis in "Making Abstraction Less Abstract: The Logical, Psychological and
Metaphysical Dimensions of Avicenna's Theory of Abstraction," in *Proceedings of the
American Catholic Philosophical Association* 80 (2006), pp. 169–183.

   [4] Deborah Black, "Consciousness and Self-Knowledge in Aquinas's Critique of
Averroes's Psychology," Journal of the History of Philosophy 31 (1993), pp. 349–385;
"Memory, Individuals, and the Past in Averroes's Psychology. Medieval Philosophy
and Theology" 5 (1996), pp. 161–187; "Conjunction and the Identity of Knower and
Known in Averroes," American Catholic Philosophical Quarterly 73 (1999), pp. 159–184;
and "Models of Mind: Metaphysical Presuppositions of the Averroist and Thomistic
Accounts of Intellection," *Documenti e studi sulla tradizione filosofica medievale* 15
(2004), pp. 319–352. For a impressive account of Averroes' noetics in an important
Averroist follower, see Jean-Baptiste Brenet, *Transferts du sujet: la noétique d'Averroès
selon Jean de Jandun* (Paris: Vrin, 2003).

   [5] See Richard C. Taylor, "Averroes' Epistemology and Its Critique by Aquinas,"
Thomistic Papers VII. Medieval Masters: Essays in Memory of Msgr. E. A. Synan, R. E.
Houser, ed. (Houston, 1999), pp. 147–177; "Cogitatio, Cogitativus and Cogitare: Remarks
on the Cogitative Power in Averroes," in *L'elaboration du vocabulaire philosophique
au Moyen Age*, J. Hamesse et C. Steel, eds., pp. 111–146. [Rencontres de philosophie
Medievale Vol. 8.] Turnhout, Brepols, 2000; "Separate Material Intellect in Averroes'

INTELLECT AS INTRINSIC FORMAL CAUSE IN THE SOUL   189

There are at least 14 characteristics Aristotle attributes to the intellect or its activity in *De Anima* 3.4. Among them are: (1) being without any character except that of the ability to receive (a21–22); (2) being what allows the soul to think and judge (a23); (3) not existing before it thinks (a24); (4) being unmixed with body and without a bodily organ (a24–27); and (5) being the place of forms potentially (a27–29), just to mention five. As I have shown elsewhere,[6] Averroes coherently addresses all 14 in his *Long Commentary on the De Anima* and weaves his way among the issues and problems in largely successful explication of the matters at stake.

Still, as interesting and insightful as Averroes is, it is difficult to see how this famous Aristotelian can escape all the devastating arguments which Aquinas brings to bear on the novel interpretation of Aristotle which Averroes sets out. The doctrine of the separate and transcendent Agent Intellect was common to the tradition of the philosophers, as Aquinas rightly states in his early *Commentary on the Sentences*,[7] for the

---

Mature Philosophy," in *Words, Texts and Concepts Cruising the Mediterranean Sea. Studies on the sources, contents and influences of Islamic civilization and Arabic philosophy and science, dedicated to Gerhard Endress on his sixty-fifth birthday*, Ruediger Arnzen and Joern Thielmann, eds., pp. 289-309. [Orientalia Lovaniensia Analecta series] Leuven: Peeters, 2004; "Improving on Nature's Exemplar: Averroes' Completion of Aristotle's Psychology of Intellect" in *Philosophy, Science and Exegesis in Greek, Arabic and Latin Commentaries*, edited by Peter Adamson, Han Baltussen and M. W. F. Stone, eds., in 2 vols., v. 2, pp. 107-130. [*Supplement to the Bulletin of the Insititute Of Classical Studies* 83.1-2] London: Insititute of Classical Studies, 2004; "The Agent Intellect as 'form for us' and Averroes's Critique of al-Fārābī," *Topicos* (Universidad Panamericana, Mexico City) 29 (2005), pp. 29-51, reprinted in *Proceedings of the Society for Medieval Logic and Metaphysics* 5 (2005) 18-32 http://www.fordham.edu/gsas/phil/klima/SMLM/PSMLM5/PSMLM5.pdf; "Aquinas's Naturalized Epistemology," *Proceedings of the American Catholic Philosophical Association* 79 (2005), pp. 83-102, co-author with Max Herrera; and "Intelligibles in act in Averroes," in *Averroès et les averroïsmes juif et latin. Actes du colloque tenu à Paris, 16-18 juin 2005*, ed. J.-B. Brenet, (Turnhout, 2007), pp. 111-140. The development of the notion of separate intellect as "form for us" or the issue of conjunction with separate intellect is taken up in detail by Marc Geoffroy, with particular reference to works on the possibility of conjunction extant only in Hebrew, in "Averroès sur l'intellect comme cause agent et cause formelle, et la question de la 'jonction'—I," in *Averroès et les averroïsmes juif et latin. Actes du colloque tenu à Paris, 16-18 juin 2005*, ed. J.-B. Brenet, (Turnhout, 2007), pp. 77-110.

[6] See "Improving on Nature's Exemplar: Averroes' Completion of Aristotle's Psychology of Intellect" cited in note 5.

[7] *In 2 Sent.* d. 17, q. 2., a. 1, resp. "...*fere omnes philosophi concordant post Aristotelem, quod intellectus agens et possibilis differunt secundum substantiam; et quod intellectus agens sit substantia quaedam separata, et postrema in substantiis separatis....*" *Sancti Thomae Aquinatis Commentum in secundum librum Sententiarum Magistri Petri Lombardi*, P. Mandonnet, ed., (Paris, 1929), pp. 422-423. "Nearly all the philosophers after Aristotle are in agreement that the agent intellect and possible [intellect] differ in

190   RICHARD C. TAYLOR

Greek tradition since Alexander of Aphrodisias and also the most well known of the philosophers of the Classical Rationalist Arabic tradition, al-Fārābī, Avicenna, and Averroes, all held for such a view in one form or another. But what was new to the tradition (and certainly proved difficult for the Latins to grasp) was Averroes' teaching of the separate, unique and transcendent Material Intellect which is also somehow shared by all human beings in knowing. Though at times somewhat sympathetic with the notion of a single shared Agent Intellect, Aquinas usually attacked both notions with what appears to be an irrefutable argument grounded in Aristotelian texts and frequently did so employing what I will call his *Principle of Intrinsic Formal Cause*, which can be found repeated many times in works from the early 1260's up through his late writings in Paris in the 1270's.[8]

1. *Thomas Aquinas and the* Principle of Intrinsic Formal Cause

In the *Summa Contra Gentiles* at book 2, chapter 59, in the context of a critique of the view of Averroes on a single receptive possible intellect separate in being but shared by all human beings, Aquinas uses the *Principle of Intrinsic Formal Cause* in his refutation:

> That by which something formally operates is its form, for nothing acts except insofar as it is in act. But it is not something in act except through that which is its form. Hence, Aristotle also proves that the soul is form through the fact that an animal lives and senses. A human being has understanding, and only through intellect. Hence, Aristotle, inquiring concerning the principle by which we understand, also treats of the nature of the possible intellect. It is necessary, therefore, that the possible intellect be formally united to us and not only through its object.[9]

---

substance and that the agent intellect is a certain separate substance and last among the separate substances." All translations of Latin and Arabic texts are mine unless otherwise noted.

[8] This is not raised directly in his lengthy account of the philosophers in the article, *Utrum anima intellectiva vel intellectus sit unus in omnibus hominibus, Whether the intellective soul or intellect is one in all human beings*, at *In 2 Sent.* d. 17, q. 2., a. 1, Mandonnet, ed. (1929). As will be explained below, Aquinas displays some awareness of the idea of the separate Agent Intellect as intrinsic to the human soul in the Greek and Arabic tradition at *In 4 Sent., d. 49, q. 2, a. 1*.

[9] *Summa Contra Gentiles*, 2.59, 12: *Id quo aliquid operatur, oportet esse formam eius: nihil enim agit nisi secundum quod est actu; actu autem non est aliquid nisi per id quod est forma eius; unde et Aristoteles probat animam esse formam, per hoc quod animal per animam vivit et sentit. Homo autem intelligit, et non nisi per intellectum: unde et*

INTELLECT AS INTRINSIC FORMAL CAUSE IN THE SOUL   191

As Aquinas goes on to explain in this chapter, Averroes held that human beings are joined to the possible or material intellect insofar as human beings provide to the one separate material intellect images or intentions derived from sensation and the internal sense powers. For Aquinas, however, that means only that human beings and their apprehended intentions are the object understood by the separate material intellect. As such, human beings are not themselves knowing subjects but only known objects, since knowing properly takes place only in the separate material intellect.[10] In order to be knowers themselves human beings must have present in themselves the very power in virtue of which they are properly denominated intelligent and knowing. In the present context this means that, as Aquinas clearly spells out, "It is necessary...that the possible intellect be formally united to us and not only through its object." That is, the possible intellect must be a power intrinsically and individually possessed by each human being in the formal nature of each individual.

Later in the same work Aquinas explains that the doctrine of a transcendent Agent Intellect necessarily entails that "intellectual understanding is not a natural operation of human beings" and invokes the *Principle of Intrinsic Formal Cause: nihil operatur nisi per aliquam virtutem quae formaliter in ipso est*, "nothing carries out an activity except through some power which is formally in itself." He then draws his conclusion: "Therefore, it is necessary that the principles in virtue of which these actions are attributed [to human beings], namely the possible intellect and the agent intellect, be certain powers existing formally in us (*in nobis formaliter existentes*)."[11] Insofar as Averroes

---

Aristoteles, inquirens de principio quo intelligimus, tradit nobis naturam intellectus possibilis. Oportet igitur intellectum possibilem formaliter uniri nobis, et non solum per suum obiectum. Summa contra gentiles (Rome, 1918) [*S. Thomae de Aquino Opera Omnia Iussu Leonis XIII P.M. edita Cura et studio Fratrum Praedicatorum* Tomus XIII], p. 415b Amplius.

[10] Averroes is not without a response to such a critique, however. For him both the separate intellects, the Material Intellect and the Agent Intellect, are in the soul of the human knower. See the texts in note 39 below.

[11] *Summa Contra Gentiles*, 2.76, p. 480b: *Adhuc. Si intellectus agens est quaedam substantia separata, manifestum est quod est supra naturam hominis. Operatio autem quam homo exercet sola virtute alicuius supernaturalis substantiae, est operatio supernaturalis: ut miracula facere et prophetare, et alia huiusmodi quae divino munere homines operantur. Cum igitur homo non possit intelligere nisi virtute intellectus agentis, si intellectus agens est quaedam substantia separata, sequetur quod intelligere non sit operatio naturalis homini. Et sic homo non poterit definiri per hoc quod est intellectivus aut rationalis.*

192   RICHARD C. TAYLOR

asserts that the human power for the abstraction or separation of intelligible forms in the activity of intellectual understanding is located in a separately existing entity, then the rational or intellectual power of soul as extrinsic to human beings cannot at the same time be the intrinsic natural operation in virtue of which humans are appropriately defined as rational animals. The contradiction could hardly be put in more obvious terms: the very same power which functions as the intrinsic defining characteristic of an external ungenerated substantial entity (the eternal separate Agent Intellect) cannot at the same time be intrinsic to the individual human being as the defining characteristic of the human substance which comes into being by generation and goes out of being by perishing. How can these two entities so different even share the same genus? In concluding that both powers of soul, the agent intellect and the possible or material intellect, belong (*convenit*) to human beings Aquinas easily shows that it follows that these must be powers formally existing in human beings, quite in accord with principles we find in Aristotle. At *Physics* 2.1, 193b7–8, Aristotle asserts form to be the intrinsic principle as the nature of a thing: "The form indeed is nature rather than matter; for a thing is more properly said to be what

---

Praeterea. Nihil operatur nisi per aliquam virtutem quae formaliter in ipso est: unde Aristoteles, in II de anima, ostendit quod quo vivimus et sentimus, est forma et actus. Sed utraque actio, scilicet intellectus possibilis et intellectus agentis, convenit homini: homo enim abstrahit a phantasmatibus, et recipit mente intelligibilia in actu; non enim aliter in notitiam harum actionum venissemus nisi eas in nobis experiremur. Oportet igitur quod principia quibus attribuuntur hae actiones, scilicet intellectus possibilis et agens, sint virtutes quaedam in nobis formaliter existentes.

"Furthermore. If the agent intellect is a certain separated substance, it is evident that it is beyond the natures of human beings. An operation which human beings exercise only in virtue of some supernatural substance is a supernatural operation, such as to make miracles and to prophesy, and things of this sort which human beings carry out by divine gift. Therefore since human beings are able to understand only in virtue of the agent intellect, if the agent intellect is a certain separate substance, it would follow that to understand is not a natural operation belonging to human beings. And in this way human beings would not be able to be defined through the fact that they are intellectual or rational.

Moreover. Nothing operates except through some power which is formally in it. Hence, Aristotle shows in Book 2 of the *De Anima* that that by which we live and sense is the form and act. But the action of each, of the possible intellect and of the agent intellect, belongs to human beings. For human beings abstract from phantasms (scil., images in the soul) and receives in the mind intelligibles in act; for we would not have come to awareness of these actions unless we were to experience these in ourselves. It is necessary, therefore, that the principles to which these actions are attributed, the possible intellect and the agent [intellect], be certain powers existing formally in ourselves."

INTELLECT AS INTRINSIC FORMAL CAUSE IN THE SOUL   193

it is when it exists in actuality than when it exists potentially."[12] And at *Metaphysics* 7.13, 1038b9–14, he states that "primary substance is that kind of substance which is peculiar to an individual which does not belong to anything else...for things whose substance is one and whose essence is one are themselves also one."[13] For Aquinas one might make sense of what Averroes asserts if it is conceived as some sort of gift from a supernatural power such as the power of prophesy or performing miracles, though in that case it would still not be a natural human operation. For, as the natural operation essentially defining human beings as rational animals, the operation of reason must be a power belonging formally, essentially and individually to each human being.[14]

The *Principle of Intrinsic Formal Cause* is used in chapter 85 of the *Compendium theologiae* (ca. 1265–67) in the course of another attack on the noetics of Averroes, a noetics rightly argued by Aquinas to entail that after the death of the bodies of human beings there would remain only the single material intellect for all. After brief attempt at logical refutation of Averroes,[15] Aquinas writes

> However, if this [determinate particular] human being understands, it is necessary that that by which he formally understand be his form. [This is] because nothing acts except insofar as it is in act. Therefore,

---

[12] *The Complete Works of Aristotle. The Revised Oxford Translation*, Jonathan Barnes (ed.), 2 vol. (Princeton, 1984). Translation from v. 1, p. 330.

[13] "For primary substance is that kind of substance which is peculiar to an individual which does not belong to anything else; but the universal is common, since that is called universal which naturally belongs to more than one thing. Of which individual then will this be the substance? Either of all or of none. But it cannot be the substance of all; and if it is to be the substance of one, this one will be the others also; for things whose substance is one and whose essence is one are themselves also one." *The Complete Works of Aristotle*, v. 2, p. 1639.

[14] See the text cited in note 9.

[15] *Hoc autem quod impossibile sit, euidenter apparet. Ad quod ostendendum, procedendum est sicut proceditur contra negantes principia, ut ponamus aliquid quod omnino negari non potest. Ponamus igitur quod hic homo, puta Sortes uel Plato, intelligit: quod negare non posset respondens nisi intelligeret esse negandum; negando igitur ponit, nam affirmare et negare intelligentis est. Compendium theologiae*, c. 85, lines 42–50, p. 109. (Rome, 1979) [*S. Thomae de Aquino Opera Omnia Iussu Leonis XIII P.M. edita Cura et studio Fratrum Praedicatorum* Tomus XLII].
"That this [view of Averroes] is impossible appears in an evident way. To show this one should proceed as one proceeds against those who deny principle, so that we assert something which cannot be denied at all. Therefore, let us assert that this [determinate particular] human being, for example Socrates or Plato, understands. One responding would not be able to deny this unless he understands that it ought to be denied. Therefore, by denying he asserts, for to affirm or to deny is characteristic of one who understands."

194 RICHARD C. TAYLOR

that by which an agent acts is his form. Hence, the intellect by which a human being understands is the form of this [determinate particular] human being, and by the same reasoning for that. It is impossible that a form one and the same in number belong to [human beings] diverse in number, because the same being does not belong to [human beings] diverse in number. Each has being through his form. Therefore, it is impossible for the intellect by which a human being is intelligent to be one in all [human beings].[16]

Here the analysis is again definitional. Insofar as intellectual understanding is an act belonging properly to a determinate particular human being, it must take place through the human being's determinate and particular intrinsic form. That human form is multiplied in accord with the number of different human beings insofar as each has its own determinate particular being. Since being is determinate and particular, not shared, neither is that in virtue of which humans are intelligent. Hence, there is not just one intellect by which all human beings are intelligent. From this it also follows, writes Aquinas in c. 86, that the agent intellect too be a power individually present in each human being: "Since, therefore, the possible intellect is not separate in being from us but united to us as form and multiplied in a multitude of human beings as was shown, it is necessary that the agent intellect be something formally united to us and multiplied in accord with the number of human beings."[17]

The principle at work here is found in the *Quaestiones Disputatae De Anima* in Question 5 where Aquinas again uses the *Principle of Intrinsic Formal Cause* to conclude that the soul's powers of agent

---

[16] *Si autem hic homo intelligit, oportet quod id quo formaliter intelligit sit forma eius, quia nichil agit nisi secundum quod est actu, illud ergo quo agit agens est actus eius, sicut calor quo calidum calefacit est forma eius; intellectus igitur quo homo intelligit est forma huius hominis, et eadem ratione illius. Impossibile est autem quod forma eadem numero sit diuersorum secundum numerum, quia diuersorum secundum numerum non est idem esse; unumquodque autem habet esse per suam formam: impossibile est igitur quod intellectus quo homo intelligit sit unus in omnibus. Compendium theologiae,* c. 85, lines 50–62, p. 109.

[17] *Si autem hic homo intelligit, oportet quod id quo formaliter intelligit sit forma eius, quia nichil agit nisi secundum quod est actu, illud ergo quo agit agens est actus eius, sicut calor quo calidum calefacit est forma eius; intellectus igitur quo homo intelligit est forma huius hominis, et eadem ratione illius. Impossibile est autem quod forma eadem numero sit diuersorum secundum numerum, quia diuersorum secundum numerum non est idem esse; unumquodque autem habet esse per suam formam: impossibile est igitur quod intellectus quo homo intelligit sit unus in omnibus. Compendium theologiae,* c. 86, lines 25–32, p. 110.

INTELLECT AS INTRINSIC FORMAL CAUSE IN THE SOUL 195

intellect and possible intellect must be formally present in individual human beings.

> [I]n each and every thing operating there must be some formal principle by which it formally operates. For something is not able to operate formally through what is separate from it in being. Even if what is separate is a principle moving it to operate, still there must be something intrinsic by which it formally operates, be that a form or some sort of impression. Therefore there must be in us some formal principle by which we receive intelligibles and another by which we abstract them. Principles of this sort are called possible intellect and agent [intellect]. Therefore, each of these is something in us.[18]

Again, as Aquinas sees it, the formal principle in a thing in virtue of which that thing carries out any action or operation must be intrinsic to the thing which acts or operates. He even argues that the illuminating power of God or any other separate substance providing universal principles remains significantly distinct from the intellectual operation in human beings, saying, "There is required in us an active principle of our own through which we are made to be intelligent in act. And this is the agent intellect."[19] Neither the receptive possible or material intellect nor the active agent intellect can be distinct in substance from the individual human intellect. This is sufficiently supported for Aquinas in the human experience of abstracting and receiving intelligibles: "We

---

[18] *Oportet autem in unoquoque operante esse aliquod formale principium quo formaliter operetur. Non enim potest aliquid formaliter operari per id quod est secundum esse separatum ab ipso, set etsi id quod est separatum sit principium motiuum ad operandum, nichilominus oportet esse aliquod intrinsecum quo formaliter operetur, siue illud sit forma siue qualiscumque impressio. Oportet igitur esse in nobis aliquod principium formale quo recipiamus intelligibilia et aliud quo abstrahamus ea. Et huiusmodi principia nominantur intellectus possibilis et agens. Vterque igitur eorum est aliquid in nobis.* Thomas Aquinas, *Quaestiones Disputatae De Anima*, B.-C. Bazán, ed. (Rome: Commissio Leonina, Paris: Éditions du Cerf, 1996) q. 5, resp., pp. 42, 194–206. [S. Thomae de Aquino Opera Omnia *Iussu Leonis XIII P.M. edita Cura et studio Fratrum Praedicatorum* Tomus XXIV, 1].

[19] *Cum igitur id quod est perfectissimum in omnibus inferioribus sit intellectualis operatio, preter principia actiua uniuersalia, que sunt uirtus Dei illuminantis uel cuiuscumque alterius substantie separate, requiritur in nobis principium actiuum proprium, per quod efficiamur intelligentes in actu. Et hoc est intellectus agens. Quaestiones Disputatae De Anima*, q. 5, resp., pp. 41, 156–163.

"Therefore, although what is most perfect in all lower [entities] is intellectual operation, in addition to the universal active principles which are the power of God as illuminator or some other separate substance, an active principle is required in us through which we are made intelligent in act. And this is the agent intellect."

196 RICHARD C. TAYLOR

experience both of these operations in our very selves, for we both receive and abstract intelligibles."[20]

In the latter years of the 1260's, while in Italy composing several different works, Aquinas repeatedly invokes the same principle to the same conclusion. In his *Quaestio Disputata De Spiritualibus Creaturis*, Aquinas three times asserts the *Principle of Intrinsic Formal Cause*. In the response of Article 2, he writes, "It is therefore necessary that the principle of this operation which is intellectual understanding be formally present in this [determinant particular] human being."[21] Later in the same response, he concludes that each human being must have individually the power of soul called possible intellect: "it is necessary that the possible intellect, which is understanding in potency, be formally present in this [determinate particular] human being so that this [determinate particular] human being understands."[22] And in Article 10 he invokes this principle again in arguing that the agent intellect is in the human soul:

> Everything carrying out a given action has formally in itself the power which is the principle of such an action. Hence, just as it is necessary that the possible intellect be something formally inhering in human beings,

---

[20] *Vtramque autem harum operationum experimur in nobis ipsis, nam et nos intelligibilia recipimus et abstrahimus ea. Quaestiones Disputatae De Anima*, q. 5, resp., pp. 42, 191–193.

[21] *Oportet igitur principium huius operationis quod est intelligere formaliter inesse huic homini. Principium autem huius operationis non est forma aliqua cuius esse sit dependens a corpore, et materiae obligatum sive immersum; quia haec operatio non fit per corpus, ut probatur in III de anima; unde principium huius operationis habet operationem sine communicatione materiae corporalis. Sic autem unumquodque operatur secundum quod est; unde oportet quod esse illius principii sit esse elevatum supra materiam corporalem, et non dependens ab ipsa. Hoc autem proprium est spiritualis substantiae....*

"It is therefore necessary that the principle of this operation which is intellectual understanding be formally present in this [determinant particular] human being. The principle of this operation is not some form the being of which is dependent upon the body and bound to or immersed in matter, because this operation does not come about through the body, as is proved in Book 3 of the *De Anima*. Hence, the principle of this operation has an operation not shared with the material body. In this way any given thing operates according to what it is; hence, the being of that principle must be a being elevated above bodily matter and not dependent on it. This is a property of a separate substance...."

De spiritualibus creaturis, a. 2 resp. J. Cos, ed. (Rome: Commissio Leonina, Paris: Éditions du Cerf, 2000), p. 24.170–183 [S. Thomae de Aquino Opera Omnia *Iussu Leonis XIII P.M. edita Cura et studio Fratrum Praedicatorum* Tomus XXIV, 2].

[22] *...set oportet ipsum intellectum possibilem, qui est potentia intelligens, formaliter inesse huic homini ad hoc quod hic homo intelligat. De spiritualibus creaturis*, a. 2 resp., p. 25.227–230.

INTELLECT AS INTRINSIC FORMAL CAUSE IN THE SOUL   197

as we showed earlier, so too it is necessary that the agent intellect be
something formally inhering in human beings.[23]

The *Principle of Intrinsic Formal Cause* also appears clearly stated in
his *Commentary on the De Anima of Aristotle* written in 1267–1268. In
an excursus on the issue of the possible intellect as a separate substance
attached to his explication of *De Anima* 3.4, 429a10–b5, he writes,

> But on the basis of these words some have been deceived to the extent
> that they asserted that the possible intellect is separate from the body, as
> one of the separate substances. That is completely impossible.
>
> For it is evident that this [determinate particular] human being under-
> stands. For, if this is denied, then the one saying this does not understand
> anything and for this reason should not be listened to. However, if he
> understands, it is necessary that he undestand by something, speaking for-
> mally. But this is the possible intellect concerning which the Philosopher
> says, "But I call intellect that by which the soul understands and opines."
> Therefore, the possible intellect is that by which this [determinate par-
> ticular] human being understands, speaking formally. That by which
> something operates as by an active principle can be separated in being
> from that which operates, as if we were to say that the bailiff operates in
> virtue of the king, because the king moves him to operate. But it is impos-
> sible for that by which something formally operates to be separated from
> him in being. This is for the reason that nothing acts except insofar as it
> is in act. Therefore, something operates formally by something insofar
> as it comes to be in act by this [thing]. But something does not come to
> be a being in act by something else if [the latter] is separate from it in
> being. Hence, it is impossible that that by which something formally acts
> be separate from it in being. Therefore, it is impossible that the possible
> intellect by which a human being understands sometimes in potency,
> sometimes in act, be separate from him in being.[24]

---

[23] *Omne autem agens quamcumque actionem, habet formaliter in seipso virtutem
quae est talis actionis principium. Unde sicut necessarium est quod intellectus possibilis
sit aliquid formaliter inhaerens homini, ut prius ostendimus; ita necessarium est quod
intellectus agens sit aliquid formaliter inhaerens homini. De spiritualibus creaturis,*
a. 10 resp., p. 106.268–274.

[24] *Set horum occasione verborum quidam in tantum decepti sunt ut ponerent intellectum possibilem esse a corpore separatum, sicut una de substantiis separatis. Quod
quidem omnino inpossibile est.*

*Manifestum est enim, quod hic homo intelligit: si enim hoc negetur, tunc dicens hanc
opinionem non intelligit aliquid et ideo non est audiendus. Si autem intelligit, oportet
quod aliquo, formaliter loquendo, intelligat; hoc autem est intellectus possibilis, de quo
philosophus dicit: Dico autem intellectum quo intelligit et opinatur anima; intellectus
igitur possibilis est, quo hic homo, formaliter loquendo, intelligit. Id autem, quo aliquid
operatur sicut activo principio potest secundum esse separari ab eo quod operatur, ut
si dicamus, quod baliuus operatur per regem, quia rex movet eum ad operandum; set
impossibile est id quo aliquid formaliter operatur separari ab eo secundum esse; quod*

198 RICHARD C. TAYLOR

Again, speaking with regard to the formal principle determinate of the nature and actions of a human being, the rational principle manifested in the possible intellect, Aquinas finds that it makes no sense to assert that what is essential and formal to the human action of understanding exists in separation from the determinate particular human being carrying out the activity of intellectual understanding. The bailiff may act in virtue of the king, in behalf of the king and on the order and with the authority of the king, in an action which is accidental to the essential being of the human person employed as bailiff. But an essential activity definitive of the nature of human beings as rational animals cannot exist separate in existence from the human being.

In the same period, Aquinas wrote *Quaestio 76* of the *Prima Pars* of the *Summa Theologiae* "On the Union of the Soul to the Body," the first article of which is entitled "Whether The Intellective Principle Is United To The Body As Form." His response in that article is dominated by discussion of the *Principle of Intrinsic Formal Cause*. There he begins with the bold if not shocking statement—at least from the point of view of the Aristotelian tradition—that "the intellect which is the principle of intellectual operation is a form of the human body."[25] His justification lies in the *Principle of Intrinsic Formal Cause* which he phrases as follows: "That by which something primarily operates is its form to which the operation is attributed...."[26] The argument for this is as follows: "nothing acts except insofar as it is in act; hence, something acts by virtue of that by which it is in act...Therefore that principle by which we primarily understand, be it called the intellect

---

ideo est quia nihil agit nisi secundum quod est actu; sic igitur aliquid formaliter aliquo operatur sicut eo sit actu; non autem fit aliquid aliquo ens actu si sit separatum ab eo secundum esse; unde inpossibile est quod illud quo aliquid agit formaliter sit separatum ab eo secundum esse; inpossibile est igitur quod intellectus possibilis quo homo intelligit quandoque quidem in potencia quandoque autem in actu sit separatus ab eo secundum esse. Sentencia libri de anima (Rome: Commssio Leonina; Paris, 1984) pp. 205.277–206.305.

[25] *[I]ntellectus, qui est intellectualis operationis principium, sit humani corporis forma. Summa Theologiae, Prima Pars,* 1.76.1 resp., p. 448a (Ottawa, 1953).

[26] *Illud enim quo primo aliquid operatur, est forma eius cui operatio attribuitur, sicut quo primo sanatur corpus, est sanitas, et quo primo scit anima, est scientia; unde sanitas est forma corporis, et scientia animae.* Ibid.

"For that by which some thing primarily operates is its form to which the operation is attributed, just as that by which the body is primarily made healthy, is health, and that by which the soul primarily knows is knowledge; hence, health is the form of the body and knowledge of the soul."

INTELLECT AS INTRINSIC FORMAL CAUSE IN THE SOUL   199

or the intellective soul, is a form of the body...."[27] He argues for this conclusion by saying that, just as the body is alive by the soul by which it carries out operations of taking nutrition, sensing and moving, similarly that by which we primarily understand is the intellect: "Therefore the principle by which we primarily understand, whether it be called intellect or the intellective soul, is the form of the body." After locating the intellect in each determinate individual human being in this way, Aquinas cites as supportive authority Aristotle in *De Anima* Book 2, 414a12: "[S]ince it is the soul by which primarily we live, perceive, and think:—it follows that the soul must be an account and essence, not matter or a subject."[28] Aquinas also appeals to his argument from experience to forestall the possible objection that the intellective soul is not the form of the body, writing that the objector will have to explain "the way in which that action which is to understand is the action of this [determinate particular] human being, for each person experiences it to be himself who understands."[29] Furthermore, he adds, when we

---

[27] *Respondeo dicendum quod necesse est dicere quod intellectus, qui est intellectualis operationis principium, sit humani corporis forma. Illud enim quo primo aliquid operatur, est forma eius cui operatio attribuitur, sicut quo primo sanatur corpus, est sanitas, et quo primo scit anima, est scientia; unde sanitas est forma corporis, et scientia animae. Et huius ratio est, quia nihil agit nisi secundum quod est actu, unde quo aliquid est actu, eo agit. Manifestum est autem quod primum quo corpus vivit, est anima. Et cum vita manifestetur secundum diversas operationes in diversis gradibus viventium, id quo primo operamur unumquodque horum operum vitae, est anima, anima enim est primum quo nutrimur, et sentimus, et movemur secundum locum; et similiter quo primo intelligimus. Hoc ergo principium quo primo intelligimus, sive dicatur intellectus sive anima intellectiva, est forma corporis. Et haec est demonstratio Aristotelis in II de anima. Summa Theologiae, Prima Pars,* 1.76.1 resp. pp. 448a–b. "I respond that it should be said that it is necessary to say that the intellect which is the principle of intellectual operation is the form of the human body. For that by which something primarily operates is the form of that to which the operation is attributed, as that by which the body is primarily healthy is health and that by which the soul primarily knows is knowledge. Hence, health is the form of the body and knowledge [is the form] of the soul. The reason for this is because nothing acts except insofar as it is in act; consequently, something acts by this by which it is in act. It is evident, however, that the first thing by which the body lives is the soul. And since life is made manifest according to the diverse operations in diverse grades of living things, that by which we primarily carry out any of the activities of life is the soul. For the soul is the first thing by which we take nourishment, sense and move in location, and [it is] likewise that by which we primarily understand. Therefore this principle by which we primarily understand, be it called the intellect or the intellective soul, is the form of the body. This is the demonstration of Aristotle in book 2 of the *De Anima*."

[28] *The Complete Works of Aristotle*, v. 1, p. 659.

[29] *Si quis autem velit dicere animam intellectivam non esse corporis formam, oportet quod inveniat modum quo ista actio quae est intelligere, sit huius hominis actio, experitur enim unusquisque seipsum esse qui intelligit. Summa Theologiae, Prima Pars,* 1.76.1 resp.,

200   RICHARD C. TAYLOR

attribute understanding to a given human being, it is as something essential to the very nature of the human being: "for it is attributed to him insofar as he is a human being, because it is predicated of him in an essential way."[30] In this way "the intellect by which Socrates understands is a part of Socrates such that the intellect is united to the body of Socrates."[31] Emphasis here is on the unitary nature of the human being, Socrates, as a whole composed of form and matter: "[I]f the intellect were not his form, it would follow that [the intellect] would be outside his essence... However, understanding is an action resting in the agent, not passing through into another, as heating. Therefore understanding cannot be attributed to Socrates due to the fact that he has been moved by intellect" as something extrinsic to him.[32]

That the main concern of Aquinas here is the location of the intellect in each human being as a determinate particular human being becomes most clear when he uses the phrase *hic homo intelligit* in saying that "this [determinate particular] human being understands, because the intellective principle is his form. In this way, therefore, from the very operation of the intellect it is apparent that the intellective principle

---

p. 448b. While Averroes does not give special emphasis to the experience of oneself knowing in the same phraseology, the notion may be implicit in his repeated assertion that we carry out the activities of knowing by our will. He writes, *Et fuit necesse attribuere has duas actiones anime in nobis, scilicet recipere intellectum et facere eum, quamvis agens et recipiens sint substantie eterne, propter hoc quia hee due actiones reducte sunt ad nostram voluntatem, scilicet abstrahere intellecta et intelligere ea*: "It was necessary to ascribe these two activities to the soul in us, namely, to receive the intelligible and to make it, although the agent and the recipient are eternal substances, on account of the fact that these two activities are reduced to our will, namely, to abstract intelligibles and to understand them." *Averrois Cordubensis Commentarium Magnum in Aristotelis De Anima Libros*, F. Stuart Crawford, ed. (Cambridge, MA, 1953), p. 439. Cf. Ibid. pp. 390; 490; and 495. This edition will be cited hereafter as LCDA (*Long Commentary on the De Anima*).

[30] *Cum igitur dicimus Socratem aut Platonem intelligere, manifestum est quod non attribuitur ei per accidens, attribuitur enim ei inquantum est homo, quod essentialiter praedicatur de ipso*. Ibid.

[31] *Relinquitur ergo quod intellectus quo Socrates intelligit, est aliqua pars Socratis ita quod intellectus aliquo modo corpori Socratis uniatur*. Ibid.

[32] *Secundo quia, cum Socrates sit quoddam individuum in natura cuius essentia est una, composita ex materia et forma; si intellectus non sit forma eius, sequitur quod sit praeter essentiam eius; et sic intellectus comparabitur ad totum Socratem sicut motor ad motum. Intelligere autem est actio quiescens in agente, non autem transiens in alterum, sicut calefactio. Non ergo intelligere potest attribui Socrati propter hoc quod est motus ab intellectu. Summa Theologiae, Prima Pars*, 1.76.1 resp., p. 449a.

INTELLECT AS INTRINSIC FORMAL CAUSE IN THE SOUL   201

is united to the body as form."[33] He bolsters this by appeal to the definitional account (*ratio*) of a human being in virtue of the species. What distinguishes human beings from other animals is understanding, something Aristotle indicated to be proper to human beings and to constitute ultimate human happiness in *Nicomachean Ethics* Book 10.[34] Aquinas then adds, "Therefore, human beings must be distinguished [in species] according to that which is the principle of this operation. However, any given thing is distinguished in species through its own proper form. Therefore, it follows that the intellective principle is a proper form of a human being."[35]

Finally, in his *De unitate intellectus contra averroistas* written in 1270 Aquinas again sets forth this principle to support the necessity of his own view of the intrinsic presence of the powers of agent intellect and possible intellect in the soul when he writes the following.

> For any given thing its species derives from its form. Therefore, that through which this [particular] human being derives his species is his form. However, any given thing derives its species from that which is the principle of the operation proper to its species. But the operation proper to human beings, insofar as they are human beings, is to understand. It is in virtue of this that human beings differ from other animals....[36]

Again, in this way the very definitional difference distinguishing human beings from other animals lies in the intrinsic presence to each member of the species of the form which bears the essential and proper operations of intellectual understanding by the agent intellect and the possible intellect in each human soul. A view that locates the power of understanding properly outside the individual human being denies to

---

[33] *[H]ic homo intelligit, quia principium intellectivum est forma ipsius. Sic ergo ex ipsa operatione intellectus apparet quod intellectivum principium unitur corpori ut forma. Summa Theologiae, Prima Pars,* 1.76.1 resp., p. 449b.

[34] Aristotle, *Nicomachean Ethics* 10.7, 1177a11–1178a8.

[35] *Oportet ergo quod homo secundum illud speciem sortiatur, quod est huius operationis principium. Sortitur autem unumquodque speciem per propriam formam. Relinquitur ergo quod intellectivum principium sit propria hominis forma. Summa Theologiae, Prima Pars,* 1.76.1 resp.

[36] *Speciem autem sortitur unumquodque ex forma: id igitur per quod hic homo speciem sortitur forma est. Vnumquodque autem ab eo speciem sortitur, quod est principium proprie operationis speciei; propria autem operatio hominis, in quantum est homo, est intelligere: per hoc enim differt ab aliis animalibus... Thomas Aquinas, De unitate intellectus contra Averroistas,* cap. 3, Roma, Editori di San Tommaso, 1976 (Sancti Thomae de Aquino Opera Omnia Iussu Leonis XIII P. M. edita cura et studio Fratrum Praedicatorum, t. XLIII), pp. 306, 321–328.

202 RICHARD C. TAYLOR

that human being something essential and intrinsic to human nature and, as such, is a view that must be rejected.

The *Principle of Intrinsic Formal Cause* employed repeatedly in these texts by Aquinas, as we have seen, is unquestionably devastating to the accounts asserting that human knowing takes place in virtue of separate agent intellect and separate material intellect in the context of the Aristotelian conception of the constituitive nature of intrinsic form as cause of individual substance. If human beings are properly understood as rational animals essentially distinguished by their rational or intellectual operations, those operations must be intrinsic as essentially contained within the very substance of human beings, he argues. Otherwise human beings would be knowers only accidentally, not essentially, and the operation of intellect would belong essentially to the separate intellects and only non-essentially in human beings. If the views of Averroes must be understood within this conception of the Aristotelian framework as recounted by Aquinas, we can only marvel at this surprising mistake by Averroes regarding such a fundamental principle. The reasoning of Averroes, however, does not proceed within the confines of that framework.

2. *Averroes and the* Principle of Intrinsic Formal Cause

In Book 3, Comment 36, of his *Long Commentary on the De Anima*, Averroes is particularly concerned with the issue of conjunction or conjoining of human beings with the separate intellects[37] in the attainment of knowledge on the part of individual human beings. That conjoining, *ittiṣāl*, is not a gnostic experience or a mystical *dhawq*, "taste," of the Divine nor is it an experience related to common religious practices, notions which the term *ittiṣāl* might well convey in other contexts. Rather, in this work conjoining is an intrinsic part of Averroes's account of how intelligibles in potency gathered by sense perception and processed by the powers of the brain are transferred from the level of particular images to the level of intelligibles in act thanks to the

---

[37] This issue is discussed by Alfred L. Ivry in "Conjunction in and of Maimonides and Averroes," in *Averroès et les averroïsmes juif et latin. Actes du colloque tenu à Paris, 16–18 juin 2005*, ed. J.-B. Brenet, (Turnhout, 2007), pp. 231–247; and by Marc Geoffroy in "Averroès sur l'intellect comme cause agent et cause formelle, et la question de la 'jonction'—1," Idem, pp. 77–110.

INTELLECT AS INTRINSIC FORMAL CAUSE IN THE SOUL   203

intellectual power of the separate Agent Intellect.[38] It is in this context that Averroes writes the following:

> For, because that in virtue of which something carries out its proper activity is the form, while we carry out {500} our proper activity in virtue of the agent intellect, it is necessary that the agent intellect be *form in us.*... [I]t is necessary that a human being understand all the intelligibles through the intellect proper to him and that he carry out the activity proper to him in regard to all beings, just as he understands by his proper intellection all the beings through the intellect in a positive

---

[38] *Abstrahere enim nichil est aliud quam facere intentiones ymaginatas intellectas in actu postquam erant in potentia; intelligere autem nichil aliud est quam recipere has intentiones. Cum enim invenimus idem transferri in suo esse de ordine in ordinem, scilicet intentiones ymaginatas, diximus quod necesse est ut hoc sit a causa agenti et recipienti. Recipiens igitur est materialis, et agens est efficiens.* "For to abstract is nothing other than to make imagined intentions intelligible in act after they were [intelligible] in potency. But to understand is nothing other than to receive these intentions. For when we found the same thing, namely, the imagined intentions, is transferred in its being from one order into another, we said that this must be from an agent cause and a recipient cause. The recipient, however, is the material [intellect] and the agent is [the intellect] which brings [this] about." LCDA 439. Cf. note 45 for this notion and phraseology in al-Fārābī. Aquinas surely has this text of Averroes in mind when he writes the following in the *Summa theologiae, Prima pars,* q. 8, a. 1, ad 3: *Ad tertium dicendum quod colores habent eundem modum existendi prout sunt in materia corporali individuali, sicut et potentia visiva, et ideo possunt imprimere suam similitudinem in visum. Sed phantasmata, cum sint similitudines individuorum, et existant in organis corporeis, non habent eundem modum existendi quem habet intellectus humanus, ut ex dictis patet; et ideo non possunt sua virtute imprimere in intellectum possibilem. Sed virtute intellectus agentis resultat quaedam similitudo in intellectu possibili ex conversione intellectus agentis supra phantasmata, quae quidem est repraesentativa eorum quorum sunt phantasmata, solum quantum ad naturam speciei. Et per hunc modum dicitur abstrahi species intelligibilis a phantasmatibus, non quod aliqua eadem numero forma, quae prius fuit in phantasmatibus, postmodum fiat in intellectu possibili, ad modum quo corpus accipitur ab uno loco et transfertur ad alterum.* "To the third it should be said that colors have the same mode of existing insofar as they are in individual corporeal matter, as also in the power of sight, and for this reason they are able to impress their likeness on sight. But, since phantasms are likenesses of individuals and exist in corporeal organs, they do not have the same mode of existing which the human intellect has, as is clear from things said earlier. For this reason they are not able to impress into the possible intellect with its power. But by the power of the agent intellect a certain likeness comes about in the possible intellect from the reversion of the agent intellect upon the phantasms which [likeness] is representative of these things of which they are the phantasms, only with regard to the nature of the species. In this way the intelligible species is said to be abstracted from the phantasms, not because some form same in number which was previously in the phantasms afterwards comes to be in the possible intellect, in the manner in which a body is taken from one place and transferred to another."

204 RICHARD C. TAYLOR

disposition (*intellectus in habitu*), when it has been conjoined with forms of the imagination.[39]

This expression of the *Principle of Intrinsic Formal Cause* was written by Averroes in his *Long Commentary on the De Anima* about 35 years before the birth of Aquinas, that is around 1186. The *Long Commentary on the De Anima* was translated around 1220–1225, perhaps by Michael

---

[39] *Quoniam, quia illud per quod agit aliquid suam propriam actionem est forma, nos autem agimus per intellectum {500} agentem nostram actionem propriam, necesse est ut intellectus agens sit forma in nobis.*

Et nullus modus est secundum quem generetur forma in nobis nisi iste. Quoniam, cum intellecta speculativa copulantur nobiscum per formas ymaginabiles, et intellectus agens copulatur cum intellectis speculativis (illud enim quod comprehendit ea est idem, scilicet intellectus materialis), necesse est ut intellectus agens copuletur nobiscum per continuationem intellectorum speculativorum.

Et manifestum est quod, cum omnia intellecta speculativa fuerint existentia in nobis in potentia, quod ipse erit copulatus nobiscum in potentia. Et cum omnia intellecta speculativa fuerint existentia in nobis in actu, erit ipse tunc copulatus nobis in actu. Et cum quedam fuerint potentia et quedam actu, tunc erit ipse copulatus secundum partem et secundum partem non; et tunc dicimur moveri ad continuationem.

Et manifestum est quod, cum iste motus complebitur, quod statim iste intellectus copulabitur nobiscum omnibus modis. Et tunc manifestum est quod proportio eius ad nos in illa dispositione est sicut proportio intellectus qui est in habitu ad nos. Et cum ita sit, **necesse est ut homo intelligat per intellectum sibi proprium omnia entia,** *et ut agat actionem sibi propriam in omnibus entibus, sicut intelligit per intellectum qui est in habitu, quando fuerit continuatus cum formis ymaginabilibus, omnia entia intellectione propria.*

LCDA, 499–500. My emphasis.

"For, because **that in virtue of which something carries out its proper activity is the form,** while we carry out {500} our proper activity in virtue of the agent intellect, it is necessary that the agent intellect be form in us.

There is no way in which the form is generated in us except that. For, when the theoretical intelligibles are joined with us through forms of the imagination and the agent intellect is joined with the theoretical intelligibles (for that which apprehends [theoretical intelligibles] is the same, namely, the material intellect), it is necessary that the agent intellect be coupled with us through the conjoining of the theoretical intelligibles. It is evident [then] that, when all the theoretical intelligibles exist in us in potency, it will be joined with us in potency. When all the theoretical intelligibles exist in us in act, it will then be joined with us in act. And when certain [theoretical intelligibles] exist in potency and certain in act, then it will be joined in one part and not in another. Then we are said to be moved to conjoining.

It is evident that, when that motion is complete, immediately that intellect will be conjoined with us in all ways. Then it is evident that its relation to us in that disposition is as the relation of the intellect which is in a positive disposition (*in habitu*) in relation to us. Since it is so, **it is necessary that a human being understand all the intelligibles through the intellect proper to him** and that he carry out the activity proper to him in regard to all beings, just as he understands by his proper intellection all the beings through the intellect which is in a positive disposition, when it has been conjoined with forms of the imagination."

INTELLECT AS INTRINSIC FORMAL CAUSE IN THE SOUL   205

Scot[40] and there is no doubt that it is expressing the same rationale for the intrinsic presence of the Agent Intellect which is found in the texts of Aquinas examined earlier. The proper operation or activity of a thing proceeds from a thing per se only insofar as it proceeds from the thing's intrinsic form which constitutes the being of the thing. Insofar as intellectual understanding on the part of human beings proceeds in virtue of the abstractive power of the Agent Intellect to transfer intelligibles in potency in human beings to the level of intelligibles in act in human beings, it follows that Agent Intellect must be form in us.

In the thought of Aquinas, as we have seen, the principle is used to show that agent intellect and possible or material intellect must be intrinsic powers of the soul, powers multiplied with the multiplication of individual souls. In the mature work of Averroes, however, there is one transcendent Agent Intellect for all human beings and one transcendent Material Intellect for all human beings. Applying this *Principle of Intrinsic Formal Cause* to the teachings of Averroes on human soul and intellect, the consequence is very different from that reached by Aquinas. For Averroes its application entails simply that transcendent Agent Intellect must be not only transcendent and existing in its own right, but must also be intrinsically present and acting as an essential part of a human being insofar as human beings exercise rational and intellectual thought and are properly defined as rational beings. The separate and unique Agent Intellect must be present in individual human beings such that it is intrinsic and essential. The Agent Intellect cannot be present after the manner of an accident simply because, were it accidentally present, human beings would be only accidentally rational and intelligent by a kind of transitory participation or gift from an extrinsic source—the Agent Intellect—in which that power of rationality and intelligence exists per se and essentially.

---

[40] In his September 21, 2007 plenary address at the XIIth International Congress of Medieval Philosophy held in Palermo, Italy, Dag Nikolaus Hasse presented a paper entitled, "Latin Averroes Translations of the First Half of the Thirteenth Century." In the paper Hasse persuasively marshalls data in support of a new method for determining the translators of various works rendered into Latin from Arabic. His method indicates that the traditional attribution of the translation of the *Long Commentary on the De Anima of Aristotle* to Michael Scot is likely correct. Hasse's paper will be published in the Congress Proceedings.

206 RICHARD C. TAYLOR

In this Averroes and Aquinas are in agreement: the Agent Intellect must be in the soul as its form.[41]

From the time of his early *Short Commentary on the De Anima* (early 1260s) through the writing of the *Middle Commentary* (perhaps ca. 1280–1283) and right up through to the completion of the final version of the *Long Commentary* (perhaps around 1286), Averroes consistently held that the transcendent Agent Intellect played an important part in the realization of intellectual understanding on the part of human beings, a view common to the Greek and Arabic traditions as noted earlier. In all three works Averroes characterizes this role as one in which Agent Intellect is *ṣurah la-nā*, "form for us."[42] Such a characterization in a general way is certainly appropriate since the tradition held commonly that a transcendent Agent Intellect played a role in the actualization of the formal content of intelligibles in the human mind. In his *Long Commentary on the De Anima* Averroes saw this doctrine of the Agent Intellect as form for us in Alexander of Aphrodisias who held that perishable individual human intellects are brought to completion in knowing by the transcendent Agent Intellect which Alexander

---

[41] In the *Long Commentary on the De Anima*, Averroes says that *propalavit Aristoteles quod intellectus agens existit in anima nobis*: "Aristotle insisted that the agent intellect exists for us in the soul" at LCDA, 390; and *oportuit ponere in anima intelligentiam agentem*: "it was necessary to assert the agent intelligence to be in the soul" at LCDA, 438. He asserts that the Agent Intellect and the Material Intellect are in the soul when he writes *opinandum est, quod iam apparuit nobis ex sermone Aristotelis, quod in anima sunt due partes intellectus, quarum una est recipiens, cuius esse declaratum est hic, alia autem agens, et est illud quod facit intentiones que sunt in virtute ymaginativa esse moventes intellectum materialem in actu postquam erant moventes in potentia, ut post apparebit ex sermone Aristotelis*: "one should hold the opinion which already was apparent to us from the account of Aristotle, that in the soul there are two parts belonging to the intellect, one is the recipient whose being is explained here, the other is the agent which is what makes the intentions which are in the imaginative power to be movers of the material intellect in act after they were movers in potency, as will be apparent later from the account of Aristotle" at LCDA, 406; and also when he writes *cum necesse est inveniri in parte anime que dicitur intellectus istas tres differentias, necesse est ut in ea sit pars que dicitur intellectus secundum quod efficitur omne modo similitudinis et receptionis, et quod in ea sit etiam secunda pars que dicitur intellectus secundum quod facit istum intellectum qui est in potentia intelligere omne in actu*: "Since those three differences must be found in the part of the soul which is called intellect, it is necessary that there be in it a part which is called intellect insofar as it is made everything by way of likeness and reception. There must also be in it a second part which is called intellect insofar as it makes that intellect which is in potency to understand everything in act." at LCDA, 437.

[42] See my "The Agent Intellect as 'form for us' and Averroes's Critique of al-Fārābī," cited in note 5. Also see the article by Geoffroy cited in note 5.

INTELLECT AS INTRINSIC FORMAL CAUSE IN THE SOUL   207

identified with the highest God.[43] Averroes analyzes the teachings of Themistius and also finds that this Greek commentator holds that the transcendent Agent Intellect is form for us.[44] However, the true meaning of the teaching becomes clear when Averroes provides a critical analysis of the account of al-Fārābī.

For al-Fārābī the Agent Intellect plays a crucial role in human intellectual understanding and in the perfection of human substance at the highest levels by providing something by means of which the human intellect is able to perform the activity of abstraction or transference of intelligibles from the level of intelligibles in potency in the human imagination to the level of intelligibles in act in the individual human material or receptive intellect. For Averroes the teaching of al-Fārābī was that Agent Intellect is only an extrinsic efficient cause acting on humans in such a way as to make possible abstraction and intellectual understanding.[45] For this he criticizes al-Fārābī at length asserting that

---

[43] LCDA, pp. 484–485.

[44] LCDA, p. 445.

[45] The texts of al-Fārābī are themselves somewhat ambiguous. In the *Treatise on the Intellect* he indicates that the Agent Intellect provides a principle by which the receptive material intellect is able to carry out abstraction. "And in a similar manner there comes to be (*taḥṣulu*) in that essence (*adh-dhāt*) which is an intellect in potentiality something whose relation to it is as the relation of transparency in actuality to sight. But the Agent Intellect provides it (*yuʿṭīhi*) this thing so by it it becomes a principle for which the intelligibles which were in potentiality become intelligibles in actuality for [the intellect]. Just as the sun is that which makes the eye to be sight in actuality and visible things to be visible in actuality, insofar as it provides it illumination, so likewise the Agent Intellect is that which makes (*jaʿala*) the intellect which is in potentiality into an intellect in actuality insofar as it provides it that principle, and through this very same thing the intelligibles become intelligibles in actuality." *Alfarabi. Risalah fī al-ʿaql*, Maurice Bouyges, S.J., ed. (Beyrouth, 1983), 2nd ed. 24.6–25.3; English translation by Arthur Hyman in *Philosophy in the Middle Ages*, ed. Arthur Hyman and James J. Walsh (Indianapolis, 1973), 2nd ed., p. 218. Translation slightly modified.

In *The Political Regime* al-Fārābī seems to consider the Agent Intellect an extrinsic efficient cause of abstraction. He writes that the Agent Intellect "makes (*yajʿalu*) the things which are not in their essences intelligible to be intelligible." It raises (*yarfaʿuhā*) things which are not per se intelligibles to a rank of existence higher than they possessed naturally so that they are intelligibles for the human intellect in act. In this way the Agent Intellect causes them to become intelligibles in act for the human rational power, assisting it to reach the rank of the Agent Intellect which is the end of human beings in their perfection and happiness. (34–35) There he also writes,"In regard to what the Agent Intellect provides (*yuʿṭīhi*) to human beings there is similarity with what is the case for the heavenly bodies. For it provides (*yuʿṭī*) to human beings first a power and a principle by which it achieves or by which human beings are able by means of their souls to achieve the rest of what remains of perfection for them. This principle is the first sciences and first intelligibles which come about in the rational part of the soul. For [the Agent Intellect] provides it these notions and intelligibles

208 RICHARD C. TAYLOR

one must hold not only that the Agent Intellect is an efficient cause acting on us but also that it is "form for us" acting intrinsically in us since we are ourselves knowers.[46]

Averroes himself then clearly held that the Agent Intellect must be "form for us" such that it is somehow not merely extrinsic but in some genuine sense must be intrinsically present in human knowers. But in light of the account of Aquinas detailed earlier, it is evident that Averroes simply cannot hold for the Aristotelian account as spelled out by Aquinas. This could hardly be more obvious. On that Aristotelian account intellect must be intrinsic to human beings who have understanding since human beings are per se rational, something reflected in the definition of a human being as a rational animal. The doctrine that Agent Intellect and Material Intellect are ontologically extrinsic excludes their being intrinsic to the individual human thinker. Based on the analysis spelled out in detail by Aquinas, the account of Averroes must be considered confused and self-contradictory nonsense. In this case, however, Averroes is not working solely within that sort of Aristotelian framework detailed by Aquinas.

Averroes holds that the Agent Intellect is (i) "form for us," as (ii) intrinsic to the human soul, and yet also (iii) ontologically distinct in its own eternal existence. Further, the Agent Intellect is (iv) available to

---

after it came to be present in human beings and made to come about in them first the sensing part of the soul and the desiderative part by which the two natures of desire and aversion belong to the soul." (71–72) al-Fārābī's *The Political Regime (al-Siyāsa al-Madaniyya also known as the Treatise on the Principles of Beings)* Fauzi M. Najjar, ed. with introduction and notes (Beirut: Imprimerie Catholique, 1964), pp. 34–35. Averroes seems to understand al-Fārābī in this latter way.

In *The Perfect State* he writes, "Neither in the rational power nor in what nature provides (a'ṭī) is there something sufficient to become by itself an intellect in actuality. Rather, to become an intellect in actuality it needs something else **to transfer it** (yanqulu-hu) from potentiality to actuality. However, it becomes an intellect in actuality when the intelligibles arise in it. The intelligibles which are in potentiality become intelligibles in actuality when they come to be understood by the intellect in actuality. But they need something else **to transfer** them from potentiality to make them come to be in actuality. The agent which **transfers** them from potentiality to actuality is a certain essence the substance of which is a certain intellect in actuality and separate from matter. For this intellect provides (yu'ṭī) something like light to the material intellect which is in potentiality an intellect...." *al-Fārābī on the Perfect State. Ab Naṣr al-Fārābī's Arā' Ahl al-Madīna al-Fāḍila*, Richard Walzer, ed. and trans. (Oxford, 1985), 198–200. My emphasis.

I discuss the views of al-Fārābī in "Abstraction in al-Fārābī," *Proceedings of the American Catholic Philosophical Association* 80 (2006), pp. 151–168.

[46] For discussion of this, see my article "The Agent Intellect as 'form for us' and Averroes's Critique of al-Fārābī," cited in note 5 above.

INTELLECT AS INTRINSIC FORMAL CAUSE IN THE SOUL   209

us to be put in use by our will.[47] Elsewhere I have argued that this issue can be resolved if Averroes is understood to frame his understanding in light of his study of Themistius and notions from the Neoplatonic tradition found in Themistius.[48] In his *Paraphrase of the De Anima of Aristotle*, Themistius held that the actual intellect "has all the forms all together and presents all of them to itself at the same time" such that its essence is activity.[49] However, for Themistius the human actual intellect does not have of itself the intellectual power for abstraction but rather must be empowered by combining with, being taken over by, or being illuminated by the transcendent Productive or Agent Intellect in order to come to exist in the soul as united with the potential intellect.[50] Abstraction takes place when the Productive Intellect (Agent Intellect in the Arabic) penetrates and takes over the human actual intellect such that intelligibles in potency can be converted to intelligibles in

---

[47] For example, see LCDA, p. 439 quoted in note 29 above.

[48] See Taylor, "Intelligibles in act in Averroes," cited in note 5. There I identified the understanding of Themistius as Neoplatonic. While there is some support for holding influence from the Neoplatonic tradition, H. J. Blumenthal argues against that view in his "Themistius, the last Peripatetic commentator on Aristotle?", in *Arktouros, Hellenic Studies presented to Bernard M. W. Knox on the occasion of his 65th birthday*, Glen W. Bowersock et al., eds., (Berlin 1979), pp. 391–400, and also in a revised account under the same title in *Aristotle Transformed. The Ancient Commentators and Their Influence*, Richard Sorabji, ed., (Ithaca, 1990), pp. 113–123. In this latter version, Blumenthal adds a brief discussion of the arguments of E. P. Mahoney in favor identifying Neoplatonic language and notions in the thought of Themistius on the relationship of the human intellect and the transcendent Productive Intellect. See Mahoney's "Themistius and the agent intellect in James of Viterbo and other thirteenth-century philosophers," *Augustiniana* 23 (1973), pp. 423–67. For other articles by Mahoney touching on this issue, see Blumenthal (1990) pp. 119–121 and the notes there. I discuss the role of the *Paraphase of the De Anima* by Themistius in the thought of Averroes at greater length in "Themistius and the Development of Averroes' Noetics," in *Soul and Mind. Medieval Perspectives on Aristotle's De Anima* (Philosophes Médiévaux LII), J.-M. Counet & R. Friedman, ed. Peeters Publisher, Leuven (forthcoming).

[49] Themistius, *In Libros Aristotelis De Anima Paraphrasis*, R. Heinze (ed.). Berlin: G. Reimeri, 1899) [Commentaria in Aristotelem Graeca, 5.3], pp. 100.20–21; *Themistius, On Aristotle s On the Soul*, Robert B. Todd (trans.) (Ithaca, N.Y., 1996), p. 124. *An Arabic Translation of Themistius Commentary on Aristotle's De Anima*, M. C. Lyons (ed.), (Columbia, South Carolina, and Oxford, England, 1973), pp. 181.12–13. This may have also functioned as assuring that the abstractions made by individuals on the basis of sense perception and subsequent images formed in the soul are in accord with one another and the forms as in the Productive Intellect, though Themistius does not make mention of this.

[50] See Themistius Greek (1899), pp. 98.19–24, Themistius English (1996), p. 122, Themistius Arabic (1973), pp. 172–174; (1899), pp. 99.6–10, Themistius English (1996), p. 123, Themistius Arabic (1973), pp. 179.6–9; and (1899), pp. 103.30–33, Themistius English (1996), pp. 128–129, Themistius Arabic (1973), pp. 188.12–14.

210   RICHARD C. TAYLOR

act.[51] As indicated earlier, Averroes followed the tradition in holding that there is a single transcendent Agent Intellect and did not give serious consideration to the notion that each human being has his or her particular abstracting agent or actual intellect. Also unlike Themistius, Averroes does not consider the Agent Intellect to function as containing all forms.[52] Still, Averroes does find in Themistius this notion of the Agent Intellect functioning intrinsically in the human soul and describes this as the Agent Intellect acting as "form for us" in such as a way that it is not only an efficient cause in abstraction but is actually in us as form such that it is we who are abstracting and knowing thanks to its presence and activity intrinsic to the soul.[53]

The philosophical framework within which Averroes conceptualizes the Agent Intellect as "form for us" is one which permits a transcendent and extrinsic power of an essential sort (the power of intellectual

---

[51] Themistius writes that "...the productive intellect settles into the whole of the potential intellect, as though the carpenter and the smith did not control their wood and bronze externally but were able to pervade it totally. For this is how the actual intellect too is added to the potential intellect and becomes one with it." Themistius Greek (1899) 99.15–18; Themistius English (1996), p. 123; Themistius Arabic (1973), pp. 179.14–17.

[52] I take this to be the implication of the remarks of Themistius that (i) the potential intellect is moved to think only by an intellect that thinks all things, Themistius Greek (1899), pp. 103.31–32, Themistius English (1996), p. 128, Themistius Arabic (1973), pp. 188.12–13; (ii) "the intellect that illuminates in a primary sense is one" (1899), p. 103.32, Themistius English (1996), pp. 128–129; Themistius Arabic (1973), pp. 188.13–14; (iii) "we who are combined from the potential and the actual [intellects] are referred back to one productive intellect, and that what it is to be each of us is derived from that single [intellect]" (1899), pp. 103.36–38, Themistius English (1996), p. 129, Themistius Arabic (1973), pp. 188.18–189.1; (iv) "we would not understand one another unless there were a single intellect in which we all shared" (1899), pp. 104.2–3, Themistius English (1996), p. 129, Themistius Arabic (1973), p. 189.3; and (v) "divine intellect, which is separate and exists in actuality, thinks none of the enmattered forms" but thinks only separate forms "continuously and perpetually" (1899), pp. 114.34–115.9, Themistius English (1996), p. 141, Themistius Arabic (1973), pp. 209.16–210.10.

[53] LCDA, p. 445. Averroes seems to have read Themistius Greek (1899), pp. 99.11 ff., Themistius English (1996), pp. 123.25 ff., Themistius Arabic (1973), pp. 179.9 ff., as identifying the actual intellect with the Agent Intellect. For the Middle Commentary that seems clearly to be the case. See *Averroes. Middle Commentary on Aristotle's De Anima. A Critical Edition of the Arabic Text with English Translation, Notes and Introduction*, by Alfred L. Ivry, (Provo, Utah: Brigham Young University Press, 2002), pp. 117.8–10. There he writes, "You ought to know that Themistius and most commentators regard the intellect in us (*al-'aql alladhī finā*) as composed of the intellect which is in potency (*al-'aql bil-quwah*) and the intellect which is in act (*al-'aql alladhī bil-fi'l*), that is, the Agent Intellect (*[al-'aql] al-fa''āl*). In a certain way it is composite and does not think its essence but thinks what is here, when the imaginative intentions are joined to it. The intelligibles perish due to the passing away of these intentions, forgetting and error thus occurring to [our intellect]. They interpret Aristotle's statement in this manner, as explained in our commentary on his discourse."

INTELLECT AS INTRINSIC FORMAL CAUSE IN THE SOUL 211

abstraction and understanding) to be shared in an intrinsic way. Averroes, recognized and rejected for himself what he perceived to be Platonic elements in the thought of Themistius.[54] Yet Aristotle's account of the separate, unaffected, unmixed and essentially active Agent Intellect at *De anima* 3.5, 430a17–18 required that the Agent Intellect be intrinsic to the human soul as an essential part of the distinctive definition of human being. But the account which Averroes ultimately provides contains key components from Themistius, in particular (i) the essential combining, uniting, or sharing (scil., participating) of human intellect in the intellectual activity of the transcendent, external and ontologically distinct Agent Intellect in the activity of abstraction insofar as the Agent Intellect is "in the soul" and "form for us" such that we are active *by will* and essentially in the production of our own intellectual understanding, and (ii) the notion that there must be a single collection of intelligibles in act shared by all human beings. For Averroes the requirements that we be the agents in our thinking and that the power by which we think be intrinsic yielded the conclusion that the Agent Intellect must be present as our proper form for these activities to take place. That is, the very nature and actuality of the transcendent Agent Intellect must be shared or participated by us essentially in the fullness of its intellectual power for abstraction and understanding, though Averroes does not use the language of participation to describe this. In this quite different philosophical framework, the Aristotelian refutation by Aquinas, foundationally based on remarks by Averroes himself in his *Long Commentary on the De anima of Aristotle*, loses its efficacy for the refutation of Averroes.

3. *Aquinas's Understanding of Intellect as Intrinsic Formal Cause in the Arab Philosophers in His Early* Commentary on the Sentences of Peter Lombard

In the works of Aquinas cited thus far regarding the *Principle of Intrinsic Formal Cause*, there is no hint that Aquinas understood the

---

[54] *Et debes scire quod nulla differentia est secundum expositionem Themistii et antiquorum expositorum, et opinionem Platonis in hoc quod intellecta existentia in nobis sunt eterna, et quod addiscere est rememorari*: "You ought to know that there is no difference between the exposition of Themistius and the other ancient commentators and the opinion of Plato in regard to the fact that the intelligibles existing in us are eternal and that learning is recollection." LCDA, p. 452.

212   RICHARD C. TAYLOR

very different framework and conception of formal cause in which Averroes set forth his doctrine of the separate, eternal, and shared Agent Intellect and Material Intellect. Nevertheless, early in his career Aquinas displays a very clear understanding of the meaning of Averroes' assertions that Themistius and Theophrastus held in some fashion that the transcendent Agent Intellect is in human beings as form. In Book 2 of his *Commentary on the Sentences of Peter Lombard* Aquinas writes that Themistius and Theophrastus said that

> the intellect *in habitu* is, as it were, composed of the agent intellect and the possible [intellect] in such a way that the agent intellect is as the form [of the possible intellect] and through that conjoining with the possible intellect the agent intellect is also conjoined with us...Since, therefore, to abstract species from phantasms[55] is in our power, it is necessary that the agent intellect belong to the intellect *in habitu* as its form.[56]

Later in the same text, Aquinas writes that Averroes refutes their view as follows:

> [B]ecause it follows that the forms of natural things which are understood would exist from eternity without matter and outside the soul, hence

---

[55] *a phantasmatibus.* That is, by images of sensed things provided by the imagination.

[56] *Eorum autem qui ponunt unum intellectum possibilem in omnibus, duplex est opinio. Una est Themistii et Theophrasti, ut Commentator eis imponit in 3 de anima. Dicunt enim, quod intellectus in habitu, qui est tertius, est unus in omnibus, et aeternus,* **et est quasi compositus ex intellectu agente et possibili, ita quod intellectus agens est sicut forma ejus, et per continuationem intellectus possibilis continuatur etiam in nobis intellectus agens;** *ita quod intellectus agens est de substantia intellectus speculativi, qui etiam dicitur intellectus in habitu, per quem intelligimus: et hujusmodi signum inducunt, quia illa actio intellectus quae est in potestate nostra, pertinet ad intellectum in habitu. Cum ergo abstrahere species a phantasmatibus sit in potestate nostra, oportet quod intellectus agens sit intellectus in habitu* **sicut forma ejus.** *In 2 Sent*, d. 17, q. 2, a. 1, resp., Mandonnet, ed. (1929) pp. 424–425. The term *intellectus in habitu* corresponds to the Arabic *al-'aql bi-l-malakah* and denotes the positive disposition of intellect in a human being subsequent to abstraction.

"However, among those who set forth one possible intellect for all, there is a twofold opinion. One is that of Themistius and Theophrastus, as the Commentator imputes to them in Book 3 of [his *Commentary on*] *the De Anima*. For they say that the intellect *in habitu*, which is the third, is one for all and eternal and **is, as it were, composed of the agent intellect and the possible [intellect] in such a way that the agent intellect is as its form and through the conjoining of the possible intellect the agent intellect is conjoined also to us.** This is in such a way that the agent intellect is of the substance of the theoretical intellect which is also called the intellect *in habitu*, through which we understand. They bring forth as a sign of this sort of thing that that action of the intellect which is in our power pertains to the intellect *in habitu*. Since, therefore, to abstract species from phantasms is in our power, it is necessary that the agent intellect belong to the intellect in a positive disposition as its form." Emphasis added.

INTELLECT AS INTRINSIC FORMAL CAUSE IN THE SOUL   213

those species are not placed in the possible intellect as its form. [This is] because the form of the possible intellect is asserted by them to be the agent intellect.[57]

That is, Themistius and Theophrastus are wrong because they place the forms outside the human soul and in the agent intellect, thereby making it impossible for the human soul to have knowledge in itself. Further, since according to them, the initial perfection or actuality of each human being is through the presence of the possible intellect in each and the final perfection or actuality of each is through the development of the intellect *in habitu* in each, then the same existence and perfection would belong to all human beings. But that would mean that there would also be precisely one and the same ultimate perfection for each and every human being and no distinction between them.[58]

---

[57] *Sed hanc opinionem Commentator improbat: quia sequeretur quod formae rerum naturalium quae intelliguntur, essent ab aeterno sine materia, et extra animam, ex quo species illae non ponuntur in intellectu possibili ut forma ejus; quia forma intellectus possibilis ponitur ab eis intellectus agens. In 2 Sent*, d. 17, q. 2, a. 1, resp., Mandonnet, ed. (1929) p. 425.

[58] *Sequeretur etiam, cum ultima perfectio hominis sit secundum intellectum in habitu, et prima secundum intellectum possibilem, quod homo non differret ab homine neque secundum ultimam perfectionem neque secundum primam; et sic esset unum esse et una perfectio omnium hominum, quod est impossibile. In 2 Sent*, d. 17, q. 2, a. 1, resp., Mandonnet, ed. (1929) p. 425. Aquinas is here recounting the critique by Averroes at LCDA, pp. 392–393: *Et est secunda questio magis difficilis valde. Et est quod, si intellectus materialis est prima perfectio hominis, ut declaratur de diffinitione anime, et intellectus speculativus est postrema perfectio, homo autem est generabilis et corruptibilis et unus in numero per suam postremam perfectionem ab intellectu, necesse est ut ita sit per suam primam perfectionem, scilicet quod per primam perfectionem de intellectis sim alius a te, et tu alius a me (et si non, tu esses per esse mei, et ego per esse tui, et universaliter homo esset ens antequam esset, et sic homo non esset generabilis et corruptibilis in eo quod homo, sed, si fuerit, erit in eo quod animal). Existimatur enim quod, quemadmodum necesse est quod, si prima perfectio fuerit aliquid hoc et numerabilis per numerationem individuorum {393} ut postrema perfectio sit huiusmodi, ita etiam necesse est econtrario, scilicet quod, si postrema perfectio est numerata per numerationem individuorum hominum, ut prima perfectio sit huiusmodi.* "The second question is much more difficult. It is this: if the material intellect is the first actuality of a human being, as it is explained concerning the definition of the soul, and the theoretical intellect is the final actuality, but a human being is generable and corruptible and [yet also] one in number in virtue of his final actuality by the intellect, then it is necessary that he be so in virtue of his own first actuality. That is to say, [it must be the case] that I be other than you in virtue of the first actuality in reference to intelligibles and you be other than I. If not, you would exist in virtue of the being belonging to me and I would exist in virtue of the being belonging to you. Universally a human being would be a being before having existed, and so a human being would not be generable and corruptible inasmuch as he is a human being but, if he were [generable and corruptible], he will be [so] inasmuch as [he is] an animal. For it is thought that, just as it is necessary that the final actuality be of this sort if the first actuality will have been a determinate

214 RICHARD C. TAYLOR

Regarding the view of Averroes, Aquinas writes,

> He himself holds another view, that both the agent intellect and the possible intellect are eternal and one for all; but intelligible species are not eternal. He asserts that the agent intellect is not related to the possible intellect as its form, but as the craftsman to [his] material. The species understood and abstracted from phantasms are as the form of the possible intellect, from which the intellect in a positive disposition is acted upon by both.[59]

Here Aquinas is apparently referring to the following text in the *Long Commentary on the De Anima* by Averroes:

> Now he [Aristotle] gives the way on the basis of which it was necessary to assert the agent intelligence to be in the soul. For we cannot say that the relation of the agent intellect in the soul to the generated intelligible is just as the relation of the artistry to the art's product in every way. For art imposes the form on the whole matter without it being the case that there was something of the intention of the form existing in the matter before the artistry has made it. It is not so in the case of the intellect, for if it were so in the case of the intellect, then a human being would not need sense or imagination for apprehending intelligibles. Rather, the intelligibles would enter into the material intellect from the agent intellect, without the material intellect needing to behold sensible forms. And neither can we even say that the imagined intentions are solely what move the material intellect and draw it out from potency into act. For if it were so, then there would be no difference between the universal and the individual, and then the intellect would be of the genus of the imaginative power. Hence, in view of our having asserted that the relation of the imagined intentions {439} to the material intellect is just as the relation of the sensibles to the senses (as Aristotle will say later), it is necessary to suppose that there is another mover which makes [the intentions] move the material intellect in act (and this is nothing but to make [the intentions] intelligible in act by separating them from matter).[60]

---

particular and numerable the way individuals are, {393} so too it is necessary for the contrary, namely, that the first actuality be of this sort if the final actuality is numbered in virtue of the numbering of individual human beings."

[59] *Et ideo ipse tenet aliam viam, quod tam intellectus agens quam possibilis, est aeternus et unus in omnibus; sed species intelligibiles non sunt aeternae; et ponit quod intellectus agens non se habet ad possibilem ut forma ejus, sed ut artifex ad materiam; et species intellectae abstractae a phantasmatibus, sunt sicut forma intellectus possibilis, ex quibus duobus efficitur intellectus in habitu. In 2 Sent*, d. 17, q. 2, a. 1, resp., Mandonnet, ed., p. 425.

[60] *Modo dat modum ex quo oportuit ponere in anima intelligentiam agentem. Non enim possumus dicere quod proportio intellectus agentis in anima ad intellectum generatum est sicut proportio artificii ad artificiatum omnibus modis. Ars enim imponit formam in tota materia absque eo quod in materia sit aliquid existens de intentione*

INTELLECT AS INTRINSIC FORMAL CAUSE IN THE SOUL 215

As Aquinas understands it, Averroes here asserts that the Agent Intellect cannot be related to the possible or material intellect as form since what come to inform or to be the forms for the possible intellect are forms abstracted from phantasms. As Aquinas sees it, the concern of Averroes is the individuation of human knowers which in the context was not sufficiently accounted for by Theophrastus and Themistius as described by Aquinas's sole source, the account of their teachings in Averroes' *Long Commentary on the De Anima*.[61] While Aquinas does not accept the cogency of the account of Averroes,[62] he also seems not to attend to the purpose of Averroes here. The intention of Averroes in this passage, while related to the analysis of Themistius and Theophrasus, is also to spell out his own teaching that the transcendent Agent Intellect is "in the soul" as an abstractive power. On the analysis of Averroes, it is not right to think that the Agent Intellect directly supplies intelligibles in act since that would mean there is no need for sense or imagination. Nor are the potential intelligibles garnered by sense and imagination sufficient to provide the content of abstraction in the formation and apprehension of intelligibles in act. Thus, the Agent Intellect must be understood as supplying abstractive power and the individual human being (by way of sense, imagination, cogitation and memory)[63] as providing potentially intelligible images derived from sense. In this simile, the Agent Intellect is likened to artistry, e.g., the art of sculpture, the Material Intellect likened to the material, e.g., the clay, and the intelligibles in act received into the Material Intellect are likened to the

---

forme antequam artificium fecerit eam. Et non est ita in intellectu; quoniam, si ita esset in intellectu, tunc homo non indigeret, in comprehendendo intelligibilia, sensu neque ymaginatione; immo intellecta pervenirent in intellectum materialem ab intellectu agenti, absque eo quod intellectus materialis indigeret aspicere formas sensibiles. Neque etiam possumus dicere quod intentiones ymaginate sunt sole moventes intellectum materialem et extrahentes eum de potentia in actum; quoniam, si ita esset, tunc nulla differentia esset inter universale et individuum, et tunc intellectus esset de genere virtutis ymaginative. Unde necesse est, cum hoc quod posuimus quod proportio intentionum {439} ymaginatarum ad intellectum materialem est sicut proportio sensibilium ad sensus (ut Aristoteles post dicet), imponere alium motorem esse, qui facit eas movere in actu intellectum materialem (et hoc nichil est aliud quam facere eas intellectas in actu, abstrahendo eas a materia). LCDA, pp. 438–439.

[61] Averroes accounts for individuation by way of the particular cogitative power in each human being. See my discussions of this in "Remarks on Cogitatio in Averroes' *Commentarium Magnum in Aristotelis De Anima Libros*," in *Averroes and the Aristotelian Tradition: Sources, Constitution and Reception of the Philosophy of Ibn Rushd (1126–1198)*, Jan A. Aertsen and Gerhard Endress, eds., pp. 217–255. (Leiden, 1999).

[62] See *In 2 Sent*, d. 17, q. 2, a. 1, resp., pp. 426–427.

[63] See LCDA, pp. 416–417; 449; and 476.

216   RICHARD C. TAYLOR

shape placed into the clay through the art of sculpture. In this context,
then, the Agent Intellect functions "in the soul" as formal cause or the
power of the abstraction without supplying the intentions which make
up the quidditative or intentional content of the intelligibles received
into the Material Intellect.[64] The analogy is imperfect, however, since

---

[64] As I argue in my article "Intelligibles in Act in Averroes" cited in note 5 above, the
way in which Averroes conceives intelligibles in act is central in his development of his
mature doctrine of the intellect, in particular the doctrine of the single, shared Material
Intellect. The understanding of intelligibles in act on the part of Aquinas is altogether
different from that of Averroes right from the time of the writing of the *Commentary on
the Sentences*. For the mature Averroes of the LCDA, the intelligibles in act cannot be
in particular intellects because they would then be individuated intelligibles in potency,
not intelligibles in act. As such, this was a central concern of Averroes contributing to
his assertion of the single Material Intellect shared by all human beings. In contrast,
Aquinas found this concern to be misplaced since he held that individuation is not a
threat to intelligibility in individual human intellects. Later at *In 4 Sent.*, d. 49, q. 2,
a. 1, resp., Aquinas states, *Non enim forma existens in intellectu vel sensu, est principium
cognitionis secundum modum essendi quem habet utrobique, sed secundum rationem
in qua communicat cum re exteriori.* "The form existing in the intellect or in the sense
is not the principle of knowing according to the being it has in each, but according
to the *ratio* in which it shares with the exterior thing." Thus, for Aquinas even in this
early work the *species* by which human beings have intellectual understanding are to
be understood as *rationes* with quidditative content derived from sense experience
and yet as having differing modes of being in sense or in intellect. The Latin texts I
use here for *In 4 Sent.* are from the 1858 Parma edition in the *Corpus Thomisticum*
prepared by Robert Busa, S.J., made available by Enrique Alarcon in his collection of
the works of Aquinas at http://www.corpusthomisticum.org/.
Here at *In 2 Sent*, d. 17, q. 2, a. 1, ad 3, Mandonnet, ed. (1929) pp. 429–430, the
very different conception of Aquinas is set forth clearly:
*Ad tertium dicendum, quod secundum Avicennam species intellecta potest dupliciter
considerari: aut secundum esse quod habet in intellectu, et sic habet esse singulare; aut
secundum quod est similitudo talis rei intellectae, prout ducit in cognitionem ejus; et ex
hac parte habet universalitatem: quia non est similitudo hujus rei secundum quod haec
res est, sed secundum naturam in qua cum aliis suae speciei convenit. Nec oportet omne
singulare esse intelligibile tantum in potentia (sicut patet de substantiis separatis), sed
in illis quae individuantur per materiam, sicut sunt corporalia: sed species istae individuantur per individuationem intellectus; unde non perdunt esse intelligibile in actu; sicut
intelligo me intelligere, quamvis ipsum meum intelligere sit quaedam operatio singularis.
Patet etiam per se, quod secundum inconveniens non sequitur: quia alius individuationis
modus est per intellectum et per materiam primam.*
"To the third it should be said that according to Avicenna the understood species
is able to be understood in a twofold way: either according to the being it has in the
intellect, and in this way it has singular being; or according as it is a likeness of some
understood thing, so that it leads to its cognition. From this [latter] part it has univer-
sality because it is not a likeness of this particular thing insofar as it is this particular
thing but rather according to the nature in which agrees with others of its species. Nor
is it necessary that every singular be intelligible only in potency (as is clear regarding
separate substances), but rather [that is only] in the case of those which are individuated by matter, as are corporeal things. But those species are individuated through the
individuation of the intellect. Hence, they do not cease to be intelligible in act [because

INTELLECT AS INTRINSIC FORMAL CAUSE IN THE SOUL   217

a particular artist observes a particular subject and places a particular image into the particular clay, thereby crafting a particular work of art. In the case of the Agent Intellect, the images in the imagination are "transferred," so to speak, from their mode being as particular imagined intentions to a new mode of being as intelligibles in act.[65] Furthermore, the subject for these, the Material Intellect, is not itself a determinate particular but rather an immaterial entity and a unique species, not a member of a species.[66] However, in another passage in the *Commentary on the Sentences*, Aquinas displays a fuller understanding of the notion of separate intellect as form for human intellect in the course of exploring whether that model from the Greek and Arabic traditions can be suitably employed in understanding how there can be vision of God in the next life.[67]

At *In 4 Sent.*, d. 49, q. 2, a. 1, Aquinas confronts the question of "Whether the human intellect is able to attain to the vision of God in his essence." In his response Aquinas cites teachings of Avicenna and the pseudo-Augustinian *Liber de videndum Deum* and draws on the accounts in the *Long Commentary on the De Anima* by Averroes to cite the teachings of al-Fārābī, Avempace (Ibn Bājja), Alexander, and Averroes. In considering the latter two thinkers, Aquinas suggests that the model of the separate intellect as form for human intellect provides the most valuable way for understanding the vision of God in His essence. He writes that "the form by which the intellect is brought to see separate substances...is the separate substance itself which is conjoined to our intellect as form, so that it is what is understood and that by which it is understood." The acceptance of this model by

---

of that], as I understand that I understand, although my very understanding is some singular operation. It is also evident in itself that the second unsuitable consequence does not follow, because the mode of individuation by intellect is different from that by prime matter." That is, intelligibles received into an intellect are not particularized by their subject, as Averroes believed. This is key to the understanding of Aquinas and perhaps the most important fundamental principle over which Aquinas and Averroes disagree. Regarding this, see pp. 172–175 my article, "Averroes' Epistemology and Its Critique by Aquinas."

[65] On this see the text cited in note 38. Cf. the texts of al-Fārābī cited in note 45.

[66] For Averroes this allows the intelligibles in act to retain their natures as immaterial and unique without being individuated by their subject. On this notion, see pp. 298–299 of my article, "Separate Material Intellect in Averroes' Mature Philosophy."

[67] That issue was mentioned in passing by Aquinas at *In 2 Sent*, d. 17, q. 2, a. 1, resp., 423, where he wrote *uniri cum intelligentia agente ponunt praedicti philosophi ultimam felicitatem hominis.* "The philosophers mentioned earlier asserted that the ultimate happiness of human beings is to be united with the agent intellect."

218   RICHARD C. TAYLOR

Aquinas is clear when he writes, "Whatever is the case for other separate substances, nevertheless, we must accept that mode in the vision of God in His essence."[68] He then adds that this should be understood to come about

> because the relation of the divine essence to our intellect is as the relation of form to matter. For whenever there are some two things of which one is more perfect than the other and these are received in the same recipient, there is a relation of one of the two to the other, namely of the more perfect to the less perfect, as is the relation of form to matter. [This is] just as when light and color are received in the diaphanous [medium] for which light is related to color as form to matter. Similarly, when the intellective power is received in the soul and the divine essence itself is present although not in the same mode, the divine essence is related to the intellect as form to matter.[69]

For Aquinas this is an acceptable way of understanding how the presence of the divine essence may enhance and enable the human intellect but it requires a qualification which he provides just before the quotation immediately above. That qualification is as follows: "This ought not to be understood as if the divine essence is the true form of our intellect or that out of this and our intellect simply one thing is made, as in natural things made from natural form and matter."[70] That is, it is not the case that the divine essence comes to be form for us in the full sense that it comes to be our intrinsic and essential human form productive of the actuality of reason characteristic of the human species, as Averroes had it. Rather, one can consider the intelligible species as form to the intellect in potency as matter with the result that "the intel-

---

[68] *Et quidquid sit de aliis substantiis separatis, tamen istum modum oportet nos accipere in visione Dei per essentiam. In 4 Sent.*, d. 49, q. 2, a. 1, resp.

[69] *...quia proportio essentiae divinae ad intellectum nostrum est sicut proportio formae ad materiam. Quandocumque enim aliqua duo, quorum unum est perfectius altero, recipiuntur in eodem receptibili, proportio unius duorum ad alterum; scilicet magis perfecti ad minus perfectum, est sicut proportio formae ad materiam; sicut lux et color recipiuntur in diaphano, quorum lux se habet ad colorem sicut forma ad materiam; et ita cum in anima recipiatur vis intellectiva, et ipsa essentia divina inhabitans, licet non per eumdem modum, essentia divina se habebit ad intellectum sicut forma ad materiam. In 4 Sent.*, d. 49, q. 2, a. 1, resp. Regarding this explanation and the controversy it generated after his death, see J.-B. Brenet, "Vision béatifique et séparation de l'intellect au début du XIVe siècle. Pour Averroès ou contre Thomas d'Aquin?," *Freiburger Zeitschrift für Philosophie und Theologie* 53 (2006), pp. 310–344.

[70] *...quod quidem non debet intelligi quasi divina essentia sit vera forma intellectus nostri, vel quod ex ea et intellectu nostro efficiatur unum simpliciter, sicut in naturalibus ex forma et materia naturali. In 4 Sent.*, d. 49, q. 2, a. 1, resp.

INTELLECT AS INTRINSIC FORMAL CAUSE IN THE SOUL 219

lect understanding in act will be as it were composed of both. Hence, if there is some thing subsisting per se which does not have anything in it except what is intelligible in itself, such a thing is able per se to be a form by which it is understood."[71] That is, something immaterial and wholly intelligible per se in its essence, when understood, is itself that in virtue of which it is understood without there being any need for any intermediary activity of abstraction from sense or imagination. In the case of God, "since the divine essence is pure act, it will be able to be a form by which the intellect understands, and this will be the beatific vision."[72]

For Aquinas the notion of the abstracted immaterial intelligibles in act coming to be understood as forms for the human intellect found in Averroes was both valuable as an account of the intelligible species present in the human intellect and as a model for explaining how God could be present as form aiding the human intellect in seeing God in his essence. Yet, while employing some of the ideas and language of Averroes, this was far from the doctrine of Averroes that the Agent Intellect comes to be *form for us* in the very moment of intellectual abstraction and understanding that takes place in human intellectual knowing. That is, to use the words of Aquinas, for Averroes the Agent Intellect comes to be "the true form of our intellect," something altogether unacceptable to Aquinas on the basis of his understanding of the *Principle of Intrinsic Formal Cause.*

4. Conclusion

The *Principle of Intrinsic Formal Cause* served Aquinas well in his critique of Averroes, as we have seen in the passages I cited earlier. But that critique succeeds only if Averroes is working solely in the Aristotelian framework as conceived by Aquinas. However, driven by philosophical considerations rising to significance in his mature study of Themistius, Averroes took advantage of models and insights from Themistius. On the view of Averroes, at the heart of the *Principle of*

---

[71] *[I]ntellectus in actu intelligens erit quasi compositum ex utroque. Unde si sit aliqua res per se subsistens quae non habeat aliquid in se praeter id quod est intelligibile in ipsa, talis res per se poterit esse forma qua intelligitur. In 4 Sent.*, d. 49, q. 2, a. 1, resp.

[72] *[C]um essentia divina sit actus purus, poterit esse forma qua intellectus intelligit; et hoc erit visio beatificans. In 4 Sent.*, d. 49, q. 2, a. 1, resp.

220   RICHARD C. TAYLOR

Intrinsic Formal Cause is the assertion that what is essential to human intellectual understanding—the abstractive power of the Agent Intellect itself—cannot remain only transcendent but must also be intrinsically present in the individual human soul, and not in an accidental or incidental fashion. According to the account of Aquinas using the same principle, it was necessary that what is truly essential to human intellectual understanding—the abstractive power of the agent intellect itself—must be intrinsically present in the human soul and cannot at the same time exist separately and extrinsically. On the basis of the texts and arguments examined here, it appears that Aquinas' understanding of the teaching of Averroes on the Agent Intellect as *form for us* was only partial. Had he understood fully, there can be no doubt but that he would have rejected it as discordant with Aristotelian principles. Still, what was at issue between Averroes and Aquinas has yet to be resolved with consensus among scholars of Aristotelian thought today, namely, just how Aristotle meant "in the soul" in describing the apparently transcendent yet immanent agent intellect in *De Anima* 3.5. On this point the views of Aquinas that the agent intellect is a power multiplied in individual human souls diverged from the dominant view of the philosophers of the Greek and Arabic traditions who held there to be a single transcendent intellect Agent shared by all human knowers in the activity of abstraction and intellectual understanding.[73]

---

[73] This paper is a product of the "Aquinas and the Arabs" Project at Marquette University. In preparing it I benefitted from valuable suggestions from my Marquette colleague, David Twetten, and from Peter Adamson of King's College London, for which I am glad to express my thanks here. I must also thank Marquette University Philosophy Department graduate students Nathan Blackerby, Fuad Rahmat, Joseph Kranak for their careful readings of this paper.

BIBLIOGRAPHY

A. *Primary Texts*

'Abd al-Jabbār, Abū al-Ḥasan, *Al-Mughnī fī Abwāb al Tawḥīd wa al-'Adl*, (Cairo, 1960–68).
Aeneas of Gaza, *Teofrasto*, ed. M. E. Colonna (Naples, 1958).
Al-Kindī, *Rasā'il al-Kindī al-Falsafiyya*, ed. M. Abū Rīda, 2 vols (Cairo, 1950/1953).
Anastasius Sinaita, *viae dux*, ed. K. H. Uthemann (Corpus Christianorum. Series Graeca, 8, Turnhout, 1981).
Aquinas, Thomas, *Compendium theologiae*. (Rome, 1979). [*S. Thomae de Aquino Opera Omnia Iussu Leonis XIII P.M. edita Cura et studio Fratrum Praedicatorum* Tomus XLII].
——, *Corpus Thomisticum* prepared by Robert Busa, S.J., made available by Enrique Alarcon in his collection of the works of Aquinas at http://www.corpusthomisticum.org/.
——, *De spiritualibus creaturis*, J. Cos, ed. Rome: Commissio Leonina, (Paris, 2000). [*S. Thomae de Aquino Opera Omnia Iussu Leonis XIII P.M. edita Cura et studio Fratrum Praedicatorum* Tomus XXIV, 2].
——, *De unitate intellectus contra Averroistas*. Roma, Editori di San Tommaso, 1976. [Sancti Thomae de Aquino Opera Omnia Iussu Leonis XIII P.M. edita cura et studio Fratrum Praedicatorum, t. XLIII]. Translated in Ralph McInerny, *Aquinas Against the Averroists: On There Being Only One Intellect*, (Indiana, 1993).
——, *Quaestiones Disputatae De Anima*, B.-C. Bazán, ed. Rome, Commissio Leonina, (Paris, 1996). [S. Thomae de Aquino Opera Omnia *Iussu Leonis XIII P.M. edita Cura et studio Fratrum Praedicatorum* Tomus XXIV, 1].
——, *Sancti Thomae Aquinatis Commentum in secundum librum Sententiarum Magistri Petri Lombardi*, ed. P. Mandonnet, (Paris, 1929).
——, *Sentencia libri de anima* (*Opera omnia*, XLV, 1) R. A. Gauthier, ed. Rome, Commissio Leonina; (Paris, 1984). [S. Thomae de Aquino Opera Omnia *Iussu Leonis XIII P.M. edita Cura et studio Fratrum Praedicatorum* Tomus XLV, 1].
——, *Summa contra gentiles* (Rome: Typis Riccardi Garroni, 1918) [*S. Thomae de Aquino Opera Omnia Iussu Leonis XIII P.M. edita Cura et studio Fratrum Praedicatorum* Tomus XIII].
——, *Summa Theologiae*, ed. Commissio Piana. (Collège Dominicain d'Ottawa, Ottawa, Canada, 1953).
Aristotle, *The Complete Works of Aristotle. The Revised Oxford Translation*, ed. Jonathan Barnes, 2 vol. (Princeton, 1984).
Augustine, *Soliloquies and Immortality of the Soul*, with an introduction, translation and commentary by G. Watson (Warminster, 1990).
——, *De Genesi ad litteram*, ed. J. Zycha, CSEL 28/1. Wien 1894 *passim*.
——, *De Trinitate*, eds. François Glorie and William J. Mountain, CCSL 32. (Turnhout, 1968).
Averroes (Ibn Rushd), *Averrois Cordubensis Commentarium Magnum in Aristotelis De Anima Libros*, ed. F. Stuart Crawford, (Cambridge, MA, 1953).
——, *Averroes. Middle Commentary on Aristotle's De Anima. A Critical Edition of the Arabic Text with English Translation, Notes and Introduction*, ed. Alfred L. Ivry. (Provo, Utah, 2002).
Avicenna (Ibn Sīnā), *Kitāb Aḥwāl al-Nafs*, ed. Aḥmad Fū'ād al-Ahwānī (Cairo, 1952).
——, *Al-Shifā': Al-Ṭabī'iyyāt*, Vol. 6: *Al-Nafs*, eds. G. C. Anawātī and S. Zayed. Rev. Ibrahīm Madkour, (Cairo, 1975).

222 BIBLIOGRAPHY

Basil of Caesarea, *Homélies sur l'Hexaéméron*. Introduction, texte grec, traduction et notes par St. Giet, Sources Chrétiennes, 26bis, (Paris, 1968).

Bernard of Chartres, *The Glosae super Platonem of Bernard of Chartres*, ed. P. E. Dutton (Toronto, 1991).

Damascius *Successoris, Dubitationes et solutiones de primis principiis, in Platonis Parmenidem*, II, ed. C. E. Ruelle (Paris, 1889, repr. Amsterdam, 1966).

Dionysius Aeropagita, *Corpus Dionysiacum*, I: *Pseudo-Dionysius Areopagita, De divinis nominibus*, ed. B. R. Suchla, (Patristische Texte und Studien, 33, Berlin, New York, 1990).

Eriugena, Johannes Scottus, *Periphyseon*, Books I–V, ed. Édouard Jeauneau, CCCM 161–5. (Turnhout: Brepols, 1996–2001) (Trans. I. P. Sheldon-Williams, Books IV–V revised by J. J. O'Meara. *Periphyseon*, Montreal and Washington, 1987), Book III, 728A–B, pp. 156–57.

Al-Fārābī, *Risāla fī al-ʿAql*, ed. M. Bouyges, (Beirut, 1938).

——, *al-Fārābī's The Political Regime (al-Siyāsa al-Madaniyya also known as the Treatise on the Principles of Beings)* ed. Fauzī M. Najjār, (Beirut, 1964).

al-Ghazālī, Abū Ḥamid, *Tahāfut al-Falāsifa*, ed. S. Donīa, (Cairo, 1972).

——, *The Alchemy of Happiness*, trans. Claud Field and E. L. Daniel, (London, 1980).

Gregory of Nazianzus, *Discours 27–31 (Discours Théologiques)*. Introduction, texte grec, traduction et notes par P. Gallay (Sources Chrétiennes, 250, Paris, 1978).

Halevi, Judah, (Hebrew) In *Religion and Knowledge: Essays and Lectures*, eds. S. H. Bergman and N. Rotenstreich, (Jerusalem, 1955).

——, *Kitāb al-Radd wa al-Dalīl fī al-Dīn al-Dhalīl*, eds. David H. Baneth and Haggai Ben-Shammai, (Jerusalem, 1977).

——, *Le Kuzari: Apologie de la religion méprisée*, (Paris, 1994).

Iamblichus, *On the Mysteries*; ed. E. Des Places, Jamblique. Les Mysteres d'Egypt, (Paris, 1989).

Ibn Ezra, Abraham, *Commentary to the Torah*, ed. Asher Weiser, (Jerusalem, 1977).

——, *Sefer Yesod Mora ve sod ha-torah*, in *The Ibn Erza Reader*, ed. Israel Levin, (Tel Aviv, 1985).

Ikhwān al-Ṣafāʾ, *Rasāʾil Ikhwān al-Ṣafāʾ*, 4 vols, (Beirut, no date).

Johannes Philoponus, *Ioannis Philoponi De aeternitate mundi et contra Proclum*, ed. Rabe, H., (Leipzig, 1899).

Al-Jāḥiẓ, *Kitāb al-Tarbīʿ waʾl-Tadwīr*, ed. Charles Pellai, (Damascus, 1955).

Johannes von Damasko, *Die Schriften des Johannes von Damaskos*, II: *Expositio Fidei*, ed. B. Kotter (Patristische Texte und Studien, 12, Berlin, New York, 1973).

——, *Die Schriften des Johannes von Damaskos*, IV: *Liber de haeresibus. Opera Polemica*, ed. B. Kotter (Patristische Texte und Studien, 22, Berlin, New York, 1981).

Justin Martyr, *Dialogue with Trypho. (An early Christian philosopher) Chapters one to nine*, Introduction, Text and Commentary by J. C. M. van Winden, *Philosophia Patrum*, 1, (Leiden, 1971).

Maimonides, *Guide of the Perplexed*, trans. S. Pines, (Chicago, 1963).

Maximus the Confessor, PG 91:1084C, 1113B, 1385BC; Maximi Confessoris *Ambigua ad Iohannem iuxta Iohannis Scotti Eriugenae latinam interpretationem*, ed. Jeauneau, É., CCSG 18 (Turnhout, 1988), p. 31, pp. 48–9, p. 238.

Nemesius of Emesa, *De natura hominis*, ed. M. Morani, (Leipzig, 1987).

Origen, *De principiis*. Traité des principes: (Peri archon) Origène; traduction de la version latine de Rufin, avec un dossier annexe d'autres témoins du texte, par M. Harl, G. Dorival, A. Le Boulluec, (Paris, 1976).

Photius, *Bibliothèque*, ed. and trans. R. Henry, II (Paris, 1960).

Plato, *The Republic*, trans. Desmond Lee, 2nd rev. edn., (Harmondsworth/London, 1987).

Plotinus, *Über Ewigkeit und Zeit*, trans. and comm. W. Beierwaltes (Frankfurt, 1967).

BIBLIOGRAPHY   223

Proclus, *Diadochi In Platonis Timaeum Commentaria*, II, ed. E. Diehl (Leipzig, 1904).
Al-Rāzī, Fakhr al-Dīn, *al-Maṭālib al-ʿĀliyya*, (Beirut, 1999).
——, *al-Arbaʿīn fī Uṣūl al-Dīn*, (Beirut, 2004).
——, *al-Mabāḥith al-Mashriqiyya*, (Teheran, 1966).
——, *al-Rūḥ wa al-Nafs*, (Beirut, 1974).
Themistius, *In Libros Aristotelis De Anima Paraphrasis*, ed. R. Heinze, (Berlin, 1899). [Commentaria in Aristotelem Graeca, 5.3], pp. 100.20–21.
——, *On Aristotle's On the Soul*, trans. Robert B. Todd, (Ithaca, N.Y. 1996).
——, *An Arabic Translation of Themistius Commentary on Aristotle's De Anima*, ed. M. C. Lyons, (Columbia, South Carolina, and Oxford, 1973).
William of Conches, *Glosae super Platonem*, ed. É. Jeauneau (Paris, 1965).
Zacharias Scholasticus, *Ammonio. Introduzione, testo critico, traduzione, commentario*, ed. M. Minniti Colonna (Naples, 1973).

B. *Secondary Sources*

Adamson, P., "Vision, Light and Color in al-Kindī, Ptolemy and the Ancient Commentators," *Arabic Sciences and Philosophy* 16 (2006), pp. 207–236.
——, *Al-Kindī* (New York, 2007).
Amīn, Aḥmad, ed., *Ḥayy B. Yaqẓān li Ibn Sīnā wa Ibn Ṭufayl wa'l Suhrawardī, Dhakhā'ir al-Arab*, no. 8, (Cairo, 1952).
Annas, J., *Platonic Ethics, Old and New* (Cornell Studies in Classical Philology 57), Ithaca, (New York, 1999).
Armstrong, A. H., *The Cambridge History of Later Greek and Early Medieval Philosophy*, (Cambridge, 1979).
Arnaldez, R., "Insān." Encyclopaedia of Islam 2. (Brill online, 2008).
Arnzen, R., *Aristoteles' De Anima. Eine verlorene spätantike Paraphrase in arabischer und persischer Überlieferung*, (Leiden, 1998).
Bazán, Bernardo Carlos, "13th Century Commentaries on *De Anima*: From Peter of Spain to Thomas Aquinas", in *Commento Filosofico nell Occidente Latino (secoli XIII–XV)*, eds. Gianfranco Fioravanti, Claudio Leonardi and Stephano Perfetti, (Turnhout, 2002), pp. 119–184.
——, "Conceptions of the Agent Intellect and the Limits of Metaphysics," in *Nach der Verurteilung von 1277: Philosophie und Theologie an der Universität von Paris im letzten Viertel des 13. Jahrhunderts: Studien und Texte. After the condemnation of 1277: philosophy and theology at the University of Paris in the last quarter of the thirteenth century: studies and texts*, eds. Jan A. Aertsen, Kent Emery, and Andreas Speer, (*Miscellanea Mediaevalia* 28), (Berlin and New York, 2001) pp. 178–210.
——, "*Intellectum Speculativum*: Averroes, Thomas Aquinas, and Siger of Brabant on the Intelligible Object," *Journal of the History of Philosophy* 19 (1981), pp. 425–446.
——, "La Noetica de Averroes (1126–1198)," in *Philosophia* 38 (1972), pp. 19–49.
——, "The Human Soul: Form and Substance? Thomas Aquinas' Critique of Eclectic Aristotelianism," *Archives d'histoire doctrinale et litteraire du moyen âge* 64 (1997), pp. 95–126.
Beck, H., *Vorsehung und Vorherbestimmung in der theologischen Literatur der Byzantiner* (Orientalia Christiana Analecta, 114, Rome, 1937).
Beierwaltes, W., *Platonismus im Christentum* (Frankfurt am Main, 1998), idem, *Denken des Einen. Studien zur neuplatonischen Philosophie und ihrer Wirkungsgeschichte* (Frankfurt am Main, 1985).
——, *Identität und Differenz* (Frankfurt am Main, 1980).
——, & R. Kannicht, 'Plotin-Testimonia bei Johannes von Skythopolis', *Hermes*, 96 (1968), pp. 247–251.

224 BIBLIOGRAPHY

Berger, Michael S., "Towards a New Understanding of Judah Halevi's *Kuzari*." *Religion* 72.2 (1992), pp. 210–228.

Betz, H. D., "The Concept of the "Inner Human Being" (o(e)/sw a)/nqrwpoj) in the Anthropology of Paul', *New Testament Studies* 46.3 (2000), pp. 315–341.

El-Bizri, O. Nader, ed., *The Ikhwān al-Ṣafāʾ and their Rasāʾil: An Introduction*, (Oxford, 2008).

Black, Debora, "Al-Fārābī" in *History of Islamic Philosophy*, eds. Nasr and Leaman (London, 1997), pp. 178–97.

——, review of Ralph McInerny, *Aquinas Against the Averroists: On There Being Only One Intellect*. (West Lafayette, Indiana: Purdue University Press, 1993). *Review of Metaphysics* 49 (1995), pp. 147–48.

——, "Consciousness and Self-Knowledge in Aquinas's Critique of Averroes's Psychology," Journal of the History of Philosophy 31 (1993), pp. 349–385.

——, "Memory, Individuals, and the Past in Averroes's Psychology", in *Medieval Philosophy and Theology* 5 (1996), pp. 161–187.

——, "Conjunction and the Identity of Knower and Known in Averroes," in *American Catholic Philosophical Quarterly* 73 (1999), pp. 159–184.

——, "Models of Mind: Metaphysical Presuppositions of the Averroist and Thomistic Accounts of Intellection," in *Documenti e studi sulla tradizione filosofica medievale* 15 (2004), pp. 319–352.

Blumenthal, H. J., "Themistius, the last Peripatetic commentator on Aristotle?", in *Arktouros, Hellenic Studies presented to Bernard M. W. Knox on the occasion of his 65th birthday*, ed. Glen W. Bowersock et al., (Berlin 1979), pp. 391–400. Blumenthal also presents a revised account under the same title in *Aristotle Transformed. The Ancient Commentators and Their Influence*, ed. Richard Sorabji, (Ithaca, 1990), pp. 113–123.

Brann, Ross, *The Compunctious Poet: Cultural Ambiguity and Hebrew Poetry in Muslim Spain*, (Baltimore, 1991).

——, *Power in the Portrayal: Representations of Jews and Muslims in Eleventh- and Twelfth-Century Spain*, (Princeton, 2002).

Brenet, Jean-Baptiste, *Transferts du sujet: la noétique d'Averroès selon Jean de Jandun*, (Paris, 2003).

——, "Vision béatifique et séparation de l'intellect au début du XIVe siècle. Pour Averroès ou contre Thomas d'Aquin?," in *Freiburger Zeitschrift für Philosophie und Theologie*, 53 (2006), pp. 310–344.

Brock, S., "The Syriac Commentary Tradition," in *Burnett* (1993), pp. 3–18.

Burkert, W., "Towards Plato and Paul: The 'Inner' Human Being", in *Ancient and Modern Perspectives on the Bible and Culture. Essays in Honor of Hans Dieter Betz*, ed. A. Y. Collins, (Atlanta, 1998), pp. 59–82.

Burnett, C., ed., *Glosses and Commentaries on Aristotelian Logical Texts: the Syriac, Arabic and Medieval Latin Traditions*, (London, 1993).

Clark, E. A., *The Origenist controversy: the cultural construction of an early Christian debate* (Princeton, N.J., 1992).

Cohen, Mark R., *Under Crescent and Cross: The Jews in the Middle Ages*, (Princeton, 1994).

Colish, M. L., *The Stoic Tradition. From Antiquity to the Early Middle Ages. II: Stoicism in Christian Latin thought through the sixth century*, (Studies in the History of Christian Thought, 35, Leyden, 1985).

Courcelle, P., *Connais-toi toi-même, de Socrate à saint Bernard*, (Paris, 1974–1975).

——, *Recherches sur saint Ambroise: "vies" anciennes, culture, iconographie*, (Paris, 1973).

——, *Recherches sur les Confessions de saint Augustin*, (Paris, 1968), idem, *La consolation de philosophie dans la tradition littéraire*, (Paris, 1967).

Courtonne, Y., *Saint Basile et l'Hellénisme*, (Paris, 1934).

BIBLIOGRAPHY 225

Dillon, J., *The Middle Platonists: A Study of Platonism 80 B.C. to A.D. 220*, Revised ed. with new afterword, (London, 1996 (1977¹)).
——, 'Plutarch and the Separable Intellect', in *Estudios sobre Plutarco: Misticismo y Religiones Mistéricas en la Obra de Plutarco*, eds. A. Pérez Jiménez & F. Casadesús, (Madrid-Málaga, 2001), pp. 35–44.
——, '*Asómatos*: Nuances of Incorporeality in Philo', in *Philon d'Alexandrie et le langage de la philosophie*, ed. Carlos Lévy. (Turnhout, 1998).
——, 'How does the Soul direct the Body, after all? Traces of a Dispute on Mind-Body Relations in the Old Academy', in *Leib und Seele in der antiken Philosophie*, eds. Dorothea Frede & Burkhart Reis, (Berlin/New York, 2009).
Dunn, J. D. G., *The Theology of Paul the Apostle*, (Edinburgh, 1998).
Elkaisy-Friemuth, Maha. *God and Humans in Islamic Thought*, (London, 2006).
——, 'al-Rūḥ wa al-Nafs', in *Encyclopaedia of Islamic Religion and Culture*, ed. I. R. Netton (London, 2007).
Engberg-Pedersen, T., "The Reception of Graeco-Roman Culture in the New Testament: The Case of Romans 7.7–25", in *The New Testament as Reception*, eds. M. Müller & H. Tronier, (Journal for the Study of the New Testament Supplement Series 230; Copenhagen International Seminar 11), (London, 2002), pp. 32–57.
Festugière, A. J., *L'idéal religieux des grecs et l'évangile* (Études bibliques), 2nd ed. (Paris, 1932).
Frank, R. M., *Beings and Their Attributes: The teaching of the Basrian School of the Mu'tazila in the Classical Period*, Studies in Islamic Philosophy and Science, (Albany, New York, 1978).
——, "The use of the Enneads by John of Skythopolis", in *Le Muséon*, 100 (1988), pp. 101–108.
Gatti, Maria Luisa, "Plotinus: The Platonic Tradition and the Foundation of Neoplatonism", In *The Cambridge Companion to Plotinus*, ed. Lloyd P. Gerson, (Cambridge, 1996).
Geoffroy, Marc, "Averroès sur l'intellect comme cause agent et cause formelle, et la question de la 'jonction'—I," in *Averroès et les averroïsmes juif et latin. Actes du colloque tenu à Paris, 16–18 juin 2005*, ed. J.-B. Brenet, (Turnhout, 2007) pp. 77–110.
Georr, K., *Les Catégories d'Aristote dans leurs versions syro-arabes*, (Beirut: 1948).
Gersh, Stephen, *From Iamblichus to Eriugena: an Investigation of the Prehistory and Evolution of the Pseudo-Dionysian Tradition*, (Leiden, 1978).
Gerson, Lloyd P., *Aristotle and Other Platonists*, (Ithaca, 2005).
Goitein, Shlomo Dov, *A Mediterranean Society*, 5 Vols, (Berkeley, 1988).
——, "The Biography of Rabbi Judah ha-Levi in Light of the Cairo Genizah Documents." *Proceedings of the American Academy of Jewish Research* 28 (1959), pp. 41–56.
Goldstein, David, *The Jewish Poets of Spain, 900–1250*, (Harmondsworth, 1971).
Goodman, L., *Avicenna*, (New York and London, 1992).
Gottheil, R. J. H., "The Syriac Versions of the *Categories* of Aristotle," in *Hebraica* 9 (1892–3), pp. 166–215.
Greive, Hermann, *Studies zum jüdischen Neuplatonismus: Die Religionsphilosophie des Abraham ibn Ezra*, (Berlin, 1973).
Grillmeier, A., Th. Hainthaler (trans. O. C. Dean), Christ in Christian Tradition, II: From the Council of Chalcedon (451) to Gregory the Great (590–604), iv: The Church of Alexandria with Nubia and Ethiopia after 451 (London, 1996).
Guidi, M. and R. Walzer, *Uno Scritto Introduttivo allo Studio di Aristotele*, (Rome: 1940).
Gutas, D., "Plato's *Symposion* in the Arabic Tradition," in *Oriens* 31 (1988), pp. 36–60.
——, "Intuition and Thinking: The Evolving Structure of Avicenna's Epistemology," in ed. Robert Wisnovsky, *Aspects of Avicenna*, (Princeton, 2001) (repr. from *Princeton Papers: Interdisciplinary Journal of Middle Eastern Studies*, Vol. IX, 1–38).
Hadot, P., *Marius Victorinus. Recherches sur sa vie et ses œuvres* (Paris, 1971).

226 BIBLIOGRAPHY

Hasse, Dag Nikolaus, "Avicenna on Abstraction," in *Aspects of Avicenna,* ed. Robert Wisnovsky, (Princeton, 2001) (rep. from *Princeton Papers: Interdisciplinary Journal of Middle Eastern Studies,* Vol. IX), pp. 39–72.

——, "Latin Averroes Translations of the First Half of the Thirteenth Century", presented at the XIIth International Congress of Medieval Philosophy held in Palermo, Italy, September 21, 2007. Revised version forthcoming.

Ḥawī, Sāmī S., *Islamic Naturalism and Mysticism: A Philosophic Study of Ibn Ṭufayl's Ḥayy Bin Yaqẓān,* (Leiden, 1974).

Heckel, Th. K., *Der Innere Mensch: Die paulinische Verarbeitung eines platonischen Motivs* (Wissenschaftliche Untersuchungen zum Neuen Testament II.53), (Tübingen, 1993).

Honigmann, E., *Évêques et évêchés monophysites d'Asie antérieure au VI siècle* (Corpus Scriptorum Christianorum Orientalium, Subsidia, 2) (Leuven, 1951).

Hughes, Aaron W., *Texture of the Divine: Imagination in Medieval Islamic and Jewish Thought,* (Bloomington, 2004).

——, "A Case of Twelfth-Century Plagiarism?: Abraham ibn Ezra's *Hay ben Meqitz* and Avicenna's *Ḥayy ibn Yaqẓān,*" in *Journal of Jewish Studies* 55.2 (2004), pp. 306–331.

——, "The 'Golden Age' of Muslim Spain: Religious Identity and the Invention of a Tradition in Modern Jewish Studies," in *Historicizing "Tradition" in the Study of Religion,* eds. Steven Engler and Gregory P. Greive, (Berlin, 2005).

Hugonnard-Roche, H., "Sur les versions syriaques des *Catégories* d'Aristote," *Journal Asiatique* 275 (1987), pp. 205–22.

——, "Remarques sur la tradition arabe de l'*Organon* d'après le manuscrit Paris, Bibliothèque nationale, ar. 2346," in *Burnett* (1993), pp. 19–28.

Iskenderoglu, Muammer, *Fakhr al-Dīn al-Rāzī and Thomas Aquinas on the Question of the Creation of the World,* (Leiden, 2002).

Ivry, Alfred L., "Conjunction in and of Maimonides and Averroes," in *Averroès et les averroïsmes juif et latin. Actes du colloque tenu à Paris, 16–18 juin 2005,* ed. J.-B. Brenet, (Turnhout, 2007), pp. 231–247.

Jeauneau, E., "Pseudo-Dionysius, Gregory of Nyssa, and Maximus the Confessor in the Works of John Scottus Eriugena", in *Carolingian Essays,* ed. U. R. Blumenthal, (Washington D.C.), pp. 138–49.

——, "L'heritage de la philosophie antique durant le Haut Moyen Age" in *Settimana di studio del centro italiano di studi sull'alto medioevo, XXII,* pp. 19–54.

Judson, L., 'God or Nature? Philoponus on Generability and Perishability', *Philoponus and the Rejection of Aristotelian Science,* ed. R. Sorabji (Leyden, 1987), pp. 179–196.

Krausmüller, D., 'Murder is good if God wills it. Nicetas Byzantius' polemic against Islam and the Christian tradition of divinely sanctioned murder', *Al-Masaq (Islam and the Medieval Mediterranean),* 16 (2004), pp. 163–176.

——, 'Divine self-invention: Leontius of Jerusalem's reinterpretation of the Patristic model of the Christian God', *Journal of Theological Studies,* 57 (2006), pp. 526–545.

Kreisel, Howard H., "On the Term *kol* in Abraham Ibn Ezra: A Reappraisal," *Revue des Études Juives* 152 (1994), pp. 29–66.

Lamberton, R., *Homer the Theologian: Neoplatonist Allegorical Reading and the Growth of the Epic Tradition* (The Transformation of the Classical Heritage 9), (Berkeley, 1986).

Langermann, Y. Tzvi, "Ibn Ezra, Abraham," *Stanford Encyclopedia of Philosophy.* (Online at http://www.science.uva.nl/~seop/entries/ibn-ezra/).

Leaman, Oliver, *Moses Maimonides,* (London, 1997).

——, "Ideals, Simplicity, and Ethics: The Maimonidean Approach", *American Catholic Philosophical Quarterly* 76, (2002), pp. 107–24.

——, "Maimonides and the development of Jewish thought in an Islamic structure," *The trias of Maimonides,* ed. G. Tamer, (Berlin, 2005), pp. 187–98.

——, *Jewish Thought: an introduction,* (London, 2006).

BIBLIOGRAPHY

227

——, (ed.) *The Qur'an: An Encyclopedia*, (London, 2006).
——, "Maimonides and the special nature of the prophecy of Moses", in, *Maimonide e il suo tempo*, eds. G. Cerchiai and G. Rota, (Milan, 2007), pp. 83–94.
Levin, Israel, *Abraham ibn Ezra: His Life and Poetry* [Hebrew], (Tel Aviv, 1969).
Lichtenberger, H., *Das Ich Adams und das Ich der Menschheit: Studien zum Menschenbild in Römer 7* (Wissenschaftliche Untersuchungen zum Neuen Testament 164), (Tübingen, 2004).
Lobel, Diana, *Between Mysticism and Philosophy: Sufi Language of Religious Experience in Judah Ha-Levi's Kuzari*, (Albany, 2000).
Louth, A., *St John Damascene* (Oxford Early Christian Studies), (Oxford, 2002).
Lubac, Henri de, *Exégèse médiévale: Les quatres sens de l'Écriture*, (Paris, 1959–64).
Mahoney, Edward P., "Aquinas's Critique of Averroes' Doctrine of the Unity of the Intellect," in *Thomas Aquinas and His Legacy*, ed. David M. Gallagher, (Washington, D.C., 1994) pp. 83–106.
——, "Themistius and the agent intellect in James of Viterbo and other thirteenth-century philosophers," *Augustiniana* 23 (1973), pp. 423–67.
Manitius, M., *Geschichte der lateinischen Literatur des Mittelalters*. 3 vols., (Munich, 1911–1931), Vol. I, pp. 22–153.
Markschies, C., "Die platonische Metapher vom 'inneren Menschen': Eine Brücke zwischen antiker Philosophie und altchristlicher Theologie", in *Zeitschrift für Kirchengeschichte* 105 (1994), pp. 1–17 (also published in: *International Journal of the Classical Tradition* 1.3 [1995] 3–18).
——, "Innerer Mensch", in *Reallexikon für Antike und Christentum*, vol. 18, (Stuttgart, 1998), pp. 266–312.
Martin, R. and J. Barresi, *The rise and fall of soul and self*, (New York, 2006).
Martinez Lorca, A., "Averroes, tafsir del De Anima: sobre el intelecto", *Endoxa* 17, (2003), pp. 9–61.
Massignon, L., "Notes sur le texte orginal arabe du De Intellectu d'al-Fārābī, in *Les sources grecoarabes de l'augustinisme avicennisant*, ed. E. Gilson (Paris, 1986).
McCallum, D., *Silence and salvation in Maimonides' Guide*, (London 2007).
McKitterick, Rosamond, "Knowledge of Plato's *Timaeus* in the ninth century: the implications of Valenciennes, B. M., Ms 293" in *From Athens to Chartres. Neoplatonism and Medieval Thought. Studies in Honour of Edouard Jeauneau*, ed. H. J. Westra, (Leiden, New York, Koln: Studien und Texte zur Geistesgeschichte des Mittelalters, 35, 1992), pp. 85–97.
Morani, M., ed., *Nemesii Emeseni De natura hominis*, (Leipzig, 1987).
Netton, Ian Richard, *Muslim Neoplatonists: An Introduction to the Thougth of the Brethren of Purity (Ikhwān al-Ṣafā')*, (London, 2002).
——, "Foreign Influences and Recurring Isma'ili Motifs in *Rasā'il* of the Brethren of Purity" in idem, *See Knowledge: Thought and Travel in the House of Islam*, (Richmond, 1996), pp. 162–164.
——, *Al-Fārābī and His School*, (Richmond, repr. 1999).
Norris, R. A., *Manhood and Christ. A Study in the Christology of Theodore of Mopsuestia* (Oxford, 1963).
Périer, A., "Un traité de Yahyā ben 'Adī. Défense du dogme de la Trinité contre les objections d'al-Kindī," in *Revue de l'orient christian* 3rd series, 22 (1920–1), pp. 3–21.
Peters, F. E., *Aristoteles Arabus: the Oriental Translations and Commentaries on the Aristotelian Corpus* (Leiden, 1968).
Pines, Shlomo, "Shi'ite Terms and Conceptions in Judah Halevi's *Kuzari*," in *Jerusalem Studies in Arabic and Islam* 2 (1980), pp. 165–251.
Pormann, P. E., "The Alexandrian Summary (*Jawāmi'*) of Galen's *On the Sects for Beginners*: Commentary or Abridgment?", in *Philosophy, Science and Exegesis in Greek, Arabic and Latin Commentaries*, *Bulletin of the Institute of Classical Studies*, eds. P. Adamson et al., Supplement 83, 2 vols (London, 2004), 2: pp. 11–33.

228 BIBLIOGRAPHY

——, "Medisch Onderwijs in de Late Oudheid: Van Alexandrië naar Montpellier," in *Geschiedenis der Geneeskunde*, 12 (2008), pp. 175–80.

Quinn, Patrick, *Aquinas, Platonism and the Knowledge of God*, (Guildford, 1996).

——, *Philosophy of Religion A-Z*, (Edinburgh, 2005).

——, "The Interfacing Image of the Soul in the Writings of Aquinas" in *Milltown Studies* No. 32, (Autumn 1993), pp. 70–75.

——, "Aquinas's Concept of the Body and Out of Body Situations" in *The Heythrop Journal*, Vol. 34, No. 4, (October 1993), pp. 387–400.

——, "Aquinas's Model of Mind" in *New Blackfriars*, (May 1996), Vol. 77 No. s904.

——, "Aquinas's Views of Mind and Soul: Echoes of Platonism" in *Verbum Analecta Neolatino*, VI/2004/1, Piliscaba.

Rahman, F., *Avicenna's Psychology: an English translation of Kitāb al-najāt, book II, chapter VI, with historical-philosophical notes and textual improvements on the Cairo edition*, (London, 1952).

Rashed, R. and J. Jolivet, *Oeuvres Philosophiques & Scientifiques d'al-Kindī: Métaphysique et cosmologie*, volume 2, (Leiden, 1998).

Riché, P., *Éducation et Culture dans l'Occident barbare, VIᵉ–VIIIᵉ siècles.* (Paris, 1962), pp. 27–92, 140–220, 353–530, also in *Education and Culture in the Barbarian West, Sixth through Eighth Centuries*, trans. Contreni, J., (Columbia, South Carolina, 1976).

——, *Écoles et enseignement dans le Haut Moyen Age. Fin du Vᵉ siècle–milieu du XIᵉ siècle.* (Paris, 1979) pp. 8–111.

Rist, J. M., "Pseudo-Dionysius, Neoplatonism and the weakness of the soul", *From Athens to Chartres. Neoplatonism and medieval thought. Studies in honour of E. Jeauneau*, ed. H. J. Westra (Studien und Texte zur Geistesgeschichte des Mittelalters, 35, Leipzig, 1992), pp. 135–161.

Roques, René, *Structures théologiques, de la gnose à Richard de Saint-Victor. Essais et analyses critiques* (Paris, 1962).

——, *L'univers dionysien. Structure hiérarchique du monde selon le Pseudo-Denys.* (Paris, 1954).

Rorem, P., *Ps-Dionysius: a commentary on the texts and an introduction to their influence*, (New York, 1993).

——, "The doctrinal concerns of the first dyonisian [sic] scholiast, John of Scythopolis", in *Denys l'Aréopagite et sa postérité en Orient et en Occident. Actes du Colloque International Paris, 21–24 Septembre 1994*, ed. Y. De Andia, (Paris, 1997), pp. 187–200.

——, & J. C. Lamoreaux, *John of Scythopolis and the Dionysian Corpus. Annotating the Areopagite* (Oxford Early Christian Studies, Oxford, 1998).

Runia, David, *On the Creation of the Cosmos according to Moses*, Introduction, translation and commentary, (Atlanta, 2001).

Russell, Bertrand, History of Western Philosophy, 2nd edn., (London, 1971).

Sambursky, Sh., "The Concept of Time in Later Neoplatonism", *Proceedings of the Israel Academy of Science and Humanities*, II.8 (1966), pp. 153–167.

Scheindlin, Raymond P., *Song of the Distant Dove: Judah Halevi's Pilgrimage*, (New York, 2008).

Schnelle, U., *The Human Condition: Anthropology in the Teachings of Jesus, Paul, and John*, trans. by O. C. Dean, Jr, (Edinburgh, 1996) (trans. of *Neutestamentliche Anthropologie: Jesus—Paulus—Johannes* [Biblisch-theologische Studien 18], Neukirchen-Vluyn, 1991).

Schrenk, L. P., "John Philoponus on the Immortal Soul", in *Proceedings of the American Catholic Philosophical Association*, 64 (1990), pp. 151–160.

Sedley, D., "The Ideal of Godlikeness", in *Plato*, vol. 2: *Ethics, Politics, Religion, and the Soul*, ed. G. Fine, (Oxford Readings in Philosophy), (Oxford, 1999), pp. 309–328.

BIBLIOGRAPHY 229

Sheldon-Williams, I. P., "Eriugena's Greek Sources", in *The Mind of Eriugena. Papers of a Colloquium Dublin, 14–18 July 1970* (Dublin, 1973), pp. 1–15, p. 5.
Shihādeh, Ayman, *Fakhr al-Dīn al-Rāzī on Ethics and Virtue*, (Oxford, 2002).
Silman, Yohanan, *Philosopher and Prophet: Judah Halevi, the Kuzari, and the Evolution of His Thought*, trans. Lenn J. Schramm, (Albany, 1995).
Suchla, B. R., 'Die sogenannten Maximus-Scholien des Corpus Dionysiacum Areopagiticum', in *Nachrichten der Akademie der Wissenschaften in Göttingen, Philosophisch-historische Klasse*, 1980, fasc. 3 (Göttingen, 1980), pp. 31–66.
——, 'Verteidigung eines platonischen Denkmodells einer christlichen Welt', in *Nachrichten der Akademie der Wissenschaften in Göttingen, Philosophisch-historische Klasse*, 1995, I (Göttingen, 1995), pp. 1–28.
——,"Das Scholienwerk des Johannes von Scythopolis zu den areopagitischen Traktaten in seiner philosophie- und theologiegeschichtlichen Bedeutung", in *Denys l'Aréopagite et sa postérité en Orient et en Occident. Actes du Colloque International Paris, 21–24 Septembre 1994*, ed. Y. De Andia (Paris, 1997), pp. 155–165.
Tībawī, A. L., "Ikhwān as-Safā' and their Rasā'il: A Critical Review of a Century and a half of Research", in *Islamic Quarterly*, vol. 2:1 (1955).
Taylor, Richard C., "Abstraction in al-Fārābī", in *Proceedings of the American Catholic Philosophical Association* 80 (2006), pp. 151–168.
——, "Averroes' Epistemology and Its Critique by Aquinas", in *Thomistic Papers VII. Medieval Masters: Essays in Memory of Msgr. E. A. Synan*, ed. R. E. Houser, (Houston, 1999) pp. 147–177.
——, & Herrera, Max. "Aquinas' Naturalized Epistemology", in *Proceedings of the American Catholic Philosophical Association* 79 (2005), pp. 83–102.
——, "Cogitatio, Cogitativus and Cogitare: Remarks on the Cogitative Power in Averroes", in *L'elaboration du vocabulaire philosophique au Moyen Age*, eds. J. Hamesse et C. Steel, [Rencontres de philosophie Medievale Vol. 8.] (Turnhout, Brepols, 2000), pp. 111–146.
——, "Improving on Nature's Exemplar: Averroes' Completion of Aristotle's Psychology of Intellect", in *Philosophy, Science and Exegesis in Greek, Arabic and Latin Commentaries*, edited by Peter Adamson, eds. Han Baltussen and M. W. F. Stone, in 2 vols., v. 2, [*Supplement to the Bulletin of the Insititute Of Classical Studies* 83.1–2] (London, 2004) pp. 107–130.
——, "Intelligibles in act in Averroes", in *Averroès et les averroïsmes juif et latin. Actes du colloque tenu à Paris, 16–18 juin 2005*, ed. J.-B. Brenet, (Turnhout, 2007), pp. 111–140.
——, "Remarks on Cogitatio in Averroes' *Commentarium Magnum in Aristotelis De Anima Libros*", in *Averroes and the Aristotelian Tradition: Sources, Constitution and Reception of the Philosophy of Ibn Rushd (1126–1198)*, eds. Jan A. Aertsen and Gerhard Endress, (Leiden, 1999), pp. 217–255.
——, "Separate Material Intellect in Averroes' Mature Philosophy", in *Words, Texts and Concepts Cruising the Mediterranean Sea. Studies on the sources, contents and influences of Islamic civilization and Arabic philosophy and science, dedicated to Gerhard Endress on his sixty-fifth birthday*, eds. Ruediger Arnzen and Joern Thielmann, [Orientalia Lovaniensia Analecta series] (Leuven, 2004), pp. 289–309.
——, "The Agent Intellect as 'form for us' and Averroes's Critique of al-Fārābī", in *Topicos* (Universidad Panamericana, Mexico City) 29 (2005) 29–51, reprinted with corrections in *Proceedings of the Society for Medieval Logic and Metaphysics* 5 (2005)18–32 http://www.fordham.edu/gsas/phil/klima/SMLM/PSMLM5/PSMLM5 .pdf.
——, "Themistius and the Development of Averroes' Noetics", forthcoming in *Soul and Mind. Medieval Perspectives on Aristotle's De Anima* (Philosophes Médiévaux LII), (Leuven, 2009).

230 BIBLIOGRAPHY

Uthemann, K. H., ed., *Anastasii Sinaitae viae dux*, (Corpus Christianorum. Series Graeca, 8, Turnhout, 1981).

Vajda, Georges, *L'amour de Dieu dans la théologie juive du Moyen Age* (Paris, 1957).

Van Kooten, G. H., "Pagan and Jewish Monotheism according to Varro, Plutarch and St Paul: The Aniconic, Monotheistic Beginnings of Rome's Pagan Cult—Romans 1:19–25 in a Roman Context", in *Flores Florentino: Dead Sea Scrolls and Other Early Jewish Studies in Honour of Florentino García Martínez*, eds. A. Hilhorst É. Puech & E. Tigchelaar, (Supplements to the Journal for the Study of Judaism 122), (Leiden/ Boston, 2007), pp. 633–651.

——, *Paul's Anthropology in Context: The Image of God, Assimilation to God, and Tripartite Man in Ancient Judaism, Ancient Philosophy and Early Christianity*, (Wissenschaftliche Untersuchungen zum Neuen Testament 232), (Tübingen, 2008).

Van Roey, A., "Un traité cononite contre la doctrine de Jean Philopon sur la resurrection", *ANTIDWRON, I, Festschrift M. Geerard* (Wetteren, 1984), pp. 123–139.

Von Balthasar, H. U., "Das Scholienwerk des Johannes von Scythopolis", in *Scholastik*, 5 (1940), pp. 16–38.

——, *Kosmische Liturgie; das Weltbild Maximus' des Bekenners* (Einsiedeln, 1961).

Von Bendemann, R., "Die kritische Diastase von Wissen, Wollen und Handeln: Traditionsügeschichtliche Spurensuche eines hellenistischen Topos in Römer 7", in *Zeitschrift für die Neutestamentliche Wissenschaft und die Kunde der Älteren Kirche* 95 (2004), pp. 35–63.

Wacht, M., *Aeneas von Gaza als Apologist. Seine Kosmologie im Verhältnis zum Platonismus* (Theophaneia, 21, Bonn, 1969).

Wasserman, E., "The Death of the Soul in Romans 7: Revisiting Paul's Anthropology in Light of Hellenistic Moral Psychology", in *Journal of Biblical Literature* 126 (2007), pp. 793–816.

——, "The Death of the Soul in Romans 7: Sin, Death, and the Law in Light of Hellenistic Moral Psychology" in (Wissenschaftliche Untersuchungen zum Neuen Testament II.256), (Tübingen, 2008).

Winter, B. W., *Philo and Paul among the Sophists: Alexandrian and Corinthian Responses to a Julio-Claudian Movement*, 2nd edn (Grand Rapids, Michigan, 2002).

Wolfson, Elliot R., "God, the Demiurge, and the Active Intellect: On the Usage of the Word *kol* in Abraham Ibn Ezra", in *Revue des Études Juives* 149 (1990), pp. 77–111.

Wolfson, Harry Austryn, "Maimonides and Halevi: A Study in Typical Jewish Attitudes toward Greek Philosophy in the Middle Ages", in *Jewish Quarterly Review* 2 (1911), pp. 297–337.

——, "Maimonides on the internal senses", in *Jewish Quarterly Review*, (1935), pp. 441–67; reprinted in *Studies in the History of Religion and Philosophy*, ed. I. Twersky and G. Williams, (Cambridge, MA, 1973) I: pp. 344–70.

al-Zurkān, Ṣāliḥ, *Fakhr al-Dīn al-Rāzī*, (Cairo, 1963).

INDEX OF NAMES

Aaron 170
Abū al-Barakāt al-baghdādī 121, 125, 132
(*al-Mu'tabir fī al-Ḥikma*) 125
Abū al-Hudhayl 137
Abū 'Uthmān 'Amr b. Baḥr al-Jāḥiẓ 109
'Alā' al-Dīn Khawārīzm 121
Adam 18–20, 44, 47, 126–127, 168–169
Aeneas of Gaza 47, 53–58
Alexander of Aphrodisias 190, 206
al-Fārābī 11, 109, 116, 129–130, 163, 166, 173, 189n5, 190, 203n38, 206n42, 207–208, 217
(*al-Madīna al-Fāḍila*) 109n11, 116, 208n45
al-Ghazālī, Abū Ḥāmid 9, 121–124, 127
Al-Kindī 7–9, 11, 13, 95–106, 109
(*On Definitions*) 105
(*On First Philosophy*) 100n11, 101n13, 105n29
(*On the Intellect*) 103
(*On the Quantity of Aristotle's Books*) 95n1, 97, 100n12
(*That There Are Separate Substances*) 8, 99, 100n12
Al-Naẓẓām 126
Al-Rāzī, Fakh al-Dīn 9–10, 121–139
(*al-Arba' īn fī Uṣūl al-Dīn*) 136–137
(*al-Maṭālib al-'Āliyya*) 121–123
(*al-Mabāḥith al-Mashriqiyya*) 121–122
(*Kitāb al-Rūḥ wa al-Nafs*) 122
(*Mafātīḥ al-Ghayb*) 124
Al-Sarakhsī 96
Al-Zurkān 121n1, 125, 128n21, 129n25, 131n31, 132, 133n33, 134n38, 135n42, 136n48, 137n53
Angels 6–7, 48, 50–52, 54–56, 58–59, 61–63, 67–69, 72–76, 85–86, 92, 127, 129–130, 149–150, 154–157, 173, 183
Animals 70, 72, 85–86, 92, 124, 130, 134, 148, 152, 192–193, 198, 201–202
Antiochus of Ascalon 17–18, 24

Aquinas, Thomas 12–13, 179–185, 187–196, 198–206, 208, 211–220
Aristotelian, Aristotelianism 8, 10–11, 20, 53n26, 70, 75n116, 87, 95–96, 98–100, 102n14, 102n17, 103n23, 109, 111, 126–128, 130–131, 137, 148n13, 171, 180–182, 188–190, 198, 202, 208, 211, 215n61, 219–220
Aristotle 3–4, 7–8, 18, 21–22, 27, 47–48, 78n3, 95, 97–100, 102–103n17, 106n30, 109–112, 127, 129–130, 135, 148n13, 154, 163, 166, 181–182, 188–190, 192–193, 197, 199, 201, 205n40, 206n41, 209–211, 214, 220
(*Categories*) 8, 95–100, 102n14, 102n16, 102n17, 103n17, 103n23
(*De Caelo*) 4, 75n116
(*De Anima*) 98–99, 102n17, 127, 163, 189, 192n11, 196n20, 196n21, 197, 199, 200n29, 202, 204, 206, 209, 210n53, 211, 212n56, 214–215, 217, 220
(*Metaphysics*) 110n20, 111n25, 111n31, 193
(*Nicomachean Ethics*) 201
(*Organon*) 95
(*Physics*) 192
Augustine 72n100, 77, 78n3, 79n6, 82–85, 89, 187
Avempace (Ibn Bājja) 217
Averroes, Averroist (see Ibn Rushd)
Avicenna (see Ibn Sīnā)

Bazán, B. C. 187n3, 188n3, 195n18
Bible 1, 5, 14, 25, 27n4, 37n14, 52n23, 80, 92, 143, 145, 163, 165–166, 171–173
Black, D. 187n1, 188
Blumenthal, H. J. 209n48
Brenet, J. B. 188n4, 189n5, 202n37, 218n69
Brethren of Purity (see *Ikhwān al-Ṣafā'*)
Buddhist, Buddha 108
Busa, Robert, S.J. 216n64

Christianity 24, 25n1, 47, 79, 82, 165–166
Cyril of Alexandria 50–52, 54, 74

232 INDEX OF NAMES

Davidson, H. 188n3
de Libera Alain 187n1

Eudorus of Alexandria 18, 24
Eunomius of Cyzicus 49–50

Flavius Josephus 25

Galen 96, 129
Genesis 47, 49–50, 56, 79–81, 84, 118, 149
Gregory of Nyssa 48n6, 49–50, 51n16, 52n24, 78n3
Geoffroy, M. 109n5, 202n37, 206n42
Gutas, D. 102n16, 188n3

Hades 23–24, 39
Halevi Judah 11, 143–147, 152–154, 158–161
Hasse, D. G. 188n3, 205n40
Ḥawī, Sāmī S. 119
Hinduism 111

Iamblichus 17n2, 77n1, 112
Ibn Ezra, Abraham 11, 143–146, 148–161
Ibn Rushd (Averroes) 11–13, 113, 187–191, 193, 200n29, 201–220
Ibn Sīnā (Avicenna) 9–11, 109n11, 119n79, 121–124, 127–130, 134–135, 147n10, 150, 152n29, 154–155, 187, 188n3, 188n5, 190, 216n64, 217
(ʿUyūn al-Ḥikma) 121
(al-Ishārāt) 121
(Ḥayy B. Yaqẓān) 119n80, 154n37, 155
Ibn Taymiyya 125
Ibn Ṭufayl 119, 154n37
(Ḥayy B. Yaqẓān) 119n79, 154n37, 155
Ikhwān al-Ṣafāʾ 9, 14, 107–109, 111, 113n42, 119, 127
(Island of the Monkeys) 117–118, 120
Indian 108
Isaiah 27
Islam, Islamic 4, 7–8, 11, 13, 74n155, 107–109, 119n80, 119n81, 121, 124–126, 128n19, 143–144, 146–148, 154n37, 159n51, 163–166, 189n5
Ivry, A. L. 202n37

John of Scythopolis 47, 53–54, 58–73, 75–76
Judaism 25n1, 42n20, 143–144, 146–147, 152, 160, 164–166

Karaites 165

Lee, D. 114n51, 115
Leontius of Byzantium 58, 97
Lombard, Peter 183, 189n7, 211–212

Mahoney, Edward P. 187n2, 209n48
Maimonides 11–12, 158n49, 163, 165–175, 202n37
Manichaean 63–64, 74–75, 108
Marius Victorinus 77n1, 82
Marquet, Yves 113
Maximus the Confessor 7, 53n30, 78n3, 84, 87, 90–92
McGinnis, J. 188n3
McInerny, Ralph 187n1
Miriam 170
Mishnah 165, 175
Moses 17–18, 20–22, 32–33, 50, 170, 173
Mishneh Torah 165, 167, 175
Muhammad 106, 109, 127
Muʿtazilites 8, 10, 126

Nemesius of Emesa 49–50, 52, 59
Neoplatonic 6, 10–11, 49, 52, 54, 58n48, 60, 77n1, 79, 80, 108, 110, 112–113, 121, 143, 148–149, 152, 163–164, 170, 209
Neoplatonism 7, 9, 25n1, 60n56, 62n64, 70n94, 77–78, 82, 84n18, 107, 109, 111, 146–148, 154
Numenius 23n13

Origen of Alexandria 24, 29, 79, 91
Origenism, Origenists, Origenist Controversy 52, 79

Persian 64n71, 108
Peters, F. E. 96n5, 109
Philo of Alexandria 17–24
Philoponus, Johannes 48n5, 52, 53n26, 69, 75n116
Plato 1–4, 18, 20–21, 27, 36–37, 39, 41–42, 47–48, 51, 56–57, 59, 78, 80–81, 91, 102–103, 109, 113–115, 118–119, 126, 130, 148n13, 154, 163, 181, 193n15, 211n54
(Euthyphro) 42
(Crito) 113
(Phaedo) 2, 97, 102n16, 110n18, 113, 181, 183
(Parmenides) 104n27
(Phaedrus) 3, 19n7, 20, 28, 48n5, 54n31

INDEX OF NAMES

233

(*Protagoras*)   35–36
(*Republic*)   2, 19n7, 37, 39, 80,
   113–115, 118–119
(*Theaetetus*)   41
(*Timaeus*)   3–4, 19–20, 22, 51–52,
   56–57, 64, 77–78, 80
(*Laws*)   27
Platonic   1–6, 14, 17, 19–20, 36–37,
   40n17, 41n18, 42, 54, 56–58, 78–80,
   98, 103, 110, 113, 117, 119, 126, 148,
   179, 211
Platonism, Platonists   2–5, 7, 11–12,
   17–20, 23–24, 42n18, 53n27, 77n1,
   80, 82, 103n23, 148n13, 179, 181,
   184–185
Plotinus   37–42, 60, 62n63, 77–78,
   82–84, 109, 111–112, 148n13
Porphyry   4, 7, 95
   Isagoge   95
   Organon   95
Proclus   7, 52, 64–65, 84n18, 184
Pseudo-Dionysius the Areopagite   7,
   52, 53n25, 70n94, 77n1, 78n3, 84
Pythagoras, Pythagorean(s)   17–18,
   23n13, 109–111

Qur'an, Qur'anic   14, 108–109,
   112–113, 118, 120, 124, 126–127, 135,
   163

Russell, Bertrand   115

Scot, Michael   204–205
Siger of Brabant   188n3
Socrates   2, 35, 37, 102n16, 103n19,
   104n27, 113, 193n15, 200
Solomon   28
Stoics, Stoicism   7, 18–20, 22, 24, 29,
   71n98, 82
Symeon of the Wondrous Mountain
   75

Talmud   11, 145, 165–167
Themistius   207, 209–213, 215, 219
Theophrastus   212–213, 215
Ṭībawī, A. L.   109
Torah   14, 149n15, 153–154, 165, 167,
   175

Wordsworth, William   110

Xenocrates   23n13

Yaḥyā ben 'Adī   95n3

Zoroastrian   108

INDEX OF CONCEPTS AND PLACES

abstraction 68, 167, 179, 188n3, 192, 207, 208n45, 209, 211, 212n56, 215–216, 219–220
actuality 5, 105, 111, 138, 166, 193, 207n45, 208n45, 210n54, 211, 213, 214n58, 218
afterlife 5–6, 8, 12, 14, 133, 152, 160, 163, 165–166, 173
Ark of Noah 118, 120
al-Andalus 10–11, 144–145, 147
al-ʿilla al-fāʿiliyya 111
al-nafs 9–10, 102, 122, 125, 126n16, 128–129, 131–133, 150n20, 152
al-rūḥ 9–10, 122, 126–129, 131
Amr ilāhī (divine influence) 159–160
anthropology
  (and ethics) 48–53
  (Lutheran) 41–42
  (Semitic) 25–27, 28, 34
  (two or three classes of man) 30, 31–32, 43, 44
ʿaraḍ (aʿrāḍ) 125, 137
Awliyāʾ Allah 117, 119–120

Basra 10, 107–108, 111
being 47, 51n20, 50, 57, 62, 65, 68, 74, 76, 81–82, 85, 89, 100, 101n13, 103n17, 112, 134, 149, 163, 170, 181–184, 190, 192, 194–198, 203, 204n39, 205, 206n41, 213n58, 216n64, 217
beings 57, 58n48, 62–64, 67n87, 68, 70–73, 81, 101, 123, 125–126, 130, 133–134, 136, 138, 152, 157, 169, 174, 182, 184, 203, 204n39, 208n45
  (class(es) of) 48, 51, 70, 123, 135
  (created) 47, 55, 69
  (eternal) 6
  (human) 13–14, 27, 44, 48, 54–55, 58, 69, 117–118, 171, 181, 190–198, 201–202, 205–208, 211–214, 216–217
  (incorporeal) 9, 59
  (intelligible) 64–65
  (invisible) 51, 64
  (spiritual) 9, 159
  (reasoning) 21, 32, 130, 205
  (temporal) 58
bipartite 2–3, 18

blood 3, 90, 110, 124
  (Lower soul as) 5, 20–21, 24, 31–32, 34
body 2, 4–14, 18n4, 19n7, 20–23, 25, 29–30, 32–35, 38, 49–50, 59, 62n66, 67, 69, 71–72, 78–83, 86–92, 97–99, 100n12, 101–105, 113, 122–133, 135–138, 148–153, 155–157, 165, 167–171, 182–183, 189, 196n21, 197–201, 203n38
  (soul and) 2–4, 7–8, 13, 23, 26, 31, 86–88, 90–91, 126, 163, 169, 171–172, 180–182, 184, 198–199
  (spiritual) 6–7, 14, 90, 185
  soma pneumatikon 29

categories 173
  (Avicennian) 147n10, 152n29
  (Arabo-Islamic) 147
  (Aristotle's) see Aristotle
  (Greco-Arabic) 160
  (Jewish) 143, 146–147, 161
China 108
cleaving (devequt) 151, 160
cognition 143, 154, 181, 183, 216n64
contingent (mumkin) 123, 134, 136
Cosmology 7–8, 47, 74, 79, 82, 134, 148n13, 164
creation 4–6, 19, 22–23, 33, 47–52, 54–57, 60–62, 65, 67–68, 76, 80, 83–84, 88–90, 113, 126, 135–136, 144, 160
creature 21–22, 32, 48, 52, 56, 58, 75–76, 81–83, 86, 90–91, 139, 146, 168–169, 172–174, 184

Dar al-Ākhira (paradise) 57, 117, 120, 126
death 4, 9–11, 22–23, 40n17, 44, 71n96, 86–88, 113, 117, 122, 124, 133, 135, 138, 149, 156, 165, 167, 170–171, 173, 179–181, 183–185, 193, 218 n.
determinate particular 193–194, 196–200
dhawq 158–159, 202
divisions of, parts of
  (arithmetic) 110
  (the body) 126, 129, 131, 137–138
  (creation) 68

INDEX OF CONCEPTS AND PLACES 235

(the divine)   74
(intellect)   62, 134
(man)   86
(nature)   57, 99
(the soul)   2–3, 5, 11, 18–19, 14,
  18–20, 24, 85–86, 88, 129–130,
  152–153, 155, 206n41
(species)   104–105

efficient cause   207–208, 210
emanation   9, 58n48, 60, 62, 109, 112,
  121, 134, 136, 170
epistles (*Rasāʾil*)   43, 96, 100n12,
  107–109, 111–114, 119
essence   2, 20–21, 32, 34, 84, 86, 88,
  89, 100n10, 101–102, 133–135,
  149–151, 156, 179–180, 182, 184,
  193, 199–200, 207n45, 208n45, 209,
  210n53, 217–219
eternity   6, 10, 23, 56, 59–64, 66–68,
  133, 184–185, 212
ex nihilo   79

fayḍ (emanation)   112
first philosophy   96, 100n11, 101n13,
  105n29
formal cause   12–13, 190–191, 193–194,
  196–198, 202, 204–205, 211–212, 216,
  219–220
forms   68, 70, 98, 103, 115, 137, 146,
  153, 156–157, 189, 192, 204, 209–210,
  212–215, 219
  (Platonic)   79, 103n19, 114
  form for us   189n6, 206–208,
    210–211, 218–220
  form in us   203–205
  intrinsic form   194, 205

Guide of the Perplexed   175

Herat   121
hermeneutics   78n3, 80
hexaemeron   47, 48n2, 48n3, 48n4, 80
hikma   119
Holy Spirit   7, 78, 83–85
human nature   14, 41n18, 86–89, 91,
  202
hypostasis/hypostases   78, 82n10, 87,
  110

illumination   119–120, 187, 207n45
imagination   4, 132, 144, 154–160,
  167–168, 170, 173, 204, 207, 212n55,
  214–215, 217, 219
imago dei   89, 92

immortality   4, 6, 14, 22–23, 56–59, 65,
  68–69, 73, 76, 91, 117
  (of the soul)   4–6, 18, 22, 55, 57, 69,
    72n100, 73, 76, 98, 135, 137
incarnation   4, 82, 91
inner man   5–6, 13, 31, 35–38, 40–44
intellect   1, 3, 9, 12–13, 19–23, 31, 38,
  43, 78, 82n10, 85, 88, 91–92, 111–112,
  115, 118, 120, 123, 131, 134, 149,
  150n19, 155–160, 163–167, 169–170,
  187–196, 198–220
  active intellect   150n19, 156,
    158–159, 164, 166
  agent intellect   13, 187–192,
    194–197, 201–217, 220
  material intellect   13, 164, 188,
    190–193, 202–208, 212–217
  possible intellect   190–192, 194–198,
    201, 203n38, 212–213, 215
intelligibles   60–61, 189n5, 192,
  195–196, 200n29, 202–211, 213–217,
  219
intelligible species   203, 214, 218–219
intention   27, 67, 191, 203n38, 206n41,
  210n53, 214–217
intentional content   216
internal sense power   191
involuntary Impulse   38–39, 40–42
Iraq   107
irrational   2–5, 18–21, 32, 39, 85–86
ittiṣāl   158, 202

jawhar   103n20, 125, 137

knowledge   6, 9–11, 13, 35, 48, 56, 58,
  78n3, 88, 99, 102n17, 108n5, 112–113,
  117, 119, 121–122, 125–126, 128–133,
  139, 147n12, 151, 153–155, 160, 165,
  175, 180–181, 183, 185, 187, 198n26,
  199n27, 202, 213

Last Day (*al-Maʿād*)   135–136
life   5–6, 9–12, 14, 20–23, 28, 30–32,
  37–38, 41, 56, 59, 62–63, 70–72, 74,
  76, 78, 80–86, 88–90, 92, 97, 101–102,
  108, 111, 114, 117, 125–126, 152–153,
  160, 165, 167–170, 180–183, 185,
  199n27, 217
  (man, archetype of)   23

matter   8, 48, 57, 66, 68, 70–71, 78–82,
  87, 89, 102n17, 111, 113, 124, 126–129,
  135–137, 157, 166–168, 183, 192,
  196n21, 199–200, 203n38, 208n45,
  212, 214, 216n64, 217n64, 218

236 INDEX OF CONCEPTS AND PLACES

Malay Peninsula 107
miracle(s) 69, 192n11, 193
mysticism 119n80, 159n51

necessary (*wājib*) 123
nefesh (soul) 11, 148–149, 151, 155–156

Organon 95

participation 43, 60–62, 66, 70, 72, 82–83, 211
particulars 121, 132, 139
perfection 169, 170, 207, 213
perishability 6, 47–49, 51–62, 64, 68–70, 73, 75–76, 136
philosophical psychology 4–7, 17, 24, 26, 40n17, 91, 129, 158, 187, 188n3, 188n4, 189n5
philosophy
  (Islamic) 7, 11, 13, 107, 109, 121, 143, 146, 148n13, 163, 169, 189n5
  (Jewish) 10–11, 13–14, 17, 143–147, 150, 152, 154, 160–161, 163, 165, 169, 171
pneuma 3, 6, 10, 14, 20–22, 24, 29–30, 43–44, 127–128
potentiality 111, 166, 207n45, 208n45
pre-existence 4, 23–24, 48, 50, 52, 54–55, 63, 79–80
prophecy 143–144, 154, 158, 160, 166, 170
pure act 219

quidditative content 216

rational 2–3, 5–6, 10–11, 14, 18–22, 48, 54–56, 58, 60, 67, 76, 82, 85–86, 88, 90, 92, 104, 108, 122, 124, 128–133, 136, 138, 143, 149, 151–153, 155, 158–160, 169, 173, 190–193, 198, 202, 205, 207–208
Rayy 121
religion 1, 12–14, 17, 31n8, 36, 41n18, 47, 107, 145n1, 146n8, 147n12, 165–166, 172–174
ruah 11, 148–149

salvation 7, 110–111, 118–120
self-movement 56, 100n12
separate substance 8, 95–97, 99–100, 190n7, 216n64, 217
separation 38, 192, 198
seven-fold 19n7, 24
ship of salvation 110, 120
society 169

sophists 36–38
soul
  (and the inner man) 5–6, 13, 31, 35–38, 40–44
  (antithesis with pneuma) 30, 32
  compound soul 39, 41
  human soul 1, 4–13, 23–25, 30, 47, 49, 51–56, 58–59, 61–65, 69, 71–76, 79, 86, 88–89, 91, 98, 122–123, 125–130, 132–136, 139, 144, 150, 152–154, 156, 169, 179, 182–185, 188n3, 190n8, 196, 201, 205, 208, 210–211, 213, 220
  (trichotomy) 31, 33–34, 43
  (various Greek meanings of *psuche*) 28–29
  two souls 20, 39n15, 40, 149
Stoicism 7, 24, 29, 71n98, 82
substance(s) 3, 7, 8–10, 20, 31–32, 49–50, 55, 72, 81, 83, 87, 96–99, 100n11, 100n12, 101–106, 111, 114, 123–126, 128, 130–132, 136–137, 153–154, 156, 182–184, 188n3, 190n7, 192–193, 195–197, 200n29, 202, 207–208, 212n56, 216n64, 217–218
  separate substance 8, 96, 99–100, 190n7, 95, 96, 97, 216n64, 217

ta'āwun (co-operation) 110, 116
terrestrial world 117
theologians (*mutakalimun*) 1, 4–11, 13–14, 52, 80, 123, 125–126, 131, 126–138
theology 1, 9, 12, 14, 77–79, 84–85, 108, 121, 173, 175, 184, 188n3, 188n4
time 6, 23, 47–50, 55–57, 59–64, 66, 68, 79, 136, 184
Torah 14, 148n14, 149n15, 153–154, 165, 167, 175
transfer 10, 97, 131, 158, 202, 203n38, 205, 207–208, 217
Trinity 64, 83–85, 89, 95, 99
tripartite 2–3, 5, 14, 19–20, 25n1, 43, 129–131, 155

understanding 5–7, 12–13, 88, 122, 132, 149, 151–152, 154, 156, 160, 174, 179–180, 190, 192, 196, 198, 200–201, 205–207, 211, 216n64, 217–220
universal concepts 132

voluntarism 54, 74n115

will 6–7, 28, 40–42, 50–52, 54, 58, 65–68, 72, 74n115, 126, 146, 200n29, 209, 211

Printed in the United States
By Bookmasters